Courtroom DRAMA

120 of the World's Most Notable Trials

CONTRIBUTORS

John S. Bowman

Rodney Carlisle

Stephen G. Christianson

Kathryn Cullen-DuPont

Teddi DiCanio

Colin Evans

Michael Golay

Bernard Ryan Jr.

Tom Smith

Eva Weber

Janet Bond Wood

NEW ENGLAND PUBLISHING ASSOCIATES

Edited and prepared for publication by New England Publishing Associates, Inc.

GENERAL EDITORS
Elizabeth Frost-Knappmann,
Edward W.Knappmann, and
Lisa Paddock

EDITORIAL ADMINISTRATION
Ron Formica and Christopher Ceplenski

PICTURE EDITOR
Victoria Harlow

Courtroom
DRAMA

120 of the World's
Most Notable Trials

Elizabeth Frost-Knappman,
Edward W. Knappman,
and Lisa Paddock, Editors

Victoria Harlow, Picture Editor

VOLUME 3
MILITARY TRIALS
AND COURTS-MARTIAL
RELIGION AND HERESY
TREASON
WAR CRIMES

U·X·L®
AN IMPRINT OF GALE

Detroit   New York   Toronto   London

Courtroom Drama:
120 of the World's Most Notable Trials

Staff

Jane Hoehner, *U•X•L Senior Editor*
Carol DeKane Nagel, *U•X•L Managing Editor*
Thomas L. Romig, *U•X•L Publisher*

Mary Beth Trimper, *Production Director*
Evi Seoud, *Assistant Production Manager*
Shanna Heilveil, *Production Associate*

Cynthia Baldwin, *Product Design Manager*
Barbara J. Yarrow, *Graphic Services Supervisor*
Tracey Rowens, *Senior Art Director*

Margaret Chamberlain, *Permissions Specialist (Pictures)*

Library of Congress Cataloging-in-Publication Data

Courtroom drama : 120 of the world's most notable trials / Elizabeth
  Frost-Knappman, Edward W. Knappmann, and Lisa Paddock, editors.

    p.   cm.
  Includes bibliographical references and index.
  Summary: Covers 120 notable trials that occurred around the world,
from the Salem witchcraft cases to O. J. Simpson.
    ISBN 0-7876-1735-0 (set). — ISBN 0-7876-1736-9 (v. 1) — ISBN
0-7876-1737-7 (v. 2) — ISBN 0-7876-1738-5 (v. 3)
    1. Trials—Juvenile literature. [1. Trials.] I. Frost
-Knappmann, Elizabeth. II. Knappmann, Edward W. III. Paddock, Lisa.

K540.C68 1998

347'.07—dc21   97-23014
                                                CIP
                                                AC

Contents

Contents

Contents

VOLUME 2:

ASSASSINATIONS

Contents

MURDER

Contents

VOLUME 3:

MILITARY TRIALS AND COURTS MARTIAL

RELIGION AND HERESY

Contents

Contents

Contents

Trials Alphabetically

A

B

Trials Alphabetically

I

J

K

L

M

**Trials
Alphabetically**

S

T

U

**Trials
Alphabetically**

**Trials
Alphabetically**

V

W

Trials Chronologically

Trials Chronologically

Trials Chronologically

Reader's Guide

Courtroom Drama: 120 of the World's Most Notable Trials presents twenty-five centuries of intriguing and influential trials that helped shape the course of world history. Falling into thirteen categories, the cases cover assassinations, murders, war crimes, court martials, religious crimes, espionage, treason, negligence, political corruption, freedom of speech, family law, and constitutional cases.

The earliest featured courtroom drama dates from 399 B.C. For refusing to worship the gods of the city of Athens, the philosopher Socrates was sentenced to death. The Timothy McVeigh trial, which deals with the worst act of terrorism in American history—the bombing of the Oklahoma City Federal Building in 1995—is among the more recent trials. Others are the *Jones v. Clinton and Ferguson* lawsuit brought by Paula Jones against President Bill Clinton for sexual harassment that allegedly occurred when he was governor of Arkansas. *Vacco v. Quill* and *Washington v. Glucksberg* together make up the Right to Die test cases heard by the Supreme Court in 1997.

Most of the cases in this book resulted in true trials, meaning that a court—usually a judge or a panel of judges—followed established rules and procedures and impartially examined disputes between parties over fact or law. Others are jury trials in which lawyers presented evidence to a jury that delivered a verdict.

Others are not real trials at all. The Salem witchcraft persecutions, for example, were not true trials since no attorney was present to represent the accused. Still, they were among the greatest social upheavals in colonial New England. Communist dictator Joseph Stalin's "show trials" made a mockery of justice since their verdicts were foregone conclusions.

The trials are arranged chronologically by category. There is an alphabetical listing as well. For easy reference, a Words to Know section at the beginning of each volume defines key terms. More than 120 sidebars provide related information while 172 photos enliven the text. A cumulative index concludes each volume.

Special Thanks

Our special thanks go to the following people for their help in preparing this book:

Colin Evans, for writing the essays on *Jones v. Clinton and Ferguson,* the Markus Wolf trials, the Right to Die case, the Steven Biko Inquest, the Roh Tae-woo and Chun Doo-hwan trials, and the Timothy McVeigh trial; Victoria Harlow, for obtaining all of the illustrations; Ron Formica, for trustworthy and meticulous editorial assistance; Tom Romig, for developing this three-volume set and asking us to prepare it; Jane Hoehner, for her high spirits, flexibility, and editorial advice; Rachael Kranz, for the lively sidebars; Carl Rollyson, for suggestions and support; Christopher Ceplenski, for general assistance and help in preparing the index; Amanda Frost-Knappman, for her independence, which allowed her parents to complete this project; John S. Bowman, for the Martin Guerre Trials and Reichstag Fire Trial essays; Rodney Carlisle, for the Peter Wright (Spycatcher) Trials and Boston Massacre Trials essays; Stephen G. Christianson, for the William "Big Bill" Haywood Trial, *Marbury v. Madison, Cherokee Nation v. Georgia,* Dred Scott Decision, *Reynolds v. U.S., Plessy v. Ferguson, Brown v. Board of Education, U.S. v. Nixon, Bakke v. University of California . . . Appeal, New York Times Company v. Sullivan, U.S. v. Cinque, U.S. v. Berrigan,* Harry Thaw Trials, Leo Frank Trial, Haymarket Trial, The Triangle Shirtwaist Fire Trial, Samuel Chase Impeachment, President Andrew Johnson Impeachment Trial, Aaron Burr Trial, John Brown Trial, and Tokyo Rose Trial essays; Kathryn Cullen-DuPont, for the *Packard v. Packard, Buck v. Bell, Roe v. Wade,* Anne Hutchinson's Trials, Mary Dyer Trials, *U.S. v. Susan B. Anthony,* The Trials of Alice Paul and Other National Woman's Party Members, *In the Matter of Karen Ann Quinlan,* and Hester Vaughan Trial essays; Teddi DiCanio, for the Alien and Sedition Acts, The "Great Negro Plot" Trial, Major John Andre Trial, and Salem Witchcraft Trials essays; Colin Evans, for the Sirhan Bishara Sirhan Trial, Edith Cavell Trial, *O'Shea v. Parnell and O'Shea, In the Matter of Baby M,* Chicago Seven Trial, Oscar Wilde Trials, Clarence Earl Gideon Trials, Ernesto Miranda Trial, Los Angeles Police Department Officers' Trials, *Bounty* Mutineers Court-Martial, William Calley Court-Martial, Samuel Sheppard Trials,

Angela Davis Trial, Guildford Four Trial, *Titanic* Inquiry, *Silkwood v. Kerr-McGee,* Oliver North Trial, Manuel Noriega Trial, Thomas More Trial, Mary Queen of Scots Trial, Walter Raleigh Trials, Gunpowder Plot Trial, Charles I Trial, Roger Casement Trial, and John Demjanjuk Trial essays; Michael Golay, for the Charlotte Corday Trial, Red Brigades Trial, Joan of Arc Trial, Giordano Bruno Trials, Galileo Galilei Trial, Louis XVI and Marie Antoinette Trials, Alfred Dreyfus Trials, The Moscow Purge Trials, József Cardinal Mindszenty Trial, The Nuremberg Trial, and Klaus Barbie Trial essays; Edward W. Knappman, for the John Peter Zenger Trial and John Thomas Scopes Trial (The "Monkey" Trial) essays; Bernard Ryan Jr., for the Alger Hiss Trials, Trial of Julius and Ethel Rosenberg and Morton Sobell, *Schenck v. U.S. Appeal, Ulysses* Trial, Hollywood Ten Trials, The Scottsboro Trials, Sacco-Vanzetti Trial, Bruno Richard Hauptmann Trial, Baader-Meinhof Trial, O. J. Simpson Trial, The Teapot Dome Trials, Socrates Trial, Martin Luther Trial, Vidkun Quisling Trial, Henri Philippe Pétain and Pierre Laval Trials, Ezra Pound Trial, Jiang Qing and the Gang of Four Trial, Tiananmen Square Dissidents Trial, Tokyo War Crimes Trial, and Adolf Eichmann Trial essays; Tom Smith, for the Alexander II's Assassins Trial, Rosa Luxemburg's Assassins Trial, Indira Gandhi's Assassins Trial, Argentina's "Dirty War" Trial, Jean-Bédel Bokassa Trial, Isabel Perón Trial, Milovan Djilas Trial, Cuban Revolutionary Tribunals, Václav Havel Trials, and Anatoly Shcharansky and Alexandr Ginzburg Trials essays; Eva Weber, for the Archduke Franz Ferdinand's Assassins Trial, Anti-Hitler Conspirators Trial, Assassins of Gandhi Trial, Jomo Kenyatta Trial, The Sharpeville Six Trial, and Nelson Mandela Trial essays; and Janet Bond Wood, for the Leon Trotsky's Assassin Trial and Jesus of Nazareth Trial essays.

Comments and Suggestions

We welcome your comments on this work as well as your suggestions for trials to be featured in future editions of *Courtroom Drama: 120 of the World's Most Notable Trials.* Write: Editors, *Courtroom Drama,* U•X•L, 835 Penobscot Bldg., Detroit, Michigan 48226-4094; Call toll-free: 1-800-877-4253; or fax: (313)877-6348.

Words to Know

Note: References to other defined terms are set in **bold**

A

Abortion: a medical term meaning the termination of a fetus or pregnancy

Accessory after the fact: one who obstructs justice by giving comfort or assistance to the felon (*see* **felony**), knowing that the felon has committed a crime or is sought by authorities in connection with a serious crime

Accessory before the fact: one who aids in the commission of a felony by ordering or encouraging it, but who is not present when the crime is committed

Accomplice: a person who helps another to commit or attempt to commit a crime

Acquit: to find a criminal defendant not guilty

Affirmative action: preferences given to one group over another to ease conditions resulting from past discrimination

Alibi: a Latin term meaning "elsewhere"; a criminal defense which shows that the defendant was unable to commit an act because he or she was at some other place

Alimony: an agreement or court order for support payments to either husband or wife after their marriage has ended

Amicus curiae: a Latin term meaning "friend of the court;" a person or organization not party to the lawsuit who provides the court with information

Annulment: to make void; to wipe out the effect of an action or agreement, such as an annulment of a marriage so that it never existed legally

Anti-Semitism: discrimination against or dislike of Jewish persons

Apartheid: a governmental policy of strict racial discrimination and **segregation**

Appeal: a legal request for a new trial or reversal of conviction

Appellant: a party which appeals a decision or a case to a higher court

Appellate jurisdiction: the power of a higher court or other tribunal to review the judicial actions of a lower court

Appellee: the party opposing the party which appeals a decision or case to a higher court; the opponent of the appellant

Arraignment: the procedure by which a criminal defendant is brought before the trial court and informed of the charges against him or her and the pleas (guilty, not guilty, or **no contest**) he or she may enter in response

Asylum: any place that provides protection or safety

Authoritarian: not questioning authority

B

Bench warrant: an order from the court giving the police or other legal authority the power to arrest an individual

Bigamy: having more than one legal spouse

Brief: a written argument a lawyer uses in representing a client

C

Cartel: an association between countries or other financial interests to fix prices of a resource or product to create a **monopoly**

Change of venue: the removal of a lawsuit from a county or district to another for trial, often permitted in criminal cases where the court finds that the defendant would not receive a fair trial in the first location because of adverse publicity

Circumstantial evidence: indirect evidence which can lead a jury or judge to conclude the existence of a fact by inference

Civil disobedience: breaking a law in order to draw attention to its unfairness

Civil liberties: rights reserved for individuals that are protections from the government

Civil rights: rights that civilized communities give to people by enacting positive laws

Claimant: the party, customarily the **plaintiff,** asserting a right, usually to money or property

Class action: a lawsuit a person brings on behalf of all members in a group sharing a common interest

Clemency: the act, usually by a chief executive such as a president or governor, of forgiving a criminal for his or her actions, as when **pardon** is granted

Co-conspirator: one who engages in a **conspiracy** with others; the acts and declarations of any one conspirator are admissible as evidence against all his or her co-conspirators

Cold war: the period of tense relations, from 1945–1990, between the former Soviet Union (and its Eastern allies) and the United States (and its Western European allies)

Common law: principles and rules established by past judicial decisions

Communism: an economic system in which all property and means of production are owned by the community or society as a whole, and all members of the community or society share in the products of their work

Communist Party: the political party that believes, supports, and advances the principles of **Communism**

Community property: everything acquired by a wife or husband after marriage, except for gifts and inheritances

Commutation: change or substitution, such as when one criminal punishment is substituted for another, more severe one

Compensatory damages: monetary damages the law awards to compensate an injured party solely for the injury sustained because of the action of another

Conspiracy: the agreement of two or more people to jointly commit an unlawful act

Contempt of court: an act that obstructs or attempts to obstruct the administration of justice, such as when someone fails to follow a specific court order

Coroner: a public official who investigates the causes of death

Coroner's inquest: an examination by the coroner, often with the aid of a jury, into the causes of a death occurring under suspicious circumstances

Corpus delicti: proof that a crime has been committed, which ordinarily includes evidence of the criminal act and evidence of who is responsible for its commission

Coup: the sudden, forcible, sometimes violent overthrow of a government

Words to Know

Court of chancery: courts that follow rules of **equity,** or general rules of fairness, rather than strictly formulated **common law;** distinctions between courts of equity and courts of law have essentially disappeared at both the state and federal levels

Cross-examination: questioning a witness, by a party or a lawyer other than the one who is called the witness, about testimony the witness gave on **direct examination**

D

Declarative judgment of relief: a binding decision of the rights and status of parties that does not require any further action or relief

Defamation: speech (**slander**) or writings (**libel**) that damages the reputation of another

Deliberations: any method used to weigh and examine the reasons for and against a verdict, usually by a jury

Deposed: one who is removed from a high office of government

Direct evidence: testimony at trial by a witness who actually heard the words or saw the actions in question

Direct examination: initial questioning of a witness by the lawyer who called him or her

Dissent: a legal opinion of one or more judges in a case who disagree with the legal opinion of the majority of judges; to disagree with

Dissenter: one who voices disagreement with the opinion of the majority

Dissident: one who expresses disagreement with the policies of a government or other ruling authority

Diversity jurisdiction: one basis for granting federal courts the power to hear and determine cases, applicable to cases arising between citizens of different states or between a citizen of the United States and a citizen of a foreign country

DNA: deoxyribonucleic acid; a molecule that appears in all living cells, and is the "building block" of life

Double jeopardy: in criminal law, the Constitutional prohibition against putting a person on trial more than once for the same offense

Due process: relevant only to actions of state or federal governments and their officials; it guarantees procedural fairness when the state deprives an individual of property or liberty

E

Emancipated: freedom from control by another

Equity: legal principle of general fairness and justice

Ex parte: a Latin term meaning "without a party"; a judicial proceeding brought for the benefit of one party without the participation of the opposing party

Excommunicated: one who is expelled from membership in a church by church authority

Executive priviledge: the right of the executive branch to keep matters confidential

Exile: being ordered to leave one's country and being prohibited to return

Expert witness: a witness, such as a psychiatrist or ballistics expert, with special knowledge concerning the subject he or she will testify about

Extenuating circumstances: factors which would reduce a defendant's criminal punishment

Extortion: a criminal offense, usually punished as a felony, consisting of obtaining property from another through use or threat of force, or through illegitimate use of official power

Extradition: the surrender by one state or country of an individual accused or convicted of an offense outside its borders and within those of another state or country

Words to Know

F

Fascism: a system of government (first established by Benito Mussolini in Italy in 1922) usually characterized by one ruling political party led by a strong leader that forcibly holds down any opposition, controls its people very closely, and advocates war

Fascists: individuals who believe, support, and advance the priciples of **fascism**

Felony: high crimes, such as burglary, rape, or homicide, which unlike **misdemeanors,** are often punishable by lengthy jail terms or death

G

Gag order: a court order restricting attorneys and witnesses from talking about or releasing information about a case; also, an order to restrain an unruly defendant who is disrupting his or her trial

Genocide: the intentional and systematic destruction, in whole or in part, of a racial, ethnic, or religious group

Grand jury: traditionally consisting of twenty-three individuals empaneled to determine whether the facts and accusations presented by prosecutors in a criminal proceeding require an **indictment** and trial of the accused

Guardian ad litem: a person appointed by the court to represent the interests of a child or one not possessing legal capacity in legal proceedings

Guerilla: a member of a small military force who make surprise attacks against an enemy army

H

Habeas corpus: a Latin term meaning "you have the body"; a procedure for a judicial ruling on the legality of an individual's custody. It is used in a criminal case to challenge a convict's confinement, and in a civil case to challenge child custody, deportation, and commitment to a mental institution (see **Writ of *habeas corpus***)

Hearsay: a statement, other than one made by a witness at a hearing or trial, offered to prove the truth of a matter asserted at the hearing or trial

House arrest: confinement under guard to quarters other than a prison

Hypocrisy: pretending to be what one is not

I

Immunity: exemption from a duty or penalty; witnesses are often granted immunity from prosecution in order to compel them to respond to questions they might otherwise refuse to answer based on the Fifth Amendment's privilege against self-incrimination

Impeach: to charge a public official with a wrongdoing while in office

Impeachment: criminal proceedings against a public official, such as a president or a supreme court justice, accused of wrongdoing while in office

In re: a Latin term meaning "in the matter of"; used to signify a legal proceeding where there are no adversaries, but merely a matter, such as an estate, requiring judicial action

Indicted: when someone is charged with a crime by a **grand jury**

Indictment: a formal written accusation drawn up by a public prosecuting attorney and issued by a grand jury against a party charged with a crime

Injunction: a judicial remedy requiring a party to cease or refrain from some specified action

Interspousal immunity: a state common law rule, now largely abolished, prohibiting tort actions, or lawsuits concerning certain civil wrongs, between husbands and wives

J

Judicial notice: recognition by a court during trial of certain facts that are so universally acknowledged or easily verifiable (for example, historical facts, geographical features) that they do not require the production of evidence as proof of their existence

Jurisdiction: a court's authority to hear a case

L

Libel: a method of **defamation** expressed by false and malicious publication in print for the purpose of damaging the reputation of another

M

Manslaughter: unlawful killing of another without malice or an intent to cause death. It calls for less severe penalties than murder. Most jurisdictions distinguish between voluntary, or intentional, manslaughter and involuntary manslaughter, such as a death resulting from an automobile accident

Martial law: the law enforced by military forces in substitution for the ordinary government and adminstration of justice when a state of war, rebellion, invasion, or other serious disturbance exists

Martyr: a person who chooses to suffer or die rather than give up his or her faith or principles

Marxism: economic and political philosophy founded by Karl Marx, also known as Socialism

Misdemeanor: any criminal offense less serious than a felony. It is generally punished by a fine or jail (not a penitentiary) and for a shorter period than would be imposed for a felony

Mistrial: a trial terminated and declared void before a verdict is reached because of serious error in procedure or other major problem

Monopoly: an organization, such as a corporation or **cartel,** that has exclusive control of a service or product in a given market

Mutiny: an act of defiance or resistance to a lawful authority, usually by a member or members of one of the armed forces against a higher ranking officer or officers

N

Nationalized: the transfer of ownership or control of land, resources, and industries from private interests to the government

No contest: a type of plea available in a criminal case that does not require a defendant to admit responsibility to the charge, however, the consequences are the same as a guilty plea

O

Opportunism: acting in a way to further one's own interest without any regard to the consequences

P

Pacifist: one who opposes war or the use of force to settle disputes

Pardon: an act, usually of a chief executive such as a president or governor, that relieves a convict from the punishment imposed for his or her crime

Parole: a conditional release of a prisoner after he or she has served part of a sentence

Patriotism: love and loyal support for one's own country

Perjury: the criminal offense of making false statements or lying while under oath

Pernicious: having the power of killing, destroying, or injuring

Plaintiff: the party who initiates a lawsuit, seeking a remedy for an injury to his or her rights

Police power of the state: the power of state and local governments to impose upon private rights restrictions that are necessary to the general public welfare

Precedent: a court decision which serves as a rule for future cases involving similar circumstances

Pro bono: a Latin term meaning "for the good of the people"; when an attorney takes a case without charging a fee

Pro se: a Latin term meaning "for oneself"; representing oneself without an attorney

Prosecution: the act of conducting a lawsuit or criminal case

Prosecutor: a person who handles the **prosecution** of persons accused of crime

Punitive damages: compensation above actual losses awarded to a successful plaintiff who was injured under circumstances involving malicious and willful misconduct on the part of the defendant

R

Reasonable doubt: the degree of certainty required for a juror to find a criminal defendant guilty. Proof of guilt must be so clear that an ordinary person would have no reasonable doubt as to the guilt of the defendant

Redress: to correct or compensate for a fault or injustice

Regime: a political system in power

Repression: strict control of another

Reprieve: a temporary relief or postponement of a criminal punishment or sentence

Republicanism: belief in a republican form of government in which all power rests with the citizens who are entitled to vote, as in the United States

Resistance fighters: members of an organization that secretly work against a government or army in power

S

Sedition: a form of treason consisting of acts intending to overthrow or disrupt the government

Segregation: practice of separating groups of people in housing, public accomadations, and schools based on race, nationality, or religion

Show trial: a trial whose outcome has been decided before it starts

Slander: false and malicious words spoken with the intent to damage another's reputation

Stalemate: any situation making further action impossible; a deadlock

Subpoena: a Latin term meaning "under penalty"; a written order issued by a court authority requiring the appearance of a witness at a judicial proceeding

T

Temporary insanity: a criminal defense which asserts that, because the accused was legally insane at the time the crime was committed, he or she did not have the necessary mental state to commit it, and is therefore not legally responsible

Totalitarian: a government in which one political party or group has complete control and refuses to recognize any other political party or group

Tribunal: an officer or body having authority to judge a case

U

Unanimous: complete agreement

Words to Know

V

Voir dire: a Latin term meaning "to speak the truth"; the examination of possible jurors by lawyers to determine their qualifications to serve

W

Writ of *habeas corpus:* a procedure used in criminal law to bring a petitioning prisoner before the court to determine the legality of his or her confinement (*see* ***Habeas corpus***)

Writ of *mandamus:* an order issued by a court, requiring the performance of some act or duty, or restoring rights and privileges that have been illegally denied

Picture Credits

The photographs and illustrations appearing in *Courtroom Drama: 120 of the World's Most Notable Trials* were received from the following sources:

On the cover, clockwise from upper left: Crowds at the Bruno Richard Hauptmann Trial (**National Archives and Records Administration**); Salem Witchcraft Trials (**The Library of Congress**); John Demjanjuk (**AP/Wide World Photos**). On the back cover: Scottsboro Trial defendant Haywood Patterson (**National Archives and Records Administration**).

United States Supreme Court. Reproduced by permission: 4, 31, 37, 120, 212; **The Library of Congress:** 6, 11, 12, 16, 17, 25, 106, 107, 108, 113, 124, 138, 158, 173, 174, 178, 184, 191, 192, 198, 252, 253, 256, 303, 336, 342, 382, 387, 425, 518, 524, 531, 532, 580, 604, 642, 643, 649, 650, 651, 669, 695, 700, 701, 707, 749; **Utah State Historical Society. Reproduced by permission:** 24; **Reproduced by permission of Elizabeth Frost-Knappman:** 41; **Official White House photo:** 44; **Photograph by Bettye Lane. Reproduced by permission:** 48, 98; **AP/Wide World Photos. Reproduced by permission:** 55, 142, 149, 211, 222, 228, 235, 236, 337, 369, 374, 412, 440, 448, 468, 498, 500, 504, 543, 760, 783, 789, 794, 833; **Illinois State Historical Society. Reproduced by permission:** 72, 406, 407; **Virginia State Library & Archives. Reproduced by permission:** 85; **Mrs. A. T. Newberry. Reproduced by permission:** 86; **Reproduced by permission of Sarah Weddington:** 90; **National Archives and Records Administration:** 114, 197, 298, 324, 328,

**Picture
Credits**

399, 401, 424, 432, 581, 705, 751, 806, 808, 819; **Hearst Newspaper Collection, University of Southern California. Reproduced by permission:** 130; **The Supreme Court Historical Society. Reproduced by permission:** 137; **Massachusetts Art Commission. Reproduced by permission:** 164; **Hulton-Deutsch Collection. Reproduced by permission:** 205, 316, 454, 460, 474, 492, 725, 739, 744, 756, 770, 775, 825, 837; **Connecticut State Police. Reproduced by permission:** 216; **U.S. Department of Justice:** 237; **U.S. Navy Hydrographic Office:** 260; **The Bettmann Archive. Reproduced by permission:** 292; **United States Air Force. Reproduced by permission:** 358; **Georgia Department of Archives and History. Reproduced by permission:** 417; **The Maryland Historical Society. Reproduced by permission:** 514; **Ronald Reagan Library. Reproduced by permission:** 537; **Columbus Ledger-Enquirer. Reproduced by permission:** 594; **Archive Photos, Inc. Reproduced by permission:** 499, 660, 665.

Courtroom
DRAMA

**120 of the World's
Most Notable Trials**

MILITARY TRIALS AND COURTS MARTIAL

Major John Andre Trial: 1780

Defendant: Major John Andre

Crime Charged: Espionage

Board of Enquiry: Fourteen generals of George Washington's staff headed by Major General Nathanael Greene

Place: Tappan, New York

Date of Trial: September 29, 1780

Verdict: Guilty

Sentence: Death by hanging

SIGNIFICANCE: Andre's espionage (spying) was connected to the treason of Benedict Arnold—treason that shook the country.

On October 2, 1780, Major John Andre, a British officer, was hanged for espionage. The men who killed him would have liked instead to hang Andre's co-conspirator, the American General Benedict Arnold.

Arnold was a talented military commander and one of the group of men whom George Washington treated like his own sons. Yet Arnold was good at making enemies. Washington appointed him to command military forces in Philadelphia while he recovered from war wounds, but the greed and ambition Arnold displayed there led to complaints to Congress that he was abusing his power. Papers found later indicated that Arnold was even more dishonest than local authorities suspected at the time.

**MILITARY TRIALS
AND COURTS
MARTIAL**

*An etching of Major
John Andre from an
English textbook.*

Courtroom Drama

Benedict Arnold Court-Martialed

A list of eight charges against Arnold was sent to Congress. A court-martial determined that there was enough evidence to support two of the accusations. Arnold was found guilty of having used public wagons for private purposes and of having improperly issued a pass allowing the ship *Charming Nancy* to leave port when all other vessels were under orders not to do so. Arnold was then sentenced to "receive a reprimand" from General Washington.

Arnold himself asked for a trial. "I ask only for justice," he wrote Washington. He complained about his countrymen's treatment of him after all of his wartime sacrifices, adding that he hoped Washington would not be eventually treated the same way.

General Benedict Arnold, American soldier and traitor.

Arnold Contacts Andre

In the fall of 1779, at the same time he was trying to seek Washington's aid, Arnold began writing secretly to Major John Andre, the head of British intelligence. Arnold offered either to join the British war effort immediately or to "cooperate on some concealed plan with Sir Henry Clinton." Arnold asked to be paid at least 10,000 pounds (British currency) for his "services." Negotiations between Arnold and Andre went on for some time—at one point they broke off entirely.

Arnold Plots to Betray American Forces at West Point

Eventually Arnold was assigned to command the American forces at West Point and the area around it on the Hudson River in New York. He then agreed to hand West Point over to British forces under Clinton. For this treasonous act, he asked to be paid the large sum of 20,000 pounds if successful and 10,000 if not.

To plan the details of the surrender, Arnold and Andre met. Clinton reluctantly agreed to their plan, but he insisted on three conditions: 1) Andre would not go behind enemy lines; 2) Andre would not carry any incriminating documents; and 3) Andre would never wear a disguise, instead remaining in uniform. If Andre were captured, he could not be charged with spying.

On September 20, 1780, Joshua Smith, a friend of Arnold who was loyal to the British, escorted Andre from the British ship, the H.M.S. *Vulture.* The terms of the passes Smith carried allowed only one man to come with him. Colonel Beverly Robinson, who was to accompany Andre, was left behind.

Rather than going to Smith's house as originally planned, Andre and Arnold met six miles up the river, at the foot of Long Clove Mountain. The British were to attack West Point, and the moves of the opposing forces had to be mapped out in advance. Each order Arnold gave his men had to appear reasonable at the time, yet they had to lead ultimately to the loss of the fort.

The Plan Falls Apart

Two farmers had been forced to row Andre across the river to the meeting. Now they refused to take him back when his meeting with Arnold was over. As daylight broke, Arnold and Andre, whose uniform was covered with a cloak, rode to Smith's home, which was located on the Hudson River within sight of the *Vulture.* They passed an American soldier on their way; Andre had crossed enemy lines. Several hours later, any hope of slipping Andre back aboard ship was lost when James Livingston, an American colonel, shelled the British ship. Because it was damaged, the *Vulture* sailed two miles away.

The simplest and safest action for Andre to take would be to ride across enemy lines in his British uniform carrying a flag of truce. Such actions were common, as both sides made frequent attempts to negotiate the exchange of prisoners. But Andre went along with Smith's idea that he switch to civilian clothes. Worse still, Andre carried a map and other incriminating documents.

Before leaving for West Point, Arnold wrote out three passes, one of which allowed Smith to transport Andre across the Hudson. But Smith was unwilling to go out on the river again. Instead, he and Andre rode toward White Plains. A day and a half later, as Andre entered the no-man's-land (land not held by either army) between the American and British lines, Smith left him.

Andre's Capture

A few miles later Andre encountered three Patriot "skinners," or mule drivers. Andre mistook them for Loyalists (people who supported the British) and introduced himself as a British officer "on business of importance." He soon realized his mistake and showed them Arnold's pass made out to John Anderson, the name Andre had used in his letters to Arnold. Andre then tried to threaten the Patriots (people who supported the American government) with warnings that Arnold would be displeased if he were detained. He indicated that his first statement had only been a ploy to protect himself, since some Loyalists had been known to rob enemies from the other side.

The Patriots, John Paulding, David Williams, and Isaac Van Wert, of the New York militia, stripped and searched Andre. They found papers between his stocking and boot. Only Paulding could read and he realized that Andre was a spy. After some talk of delivering Andre into British hands in exchange for money, the men took Andre to the American Lieutenant Colonel John Jameson at North Castle.

Jameson had received orders several days earlier to permit a John Anderson to pass through to West Point to visit Arnold. However, this Anderson was headed in the wrong direction. The handwriting on all the papers, including the pass, was the same. However, Jameson did not know Arnold's handwriting. Andre insisted he be taken to Arnold and Jameson reluctantly agreed. However, without telling Andre, Jameson sent the suspicious documents to General Washington.

Shortly after Andre left under guard, Major Benjamin Tallmadge, the head of Washington's secret service, arrived. Tallmadge convinced Jameson to call back "John Anderson" but failed to convince him to recall the messenger sent to inform Arnold of Anderson's capture. Arnold escaped to the *Vulture* shortly before Washington reached West Point. The

MILITARY TRIALS AND COURTS MARTIAL

incriminating documents caught up with Washington there, and he sent men in pursuit of Arnold. But it was too late.

Andre realized he could no longer pretend to be John Anderson. He wrote to Washington. Without naming Arnold, he stated that he had come, in uniform, to land not held by either army to meet someone who was to give him intelligence information. Andre insisted that his presence behind enemy lines was unplanned and undesired. In effect, he said, he was a prisoner of war and as such had a right to try to escape wearing civilian clothes. This would be his defense at his trial.

Washington also received a letter from Arnold, who said he had acted out of love for his country. He also said his wife had not been involved in his recent actions (although she had plotted with him) and asked Washington to protect her.

Andre's Trial

On September 29, 1780, Washington ordered Andre to be put on trial. Andre's testimony conflicted on a major point with evidence presented in letters from Arnold, Clinton, and Robinson. They all claimed that Andre had traveled to Arnold under a flag of truce. When asked directly, Andre, who did not know about the letters, denied it.

No one believed Andre's argument about being made a prisoner of war subject to Arnold's orders. Historian James Flexner has pointed out: "Had Andre been acting legally, he would have had no need for an assumed name. An officer is not obligated to obey an enemy's orders." However, the presence of a flag would also have been a reason to avoid a judgment of espionage. Andre's conduct brought him respect and sympathy, but the evidence against him was overwhelming. The verdict was unanimous, he was declared an enemy spy and was ordered to be put to death. The next day, Washington approved the verdict and ordered that Andre's execution take place the following day.

Sir Henry Clinton, under a flag of truce, sent a delegation to present the case that Andre was not a spy. Washington delayed the execution. The British produced another letter from Arnold in which he took all the blame. There were threats that if Andre were executed, American prisoners of war might suffer in the same way.

Hints reached Clinton that Andre could be exchanged for Arnold. Although Clinton despised Arnold, and Andre was his favorite aide, he rejected the idea. Arnold, fighting on the side of the British, could not be exchanged as if he were a prisoner. Moreover, returning Arnold to Wash-

BENEDICT ARNOLD: AMERICAN TRAITOR

Benedict Arnold, the indirect cause of Major John Andre's death, had a complicated history. Americans now use his name to mean "traitor." However, he was once a respected military officer. On May 10, 1775, with New Hampshire hero Ethan Allen, he led the force that took the British arsenal (ammunition storehouse) at Fort Ticonderoga. Later, he led a brave but failed attempted to capture Quebec. On April 27, 1777, he defeated the British at Ridgefield, Connecticut. In the fall of 1777, he played a key role in the important victory at Saratoga, New York. During the battle at Saratoga, he was wounded. However, when he was appointed commander of West Point on August 3, 1780, Arnold had already been secretly informing British commander Henry Clinton of General George Washington's movements. After Andre was captured, Arnold fled to a British ship. He was later made a brigadier general in the British army. He conducted raids on American forces in New England and Virginia. After the war, the British government rewarded him with a royal pension and some land in Canada.

ington would defeat the hopes of others who might wish to leave the revolutionary cause and join the British.

Eventually all negotiations fell through and Washington again set a date for Andre's execution. He rejected Andre's appeal for a soldier's death. Instead of facing a firing squad, Andre would be hanged like most other eighteenth-century captured spies. Not to follow this practice would cast doubt on Andre's guilt. If Andre was not a spy, then he was a prisoner of war and should not be executed.

Andre had been unaware that Washington had denied his request. When he saw the gallows, he turned white. Then, asked if he had any last words, he asked those present to "bear me witness that I meet my fate as a brave man." He adjusted his noose himself and pulled a handkerchief over his eyes. He also supplied the handkerchief that was used to tie his arms. When he died, many onlookers wept.

**MILITARY TRIALS
AND COURTS
MARTIAL**

Suggestions for Further Reading

Brown, Richard C. "Three Forgotten Heroes." *American Heritage* (August 1975): 25.

Flexner, James Thomas. *The Traitor and the Spy: Benedict Arnold and John André.* New York: Syracuse University Press, 1991.

Hagman, Harlan L. *Nathan Hale and John André: Reluctant Heroes of the American Revolution.* Empire State Books, 1992.

Hatch, Robert McConnell and Don Higginbotham. *Major John Andre: A Gallant in Spy's Clothing.* Boston: Houghton Mifflin, 1986.

Bounty Mutineers Court-Martial: 1792

Defendants: Thomas Burkett, Michael Byrn, Joseph Coleman, Thomas Ellison, Peter Heywood, Thomas McIntosh, John Millward, James Morrison, William Muspratt, and Charles Norman

Crime Charged: Mutiny

Chief Defense Lawyers: Stephen Barney and Edward Christian

Judge: Court-martial presided over by Lord Alexander Hood

Place: Portsmouth, England

Dates of Court-Martial: September 12–18, 1792

Verdicts: Guilty: Burkett, Ellison, Heywood, Millward, Morrison, and Muspratt. However, Heywood and Morrison were pardoned, and Muspratt's conviction overturned

Sentences: Death

SIGNIFICANCE: Much discussed and much filmed, the mutiny on the *Bounty* is one of history's most often told sea adventure stories.

On December 23, 1787, the *Bounty,* a 215-ton British merchant ship, sailed out of Spithead on the south coast of England, bound for the Pacific. Its mission was to collect breadfruit plants from the Society Islands and take them to the West Indies. It was hoped that once planted in the West Indies, the breadfruit would provide a cheap food source for enslaved people.

Captain Bligh

The master of the *Bounty* was an ambitious thirty-three-year-old lieutenant named William Bligh. Bligh saw this voyage as a chance to advance his career. He had at his command a crew of forty-five, ranging from seasoned officers to civilians forced into service. In a short period of time, Bligh managed to make them all hate him. He did so in a number of ways, but it was primarily due to his terrible temper. At times of stress—which were frequent in the confined space of a ship—Bligh would have angry outbursts. After insulting everyone around, he would flog them (hit them with a whip) to keep them in order.

Captain William Bligh had just completed his triumphant launch voyage in 1790 when this painting was done in London by artist J. Russell.

Floggings took place almost every day. The crew accepted this as a normal part of life, but they would not tolerate hunger. From the beginning, Bligh starved his crew, keeping extra food for himself and blaming the ordinary seamen for the shortages. Those who complained had their already small portions cut in half. Throughout 1788, the crew of the *Bounty* was on the verge of mutiny (revolting against the person in control) as it sailed the Pacific in search of breadfruit plants. By the following spring, the spirits of the crew had sunk to dangerous levels. On the night of April 27, 1789, Bligh accused his second-in-command, Fletcher Christian, of stealing coconuts. Christian was an honest man, and he could not stand this insult. The next day, he and half a dozen crew members seized control of the ship.

They put Bligh and eighteen others in a small boat adrift in the South Pacific. The rest, including men who had played no part in the mutiny, disappeared on the *Bounty*. Six weeks later, after traveling 3,000 miles, Bligh's tiny boat and the majority of its crew reached safety on the island of Timor in what is now Indonesia. Their survival was a miracle, as Bligh pointed out in the report he soon filed. It was harder to explain how only a handful of men were able to take away his authority on the *Bounty*. Bligh stretched the truth by claiming that all but three of the men who remained on the ship had taken part in the mutiny. A ship that was sent from England to arrest the mutineers eventually found ten of them living on the island of Tahiti in the South Pacific. They were returned to England to face charges of mutiny. Fletcher Christian, however, was not among them—neither he nor the *Bounty* could be found.

Best Seller

The distances involved were so great and communication so slow that the court-martial did not begin until three years later in 1792. By then, Bligh (who had been promoted to captain) was sailing in the Pacific and unable to testify. But he had made good use of the time between voyages, and he had written a best-selling account of the mutiny and make himself the hero. When the court-martial aboard the ship, the H.M.S. *Duke,* opened on September 12, the judges did not care what caused the mutiny. They only wanted to know who the mutineers were.

Testimony from numerous crew members soon made it clear that there was no case against Charles Norman, Joseph Coleman, and Thomas McIntosh. Bligh himself had said so in his report. The court was also sympathetic to Michael Byrn, a half-blind Irish fiddler, who had not been able to board the small boat that was set adrift from the *Bounty*.

Less clear was the case of Peter Heywood, who was charged under a law saying that to do nothing during a mutiny is to help the mutineers. William Purcell, who had been cast adrift with Bligh, testified that he had seen Midshipman Heywood standing on deck of the *Bounty*. Heywood, he claimed, appeared to be confused and was holding a sword. When Purcell cried out, "In the name of God, Peter, what do you want with that?" Heywood had dropped the sword. Lieutenant Thomas Hayward told of seeing Heywood unarmed on the deck. Although he "rather supposed [assumed]" that Heywood was on the side of the mutineers, it was clear to him that Heywood was certainly not actively involved.

Crucial evidence came from Lieutenant John Hallet. He had seen Heywood on deck, unarmed, not doing anything, merely "standing still,

looking attentively toward Captain Bligh." Then, said Hallet, Bligh said something to Heywood while Christian stood holding a bayonet to Bligh's chest. Heywood only laughed and turned away. What Hallet did not say was that at the time Bligh had been wearing only a nightshirt and was yelling like a madman. Anyone might have found the situation at least somewhat funny. Now it seemed that a single laugh would condemn Heywood to death. Other witnesses rallied to his cause, however, undoing much of the damage done by Hallet's testimony.

Thomas Burkett, giving evidence on his own behalf, described how Hayward and Hallet pleaded with Christian not to send them away in the boat with Bligh. But the case against Burkett, Thomas Ellison, and John Millward was too strong to be overcome.

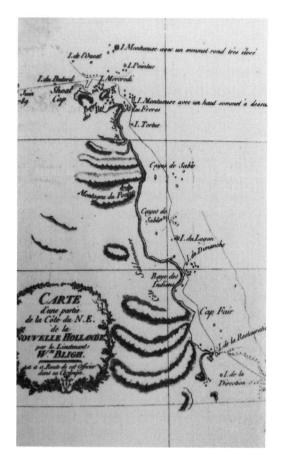

This 1790 map, published in a French translation of Bligh's voyage, tracks the path of his trip within Australia's Great Barrier Reef.

Solo Defense

Most of the defendants received at least some legal assistance. James Morrison, the boatswain's mate, was the only one of the accused who conducted his own defense. A journal he kept while on board the *Bounty* indicates that he was an intelligent man, and the thoughtful manner in which he questioned witnesses made a good impression on the court-martial. Like Heywood, he had done nothing during the revolt, but he was still accused of being among the mutineers. On September 18, 1792, when the

MUTINY AT THE MOVIES

Hollywood has continued to be fascinated by the story of the mutiny on the *Bounty.* In 1935, MGM studios released a film called *Mutiny on the Bounty,* starring Charles Laughton and Clark Gable. It went on to win the Academy Award for Best Picture. Some thirty years later, in 1962, a remake was scheduled with the British director Carol Reed selected to direct. However, Reed was removed from the picture and replaced with Lewis Milestone. This version starred Hollywood legend Marlon Brando. A third remake was supposed to be made in the 1970s, by director David Lean, but financial and studio problems prevented Lean from making the picture. Another version of the story, *The Bounty,* starring Mel Gibson and Anthony Hopkins, was released in 1984.

minutes (record of what is spoken during court proceedings) of the court were read, Peter Heywood, James Morrison, Thomas Ellison, Thomas Burkett, John Millward, and William Muspratt were found guilty and sentenced to death by hanging. The court recommended, however, that Heywood and Morrison be pardoned. As expected, Norman, Coleman, McIntosh, and Byrn were acquitted (found not guilty).

William Muspratt had a final card to play. Prompted by defense lawyer Stephen Barney, he argued that not all of the evidence had been presented. Since all of the prisoners had been tried together and could not give testimony for each other, he had not been able to call Byrn and Norman. Muspratt argued that these two would have supported his case. On October 26, 1792, Heywood and Morrison received the king's pardon, and Muspratt's conviction was overturned. For the other three there was no mercy. On October 29 they were hanged by the neck on the H.M.S. *Brunswick* as boats filled with onlookers crowded Portsmouth Harbor.

The Fate of the *Bounty*

The location of the *Bounty* remained a mystery until 1808, when the American ship *Topaz* stopped at Pitcairn Island in the East Pacific. The crew

**MILITARY TRIALS
AND COURTS
MARTIAL**

of the *Topaz* found a group of English-speaking natives, among them Alexander Smith, who claimed to be the last surviving member of the *Bounty* mutineers. The rest, he said, had either died of natural causes or had been murdered. In 1957, divers confirmed that a wreck found off the coast of Pitcairn Island was indeed the *Bounty*.

The story has one final twist. In 1808, Peter Heywood was walking down Fore Street in Plymouth Dock when he saw a man ahead of him who looked just like his old friend Fletcher Christian. The man, upset about Heywood's obvious interest, took off through the narrow cobbled alleyways, and Heywood lost him. Other reports, too, placed Christian back in England in the early nineteenth century, although there is no clear evidence that any of these claims is true.

Suggestions for Further Reading

McKee, Alexander. *H.M.S. Bounty.* New York: William Morrow, 1962.

McKinney, Sam. *Bligh: A True Account of Mutiny Aboard His Majesty's Ship Bounty.* Rockport, ME: International Marine Publishing Group, 1989.

William Calley Court-Martial: 1970–1971

Defendant: William L. Calley

Crime Charged: Murder

Chief Defense Lawyers: Brookes S. Doyle Jr., Richard B. Kay, George W. Latimer, and Kenneth A. Raby

Chief Prosecutors: Aubrey Daniel and John Partin

Judge: Reid W. Kennedy

Place: Fort Benning, Georgia

Dates of Court-Martial: November 17, 1970–March 29, 1971

Verdict: Guilty

Sentence: Life imprisonment

SIGNIFICANCE: The trial of Lieutenant William Calley for war crimes is unique in American military history. It provides an insight into the horrors of combat and the reaction of ordinary people to extraordinary circumstances.

At first light on the morning of March 16, 1968, 105 soldiers of Charlie Company, a unit of the U.S. Eleventh Light Brigade, moved into the Vietnamese village of My Lai. No one tried to stop them. By midday almost 500 villagers had been massacred. All of the victims were unarmed civilians, among them women, babies, and elderly men. By chance, the scenes of mass slaughter were recorded by an Army cameraman. It was his pictures that revealed the horror of My Lai to the world. An Army inquiry into the incident resulted in charges of murder against several of the soldiers who participated. However, evidence suggested that the majority of

Lieutenant William Calley (far right) and his attorneys leave the Judge Advocate General Building at Fort Benning, Georgia, on October 13, 1970. Calley was charged with the murders of 109 people during the Vietnam Conflict.

the blame for the tragedy rested with a single platoon commander: Lieutenant William Calley.

Court-Martial Opens

When the court-martial began on November 17, 1970, Calley was charged with having murdered 109 "Oriental human beings." The prosecution charged that Calley, breaking the U.S. Military Rules of Engagement, deliberately ordered his men to murder innocent civilians. In presenting his case, chief military prosecutor Aubrey Daniel was frustrated by the reluctance of many soldiers to testify against Calley. Some refused point-blank, citing the Fifth Amendment privilege against self-incrimination (the right not to say anything that could make them look guilty). Perhaps the strangest of these holdouts was Paul Meadlo. He had given a televised interview that, along with the photographs taken by Robert Haeberle, had been responsible for the public anger over the My Lai massacre. However, Meadlo would only agree to testify after Judge Reid Kennedy had ordered him taken into custody and then granted him immunity (freedom from prosecution). Meadlo then told of standing guard over dozens of villagers when Lieutenant Calley arrived. "He [Calley] said, 'How come

they're not dead?' I said, 'I didn't know we were supposed to kill them.' He said, 'I want them dead.' He backed off twenty or thirty feet and started shooting into the people." Meadlo joined him.

"Were you crying?" asked Daniel.

"I imagine I was," replied Meadlo, confirming the statements made by other witnesses that he had tears in his eyes and a rifle in his hands. Between them, Calley and Meadlo gunned down a hundred villagers.

Brutal Action Described

Piece by piece, Daniel painted an almost unimaginable picture of murder, rape, and devastation. He described how Calley tossed a baby into a ditch and shot it, then opened fire with an M-16 rifle, first killing a monk before turning to dozens of villagers hiding in an irrigation canal.

An eyewitness, Dennis Conti, described the bloodbath:

> They [villagers] were pretty much messed-up. I saw the recoil of the rifle and the muzzle flashes and as I looked down, I saw a woman try to get up. As she got up I saw Lt. Calley fire and hit the side of her head.

Other soldiers joined in the madness. One man who had refused to participate in the slaughter, Leonard Gonzalez, told of seeing another soldier herd some women together and order them to remove their clothes. When they refused, the angry soldier fired a single round from his grenade launcher into the group, killing everyone.

Originally the defense claimed that the destruction at My Lai had been caused by helicopters and bombs. Clearly the prosecution witnesses had proven this claim to be untrue. Calley could only fall back on the defense that soldiers have always used: he was acting on orders.

Prompted by civilian attorney George Latimer, Calley told his side of the story. He told of a briefing (meeting where orders are handed out) given one day before the operation by his commanding officer, Captain Ernest Medina. Calley said Medina made it clear that everyone in the village was to be shot. Twenty-one other members of Charlie Company who attended the briefing backed up Calley's story. Others denied that any such order was given. Still more testified that although the order was left unstated, it was clearly intended.

Calley testified:

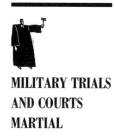

I was ordered to go in there and destroy the enemy. That was my job that day. That was the mission I was given. I did not sit down and think in terms of men, women, and children. They were all classified the same, and that was the classification that we dealt with, just as enemy. . . . I felt then and I still do that I acted as I was directed, and I carried out the orders that I was given and I do not feel wrong in doing so.

Some Refused Orders

But not everyone at My Lai that day blindly followed such terrible orders. Robert Maples told of entering the village and seeing Calley and Meadlo firing into a ditch full of civilians. "[Calley] asked me to use my machine gun."

"What did you say?" Daniel inquired.

"I refused," was the reply.

Another soldier who refused to shoot was James Dursi.

"Did Lt. Calley order you to fire?" asked Daniel.

"Yes, sir."

"Why did you not fire?"

"Because I could not go through with it."

In his final speech to the jury, Daniel said, "The defense would ask you to legalize murder." He then invoked the memory of Abraham Lincoln's order to Union troops during the Civil War: "Men who take up arms against one another in public do not cease on this account to be moral human beings, responsible to one another and to God."

Calley Found Guilty

On March 29, 1971, after almost ninety hours of deliberations (when the jury meets to decide innocence or guilt), the jury of six officers—five of whom had served in Vietnam—found Calley guilty of the premeditated (planned) murder of twenty-two villagers at My Lai.

Next came the sentencing phrase of the trial. Under military law, Calley faced possible execution by hanging. Latimer pleaded for his client's life, saying Calley had been a "good boy until he got into that Oriental situation." Latimer reminded the jurors that they had not had access to the news during the long months of the court-martial. "You'll find there's been no case in the history of military justice that has torn this country apart as this one."

Calley made a plea on his own behalf:

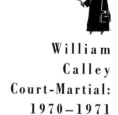
> I'm not going to stand here and plead for my life or my freedom. I've never known a soldier, nor did I ever myself, wantonly kill a human being. . . . Yesterday, you stripped me of all my honor. Please, by your actions that you take here today, don't strip future soldiers of their honor—I beg of you.

Daniel was on his feet immediately, reminding the jury, "You did not strip him of his honor. What he did stripped him of his honor. It is not honor, and never can be considered honor, to kill men, women, and children."

The jury sent Calley to prison for life. Three days later he was freed from the prison in Fort Leavenworth, Kansas, by President Richard Nixon. He was returned to Fort Benning, Georgia, where he was held under house arrest while his case was appealed. On August 20, 1971, his sentence was reduced to twenty years. Calley remained at Fort Benning until February 27, 1974, when he was released on bail. On November 9, 1974, the Army announced that Lieutenant Calley had been freed.

Following his release, Calley remained in Columbus, Georgia, where he became a successful and well respected jeweler in his community.

War Crimes

Four other people were tried for war crimes arising out of the My Lai Massacre. Besides Calley, the most visible one was his commanding officer, Captain Ernest Medina. In August 1971, Medina faced charges of murdering 175 Vietnamese civilians. He was cleared of these charges after a month-long trial. Calley remains the only man ever convicted for what happened on that morning in My Lai.

Nothing in its history had prepared the United States for the shocking slaughter at My Lai. Yet, the nation's initial horror decreased during

**MILITARY TRIALS
AND COURTS
MARTIAL**

INVESTIGATING MY LAI

In the three months before the incident at My Lai, Charlie Company had lost about 100 soldiers. These deaths came from sniper fire and booby traps. The Vietnamese were fighting a guerrilla war. This means that thousands of U.S. troops and advanced weapons were confronted by small groups of Vietnamese hiding in the jungle. U.S. soldiers were taught to consider all Vietnamese dangerous. Vietnamese civilians and soldiers alike were approached carefully by American soldiers. The image of a GI (soldier) setting a village on fire with his cigarette lighter had become famous. One U.S. officer once said: "We had to destroy this village to save it." Thus, even though there were no Vietcong (name for Vietnamese soldiers) in My Lai, nor any signs that the Vietcong were using the village as a base, the civilians there were considered enemies. Only one American tried to intervene in the massacre: a helicopter pilot saw the bodies in the ditch, flew down, and put his helicopter between a group of U.S. soldiers and some Vietnamese children. While rescuing some children, the pilot ordered his crew to shoot any GI who interfered. The army photographer present at the incident was ordered to turn in his camera. However, he had kept a second camera on which he recorded the massacre. A veteran of Charlie Company who had not been at My Lai, Ronald Ridenhour, reported the incident based on rumors he had heard from his fellow soldiers.

Calley's long trial. Many came to view him as a scapegoat (person who is blamed for the mistakes of others), even a hero who had waged war against communism. Time and distance may have dulled the extent of his crimes, but not their historical importance.

Suggestions for Further Reading

Bilton, Michael and Kevin Sim. *Four Hours at My Lai*. New York: Viking Press, 1992.

Goldstein, Joseph, Burkr Marshall, and Jack Schwartz. *The My Lai Massacre and Its Cover-Up.* New York: Free Press, 1976.

Hammer, Richard. *The Court-Martial of Lt. Calley.* New York: Coward, McCann & Geoghegan, 1971.

Unger, Craigt. "William Calley." *People* (November 20, 1989): 152–158.

William
Calley
Court-Martial:
1970 – 1971

RELIGION AND HERESY

Socrates Trial: 399 B.C.

Defendant: Socrates

Crimes Charged: Disbelief in orthodox religion, introduction of strange new divinities, and corruption of the youth

Chief Defense Lawyer: Socrates

Chief Prosecutors: Anytus, Meletus, and Lycon

Judge: The King-Archon of Athens

Place: Athens, Greece

Date of Trial: 399 B.C.

Verdict: Guilty

Sentence: Execution

SIGNIFICANCE: The trial of Socrates provides one of the earliest examples in history of scapegoating (blaming one for the mistakes of others). It also offers a powerful example of courage in the face of death.

In 399 B.C., the philosopher Socrates was seventy years old. He had served as a warrior and as a courtroom judge. His bald head, his stocky figure, and the awkward way he walked were well known throughout Athens. For more than thirty years he had entertained and sometimes irritated people in the marketplace with questions about their souls and their ideals. He was best known among the young. He had devoted much of his life to their education.

Socrates's strongest philosophical influence came from a group known as the Sophists. They were paid teachers of philosophy and rhetoric

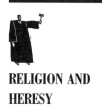
(the art of speaking and writing persuasively) who were skilled in reasoning. Socrates himself did not claim to have these skills. He simply believed, above all, in moral goodness. He could not understand how anyone could see what was right and not do what was right.

Socrates Defies Authority

In 399 B.C., an Athenian jury found Socrates guilty of impiety and corruption of youth. Athenian officials ordered Socrates to kill himself by drinking hemlock, a poison.

Six years earlier, in 406 B.C., Socrates had resisted government orders. At the time, Athens was an independent city-state, governed by a ruling class known as "the Thirty Tyrants." They ordered him and four others to recover an Athenian who had fled the city to escape government brutality. Socrates alone refused to comply, saying he would no longer participate in public affairs. He said that his internal voice, which he called a divine counselor, was telling him to pursue another calling. His mission was to lead a moral revival and establish a scientific basis for it.

By 403 B.C. the Thirty Tyrants had been removed from power. Full democracy and freedom were restored in Athens, but the people remained bitter and angry. Many citizens said that the city had been ruined by people like Socrates, who had contributed to the immorality of the Thirty

Tyrants. A movement to make Socrates a scapegoat for the people's unhappiness began.

Socrates Accused

In 399 B.C. three Athenians brought formal charges against Socrates. The three were led by Anytus, a wealthy leather dealer who had helped restore democracy in Athens. Anytus was unhappy with Socrates's criticisms of the city's politicians. Another accuser was Meletus, a young poet who resented Socrates's criticism of the new generation of Athenian poets. The third was Lycon, an orator (public speaker), who was personally insulted by what Socrates had to say about orators.

Following Athenian law, the accusations against Socrates were taken to the city's governor, known as the king-archon. He then called a hearing to determine whether the case against Socrates was serious enough to go to trial. Meletus prepared the charges, of which there were three. "Socrates is guilty of crime, first, for not worshipping the gods the city worships, and [second] for introducing new divinities of his own; next [third], for corrupting the youth. The penalty due is death."

Athenian Law

Under Athenian law, the rules prohibiting perjury during a trial only outlawed false testimony given by witnesses, not by defendants or prosecutors. They were required to swear they were telling the truth only during the preliminary hearing.

The king-archon found sufficient evidence for a trial to be held before a dikastery (a law court made up of citizen judges). This panel was like a modern jury, only larger. Its size varied from case to case. For the trial of Socrates, the number of judges was reported to have been anywhere from 500 to 567. A majority of historians put the number at 501— an odd number to avoid a final tie vote.

Socrates On Trial

Little would be known today about the trial of Socrates if it were not for a young poet who was one of his followers. The poet, named Plato, attended the trial and afterward wrote his recollection of a series of speeches Socrates made in his own defense. Plato's report on the trial became known as the *Apology*.

RELIGION AND HERESY

Socrates began by describing his call: to convince his fellow citizens of their ignorance and to inspire them. He assured the jury that if he were found not guilty, he would continue his practices. He added that he looked on the possibility of a death sentence without alarm.

To the jury, this defense sounded ridiculous. It violated the ethical and religious principles the restored Athenian democracy was eager to put back into place. A narrow majority of the jury found Socrates guilty on all three charges.

Prison and Execution

While awaiting his death, Socrates met each morning in his cell with his wife, three sons, and friends. He talked with them as he always had. Friends proposed various plans for escape, but Socrates turned them all away. His duty as a citizen, he said, required him to follow the law.

On his last day, the philosopher's friends stayed with him until nightfall. Then the jailer came in, saying the time had come. He handed Socrates a cup of hemlock (poisonous weed). Taking the cup, Socrates said, "What do you say about making a libation [offering] out of this cup to any god? May I, or not?"

The jailer answered, "We only prepare, Socrates, just so much as we [think] enough."

"I understand," Socrates responded. Then he drank the contents of the cup. As his friends stood by weeping, he strolled around the cell, then lay down, covered himself with his cloak, and died.

"Thus died the man," Plato later wrote, "who of all with whom we are acquainted was in death the noblest, in life the wisest and most just."

Suggestions for Further Reading

Brickhouse, Thomas C. and Nicholas D. Smith. *Socrates on Trial.* Princeton, NJ: Princeton University Press, 1989.

Stone, I. F. *The Trial of Socrates.* Boston: Little, Brown and Co., 1988.

Vlastos, Gregory. *Socrates.* Ithaca, NY: Cornell University Press, 1991.

Socrates
Trial:
399 B.C.

Jesus of Nazareth Trial:
A.D. 33

Defendant: Jesus of Nazareth

Crimes Charged: Blasphemy (that he presented himself as the Messiah, the Son of God) and high treason (that he defied the authority of Rome)

Chief Defense Lawyer: None

Chief Prosecutors: The high priests

Judges: Caiaphas (high priest), Pontius Pilate (Roman governor), and in one account, Herod Antipas (ruler of Galilee)

Place: Jerusalem, Judea

Date of Trial: Probably just before the Passover festival, early April A.D. 33 (now regarded as about 26 in the Christian Era)

Verdict: Innocent of any crimes against the Roman state, but guilty of blasphemy

Sentence: Flogging, crucifixion

SIGNIFICANCE: Christianity has been the main religion of the Western world. So the trial and execution of Jesus has provoked historical debates and inspired creative works.

For several years, a young man named Jesus traveled through the regions of Judea and Galilee in the land of Palestine. There he preached his message of a new kingdom of God. He was said to have performed miracles. His activities disturbed the leaders of the Jewish community. They were even more troubled when Jesus made a triumphant entry into the city of Jerusalem on the Sunday before the Passover holiday.

The last straw came when Jesus disrupted the order of the Great Temple. He charged that the money changers and animal sellers there made the temple a "den of robbers." He then threw chairs and tables about and drove away all those involved in commercial activity. The Sadducees (SAD-jew-sees), high Jewish priests who controlled the Temple, were outraged. The activities Jesus objected to fell within Jewish tradition. Only the attentive crowd that had gathered around Jesus in the Temple prevented the priests from stoning him to death on the spot. They would not forget his defiant act.

Priests Take Revenge

Jesus rebelled against organized Judaism. On the strength of his own personal authority, he wanted to deliver a new message about God. To the old priests, he was only a carpenter's son from Galilee. He challenged their authority, as well as that of their religious laws.

Jesus's defiance was especially irritating to the Pharisees, highly devout Jews. Their strict laws regulated every aspect of life, including fasting, hand washing, and working on the Sabbath. Even before the incident in the Temple, Jesus broke these laws. He healed the sick on the Sabbath,

This sixth-century mosaic (from the basilica of Sant' Apolinaire Nouvo in Ravenna, Italy) shows Jesus of Nazareth standing before Pilate as a riotous crowd gathers around him.

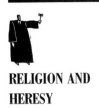

RELIGION AND HERESY

and he did not wash his hands before meals. He also pardoned people's sins, something the Pharisees said only God could do. Some said he claimed to have brought the dead back to life. Worst of all, there were rumors that he called himself the Messiah. Something needed to be done. The supreme court of chief priests and other important religious leaders, called the Sanhedrin, decided that Jesus had to be arrested and tried.

Jesus On Trial

The priests paid Judas, one of Jesus's disciples, thirty pieces of silver to lead them to him. On a night before the Jewish festival of Passover, they arrested him. Jesus was praying in the garden of Gethsemane when Judas, along with several priests and Pharisees, approached him. Judas then kissed Jesus to point out to the others who Jesus was. Immediately, Jesus was arrested and taken to the house of Caiaphas, a high priest, who lived in Jerusalem.

Under Jewish law, the Sanhedrin were not supposed to conduct trials in private homes, or at night, or during Passover. Nevertheless, Jesus was tried that night. He was accused of boasting that he would destroy the Temple and then rebuild it. Evidence of other blasphemies was presented. The priests, however, could find no witnesses to testify truthfully as to Jesus's acts.

Then Caiaphas questioned Jesus: "I put you under oath before the living God; tell us if you are the Messiah, the Son of God."

Jesus responded, "You have said so. But I tell you, from now on you will see the Son of Man seated at the right hand of Power and coming on the clouds of heaven."

Caiaphas, very excited, said, "He has blasphemed! Why do we still need witnesses? You have now heard his blasphemy. What is your verdict?"

The Sanhedrin responded, "He deserves death."

In the morning the Sanhedrin again met to conduct a legal trial. Some authorities say the Sanhedrin did not have the power to carry out a death sentence because Palestine was under Roman rule. Others say the Sanhedrin could put a Jew to death by stoning, but that they could not agree about Jesus's guilt. Whatever the reason, Jesus was taken the next morning to Pontius Pilate, the Roman governor of Judea.

The chief priests told Pilate, "We found this man perverting our nation, forbidding us to pay taxes to the emperor and saying that he himself is the Messiah, a king."

*The trial of Jesus
before Pilate
(Illumination from
the sixth-century
Rossano Gospels).*

Pilate asked Jesus, "Are you the King of the Jews?"

"You say so," was Jesus's only response. He would not respond to
the other charges the priests made against him when Pilate asked about
them. His refusal to cooperate with this representative of the Roman emperor amazed Pilate.

Pilate told those gathered around that he saw no basis in Roman
law for prosecuting Jesus. But the chief priests insisted: "He stirs up
people by teaching throughout Judea and Galilee, where he came from
originally."

Pilate did not want to make a decision. When he heard that Jesus was from Galilee, he sent the prisoner to be examined by Herod Antipas, the Roman ruler of Galilee, who also happened to be in Jerusalem.

Herod had heard of Jesus and was excited to meet him. He hoped, in fact, to be entertained by some miracles. Jesus, however, refused to answer any of Herod's questions. After Herod and his guards belittled him, Jesus was returned to Pilate.

Jesus Crucified

With the fate of Jesus back in his hands, Pilate rendered his judgment: "You brought me this man as one who was perverting the people, and here I have examined him in your presence and have not found this man guilty of any of your charges against him. Neither has Herod, for he sent him back to us. Indeed, he has done nothing to deserve death. I will therefore have him flogged and release him."

The priests would not accept such easy treatment of Jesus. As it was the custom for the Roman rulers to release a prisoner during the Passover festival, Pilate then asked a crowd gathered outside, "Whom do you want me to release for you—Barabbas or Jesus of Nazareth?" The priests had already convinced the crowd that it should choose Barabbas, who had been found guilty of treason and murder. When Pilate asked, "Then what should I do with Jesus?" the crowd responded, "Let him be crucified!"

Pilate had concluded that Jesus was not guilty of any crime against Rome. He was, however, less concerned about justice than about keeping the peace in Jerusalem. Fearing the crowd might riot if he did not crucify Jesus, he washed his hands in a bowl of water as the crowd looked on. "I am innocent of this man's blood; see to it yourselves," he said.

Pilate had Jesus flogged (beaten), as was the tradition before a death sentence was carried out. Jesus was then turned over to Roman soldiers to carry out the crucifixion. The crucifixion took place at a place called Golgotha (called Calvary in the Latin version of the New Testament). On Jesus's cross was written, "This is Jesus, King of the Jews." The soldiers gambled for the dying man's clothing, then left his body to be taken away by his followers.

The trial of Jesus went unnoticed in the official records of the time. But it was set down in the Four Gospels: the New Testament books of Matthew, Mark, Luke, and John. Although the details differ from one account to the next, all tell essentially the same story, one that has inspired people across the centuries.

THE LAST SUPPER

The Jewish holiday of Passover traditionally begins at sunset and lasts for the next eight days. Thus the "Last Supper" that Jesus attended with his disciples is actually a Passover seder (SAY-der). A seder is a Jewish ceremony. In it the story of Moses leading the Jews out of Egypt is traditionally told and retold. This way Jews will remember their story of liberation (gaining freedom) and their commitment to the Ten Commandments, which Moses is supposed to have brought from God after the Jews left Egypt. At the seder, people eat matzo (unleavened bread). They do this to to remember the bread that the Jews took out of Egypt before it had time to rise. It is also traditional to drink four cups of wine. According to the gospels, at the seder, Jesus offered bread and wine to his disciples, saying that they represented his body and his blood. Thus he began the Christian ritual of communion.

Suggestions for Further Reading

Brown, Raymond E. *The Death of the Messiah*. Vols. I and II, The Anchor Bible Reference Library. New York: Doubleday, 1994.

Reader's Digest. *Jesus and His Times*. Pleasantville, NY: The Reader's Digest Association, 1987.

Watson, Alan. *The Trial of Jesus*. Athens: The University of Georgia Press, 1995.

Joan of Arc Trial: 1431

Defendant: Joan of Arc

Crimes Charged: Heresy (opinions that defied church authority) and male dress

Chief Defense Lawyers: None

Chief Prosecutor: Pierre Cauchon, bishop of Beauvais

Judge: Cauchon and his tribunal

Place: Rouen, France

Dates of Trial: January 9–March 17, 1431

Verdict: Guilty

Sentence: Death by burning at the stake

SIGNIFICANCE: Joan's trial and martyrdom (suffering or death on account of adhering to a cause) made her a hero. In life and in death, she helped create the modern French nation.

Joan of Arc began hearing voices when she was thirteen years old. From out of a dazzling light came this command: "Joan, be a good and dutiful child; go often to church." She obeyed the command. But even before she heard the voice, Joan had been a devout and obedient girl. Near the end of her life, a peasant testified that she had nursed the sick and given money to the poor. "I know it for certain," he said. "I was a child then, and she took care of me."

Joan was born in 1412 or 1413 (the historical record is uncertain) in the village of Domrémy in the Lorraine region of northeastern France. She was the third daughter of Jacques Darc (or d'Arc), a peasant, and his wife,

Isabelle Romée. Domrémy had suffered much during the long struggle of the Hundred Years' War (1337–1453). When Joan was fifteen years old, her family was forced to flee when their village was threatened by an unfriendly army. When they returned, they found the village ransacked, the church burned, storehouses looted, and livestock and crops stolen or destroyed.

The Hundred Years' War began in 1337, when the English king, Edward III, claimed the throne of France. His successors did the same. King Henry V led the English in their decisive victory over the French at the Battle of Agincourt in 1415. Then he named his heir, Henry VI, as the future king of England and France. By 1429, the English and their French allies held much of northern France, and English troops were attacking to the city of Orléans on the River Loire. Orléans was the key to the lands still under the control of the dauphin (eldest son of king of France) Charles VII, an uncle of Henry VI, who also claimed the French crown.

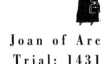
"The Maid of Orléans"

In 1429 Joan began to hear voices again. This time Saint Catherine, Saint Margaret, and the archangel Michael (who symbolized French resistance

In a scene from the Vigils of Charles VII, Joan chases out camp followers.

RELIGION AND HERESY

to the English) spoke to her. "Joan, go thou to the assistance of the king of France, and thou shalt restore his kingdom to him." The eighteen-year-old Joan had found her life mission: she would become a soldier.

Joan traveled to the fortress town of Vaucouleurs in February 1429. There she persuaded the local leader, Robert de Baudricourt, to provide her with an escort to the city of Chinon, where Charles VII held court. She arrived in Chinon dressed in men's clothing, in the company of a half dozen men-at-arms. Charles' council debated two days before allowing her to see him. Some of these councilors suspected her of sorcery (black magic). A group of religious thinkers examined her and asked for proof that her visions were a sign from heaven or a miracle. "My sign will be to raise the siege

(attack) of Orléans," Joan answered. She then told Charles it was his destiny to be crowned king of France in the cathedral in the city of Reims.

Legend has it that Joan wore white armor and rode a black horse as she set out for Orléans. The English forces there had become so weakened over the previous winter that it would not have taken a miracle to defeat them. Still, Joan's leadership had everything to do with the outcome of the French attack. By May 8, the battle had finished and the English driven off. Joan was then referred to as "The Maid of Orléans." Charles

Notice the pen drawing of Joan of Arc in the upper left margin of this page of official history. Published on May 14, 1429, it shows the blockade of Orléans and the lifting of the siege. French artist Clement de Fauquemberge created this image—the only known drawing of Joan done during her lifetime.

ops treffort reaussairut.

*Soldiers capture
Joan of Arc.*

reached Reims on July 15, and on July 17 he was crowned just as Joan had predicted.

The English regrouped and made arrangements to crown Henry VI as king of France. Meanwhile, Joan commanded a failed assault on the English troops occupying Paris. Her relationship with Charles began to suffer. Without his blessing, Joan led a party to the defense of Compiègne. She was captured in battle there on May 23, 1430, and handed over to the English. They decided to put her on trial as a sorceress in order to prove that Charles VII had gained his throne through witchcraft.

**RELIGION AND
HERESY**

The Trial

Joan's trial opened in the city of Rouen on January 9, 1431. Pierre Cauchon, the bishop of Beauvais, presided. He was assisted by one of the leaders of the Inquisition, an infamous Roman Catholic tribunal (court) responsible for persecuting thousands. From the beginning, Cauchon seemed to understand that a charge of witchcraft would not work. It was quietly changed to heresy. As the trial progressed, it became clear that the main issues were the voices Joan had heard and the men's clothing she had worn.

A long line of religious leaders and lawyers, sometimes as many as seventy at a time, interrogated Joan. She remained firm in her belief that the voices were real and of divine origin. She also refused to give up the men's clothing she had. At one point, the examiners questioned her closely about her virginity, hinting that she had not really been a military leader but only lived with the soldiers. The judges asked, too, if she had used charms to protect herself in battle. And they accused her of being unnatural in her insistence on wearing men's clothes.

Just as the English wanted to expose Charles as a false king, so the church leaders wanted to punish Joan for her apparent defiance of their authority. Throughout the trial, she insisted on putting her own conscience first. She insisted that those things that had been revealed to her through the visions were true, despite what the church said. In one of the early interrogation sessions, she challenged Cauchon: "You tell me you are my judge; ponder with great care over what you mean to do, for in very truth I was sent of God, and you are putting yourself in great jeopardy."

The examiners continued to claim that since the church had not certified the voices and visions, and they were therefore not genuine. Joan responded: "I came to the king of France sent by God, by the Virgin, by the saints and the Church *victorious* above; to *that* Church do I submit myself, my works, all I have done, all I have still to do."

"And the Church *militant?*" the judges persisted.

"I shall answer nothing further at this time."

Joan grew impatient with some of their other questions. The examiners wanted to know if Saint Michael appeared to her naked or clothed.

"Do you think," she answered, "our Lord did not have the wherewithal to clothe him?"

On another occasion, they wanted to know whether God hated the English.

"Whether He loves them or hates them and what He proposes to do with their souls, I know not; but this I know for certain, that all of them will be thrown out of France, except those who perish there."

After a while, the interrogations were moved from the public rooms at Rouen Castle to Joan's prison cell, where secret sessions were held. The final cross-examination was held on March 17. Cauchon might have believed then that he had enough evidence to prove that Joan was a heretic (one who commits heresy), but the Rouen legal experts were not convinced. Early in the case one of them, Master John Lohier, drew up a long list of legal errors that he believed should have canceled the entire trial. "This is a trial to impugn [attack] the honor of the prince whose cause this girl is supporting; you should frankly say so, and you should have a counsel appointed for her," he advised. But because this was in part a political trial intended to undermine Charles, Cauchon knew he could ignore the lawyers.

The Verdict

The tribunal convicted Joan of heresy and of wearing men's clothes. At the insistence of the English, her judges then tried to make Joan take back her own testimony as a means of undermining Charles and his claim on the French throne. She was tortured and threatened with burning. Finally, she agreed to sign a document taking back her testimony. In return, she was assured that she would be delivered to the church by the hated English who held her.

In fact, her sentence turned out to be life in an English prison. Within a few days, Joan took back her retraction, resumed male dress, and announced that the saints had again spoken to her. In doing so, she permitted the tribunal to convict her as a heretic to be burned at the stake.

On May 30, 1431, now clothed in a woman's long dress, she was taken in a cart to the Old Market Place in Rouen. An enormous pyre (pile of material to be burned) had been built there, and she was placed on top of it. The executioner lit the fire. A witness known only as the Bourgeois de Paris left this account of what happened next:

> She was soon dead and her clothes all burned. Then
> the fire was raked back, and her naked body shown
> to all the people and all the secrets that could or
> should belong to a woman, to take away any doubts
> from the people's minds. When they had stared long

RELIGION AND HERESY

THE MAID ON STAGE

Many playwrights have been inspired by the story of the Maid of Orléans and her amazing accomplishments. The Irish playwright George Bernard Shaw wrote *Saint Joan.* He wrote in his preface: "She is the most notable Warrior Saint in the Christian calendar [listing of saints], and the queerest fish among the eccentric [odd] worthies of the Middle Ages. As her actual condition was pure upstart, there were only two opinions about her. One was that she was miraculous. The other that she was unbearable." The French playwright Jean Anouilh (ah-NOO-ee) also wrote a story of Joan, called *The Lark.* Both Shaw and Anouilh wrote sympathetically of Joan; however, in *Henry VI, Part I,* the English playwright William Shakespeare portrayed her as a witch who achieves her military triumphs by means of fiends and demons who finally deserted her.

enough at her dead body bound to the stake, the executioner got a big fire going again round her poor carcass, which was soon burned, both flesh and bone reduced to ashes.

Someone claimed that just before the end a dove flew out of Joan's mouth. When the embers cooled, her ashes were scattered on the River Seine. The heresy charge did not hold up over time. Only twenty-five years after Joan's execution, the charge was removed by a decree issued by the pope. In 1920, Pope Benedict XV proclaimed Joan of Arc a saint.

Suggestions for Further Reading

Brooks, Polly Schoyer. *Beyond the Myth: The Story of Joan of Arc.* New York: J. P. Lippincott, 1990.

Gies, Frances. *Joan of Arc: The Legend and the Reality.* New York: Harper & Row, 1981.

Warner, Marina. *Joan of Arc: The Image of Female Heroism.* New York: Alfred A. Knopf, 1981.

Martin Luther Trial: 1521

Defendant: Martin Luther

Crime Charged: Heresy (opinions that defied church authority)

Chief Defense Lawyer: Jerome Schurf

Chief Prosecutor: The Archbishop of Trier

Judge: Emperor Charles V

Place: Worms, Germany

Dates of Trial: April 17–18, 1521

Verdict: Guilty

Sentence: Excommunication and ban of Empire

SIGNIFICANCE: Luther's defiance of Papal authority immeasurably advanced the cause of the Protestant Reformation.

In sixteenth century Europe, the Roman Catholic Church sold "indulgences." These supposedly allowed people to free their souls from purgatory (a place of temporary punishment after death). Actually, they were a means of raising money. Martin Luther was a monk in the Augustinian order. He was a preacher and scholar at the university in the Germany town of Wittenberg. Luther disliked selling indulgences. In 1517, the pope's representative began to sell them in Germany. He was trying to rebuild St. Peter's cathedral in Rome. Luther rebelled.

The Ninety-Five Theses

Luther quickly wrote out ninety-five theses (arguments) attacking the sales and other forms of corruption in the Catholic Church. He also chal-

lenged the authority of priests to grant the forgiveness of sins. "Doesn't it disturb you," he wrote a friend, "that Christ's unfortunate people are tormented and fooled by indulgences?" On October 31, he nailed his ninety-five theses to the door of the church.

Challenges to church corruption were fairly common in the early part of the sixteenth century. Luther found many allies (supporters) among his Augustinian brothers. Still, to question a church practice or the supreme authority of the pope was dangerous.

German reformer Martin Luther was found guilty of heresy in Worms, Germany, on April 18, 1521.

The Response

The papal authority in Rome did not take Luther seriously at first. By the summer of 1518, however, complaints had begun to reach Pope Leo X. The dispute was part of a larger struggle. Church reformers opposed defenders of the traditional way of doing things. The poor hated the rich. Germany resented Rome. The pope formally charged Luther with heresy, or contradicting a traditional belief. A church official, Sylvester Prierias, prepared an answer to the ninety-five arguments.

Prierias wrote the pope was "the oracle of God." He asserted that the authority of the church was more powerful than that of even the holy scriptures. It attacked Luther directly, calling him "a leper and a loathsome fellow."

On August 7, 1518, Luther received this response as well as a command to appear in Rome. He asked, instead, that his supporters work to have his case tried in Germany. Rome agreed, and he was ordered to appear in Augsburg for a hearing before Thomas de Vio Cajetan.

Cajetan, himself a church reformer, agreed with many of the arguments Luther had set down in the ninety-five theses. Still, church authority had to be upheld. Cajetan made it clear that Luther had been summoned to Augsburg to recant (take back) his objections, not to debate them. The two met three times in mid-October.

"He [Cajetan] promises to handle everything leniently and in a fatherly way," Luther wrote a supporter. "He continually repeated one thing: recant, acknowledge that you are wrong; that is the way the Pope wants it and not otherwise whether you like it or not."

However, Luther was committed to his beliefs. He denied the necessity of having a priest act as a go-between for man and God. And faith alone, he believed, was the way to achieve salvation. He increased his attack on the pope's authority. In 1519, he publicly denied the pope's supremacy.

Rome did not want to anger the Germans, so it acted cautiously and quietly. Cajetan continued to hope that the Germans themselves would move against Luther. Yet the ruler of Luther's home province, Saxony, backed Luther and refused to surrender him to Rome. For more than a year, matters were at a standstill.

The Message Travels

Luther published his opinions widely in 1519, and his influence increased. New editions of his work appeared. Inspired, even possessed, Luther worked himself into a state of near exhaustion. "God is pushing me—he drives me on, rather than leading," he wrote to his Augustinian mentor, Johann Staupitz. "I cannot control my own life. I long to be quiet but am driven to the middle of the storm." In March 1520, he wrote, "Confidentially, I do not know whether the Pope is the Antichrist himself or whether he is his apostle, so miserably is Christ corrupted and crucified by the Pope."

The Vatican in Rome reopened the case against Luther in January 1520. Matters came to a head that year when Luther published three new arguments. One invited the German princes, including Luther's protector, Frederick III, to take church reform into their own hands. A second attacked aspects of the Mass, such as the religious service. It criticized church doctrine that during church services, common bread and wine were transformed into the body and blood of Christ. The third proclaimed that

RELIGION AND HERESY

faith freed Christians from the doctrine of good works, which held that man could somehow earn God's grace.

On June 1, the cardinals formally approved a papal decree declaring that Luther was a heretic (one who is guilty of heresy). Forty-one of the ninety-five theses were condemned, and Luther was given sixty days to retract them or be excommunicated (banned) from the church.

On September 6, Luther petitioned the pope for a hearing. In late September, papal authorities posted the papal decree in public places all over Germany. Luther's supporters tore it down and burned it. Luther himself treated it with contempt.

On December 10, 1520, having failed to recant, Luther was declared a heretic. In the German towns of Cologne and Louvain, conservatives made bonfires of his books. Still in many other towns, Luther's supporters burned papal books.

The Trial

Frederick continued to protect Luther. The prince told the pope's messengers that Luther should be allowed to appear before an independent tribunal, as he had offered to do. And, Frederick declared, Rome should use the scriptures to demonstrate exactly how Luther was wrong.

Early in 1521, Charles V, the secular ruler of the Holy Roman Empire that included Germany, summoned Luther to appear before the diet (the formal assembly) of German leaders meeting in the city of Worms. Luther reached Worms on April 16, after a long journey, much of it made on foot. An order awaited him to appear before the emperor, the archbishop of Trier, and other high officials at 4 P.M. the next day. Dressed in the clothing of an Augustinian monk, Luther went to the imperial chambers, accompanied by a Wittenberg lawyer, Jerome Schurf.

Luther began by saying that he stood ready to be shown where he was wrong. Motioning towards a stack of books, one of the archbishop's men asked Luther whether he had written them. If so, was Luther prepared to disavow them? Luther asked for twenty-four hours to consider the question. Charles granted his request.

The hearing resumed the next day, April 18, in a hot, overcrowded palace chamber. Luther, who had been ill, broke out in a soaking sweat, but his nerves and voice were steady. He apologized for any offense he might have given. Yes, he admitted, he had written the books in question. They could be taken altogether as an attack "against some private and (as they say) distinguished individuals—those, namely, who strive to preserve the Roman tyranny and to destroy the godliness which I teach."

The archbishop's representative, Johann von Eck, laid out the church's unanswerable case against heresy. "What the doctors have discussed as doctrine, the church has defined as its judgment, the faith in which our fathers and ancestors confidently died and as a legacy have transmitted to us," Von Eck reminded the court. "We are forbidden to argue about this faith by the law of both pontiff and emperor. Both are going to judge those who with headlong rashness refuse to submit to the decisions of the Church."

Luther replied plainly. "Unless I am convinced by the testimony of the scriptures or by clear reason, I am bound by the scriptures I have quoted and my conscience is captive to the word of God. I cannot and I will not retract anything. Here I stand, may God help me, Amen."

Martin
Luther
Trial: 1521

The Outcome

The emperor left to prepare a statement to deliver to the diet the next day, April 19. "I am determined to proceed against him as a notorious heretic,"

*Martin Luther,
shortly before his
death on February
18, 1546.*

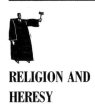

THE PROTESTANT REFORMATION

Martin Luther's criticism of the Catholic Church was the beginning of a long process known as the Reformation. As the name suggests, the Reformation originally began as a movement to reform the Catholic Church. By the time of Luther's excommunication, however, protestors had moved from dissenting within the Catholic Church to developing new forms of Christianity. These came to be known as Protestant denominations. Besides the Lutherans of Germany and Scandinavia, Protestants included the followers of John Calvin in Geneva, Switzerland. Followers of Calvin included the French Huguenots and much later, the English Puritans, many of whom eventually came to America. In England, meanwhile, King Henry VIII broke from the Catholic Church in 1534, when he issued the Act of Supremacy. This created a new national church—the Church of England—headed by the king rather than the pope. Although Protestant religions differ from one another, all are characterized by the belief that individuals can communicate directly with God. They need no interpretation, intervention, or authorization by a church.

Charles announced. He directed the diet to do its duty and get on with the punishment. The members of the diet, in order to avoid a confrontation with their emperor, reluctantly approved the Edict of Worms, the document formally condemning Luther.

There was, in the end, no punishment to speak of, because Luther had become too powerful. No German would hand him over to Rome. Leaving Worms, he conspired in his own kidnapping. Friends took him away to Wartburg Castle for safekeeping. There he continued to defy church authority.

"I thought his Imperial Majesty would have got together one or fifty scholars and overcome this monk in a straightforward manner," he wrote. "But all that happened was this: Are these your books? Yes. Do you want to renounce them or not? No. Then go away!"

Luther went on with his work. In Wartburg, he began his translation of the Bible into German. Back in Wittenberg in 1522, he continued to attack traditional church practices. He left his order in 1524. The following year, he married.

Luther's teachings spread rapidly through Germany and beyond. By the close of the sixteenth century, fifty years after Luther's death, two-thirds of the German population had become Lutherans. In Scandinavia, the faith built on the great heretic's beliefs became the official state religion.

Martin Luther Trial: 1521

Suggestions for Further Reading

Bainton, Roland Herbert. *Here I Stand: A Life of Martin Luther.* Nashville, TN: Abbington Press, 1990.

Kittelson, James M. *Luther the Reformer: The Story of the Man and His Career.* Minneapolis, MN: Augsburg Press, 1986.

Todd, John M. *Luther: A Life.* New York: Crossroad Publishing Company, 1982.

Giordano Bruno Trials: 1592–1600

Defendant: Giordano Bruno
Crime Charged: Heresy (opinions that defied church authority)
Defense Lawyer: None
Prosecutor: The Holy Office of the Inquisition
Judges: The Cardinal General Inquisitors
Places: Venice and Rome, Italy
Dates: May 26, 1592–February 8, 1600
Verdict: Guilty
Sentence: Burning at the stake

SIGNIFICANCE: The Catholic Inquisition fought against the spread of the Protestant Reformation in sixteenth-century Europe. Those who did not agree with the Inquisition were forced to give up their beliefs or be punished. With the prosecution of Bruno, the Inquisitors showed how far they would go to defend the official faith.

Giordano Bruno was a traveling teacher who lived in sixteenth-century Italy. The established churches resented him, for he was not under their control. The Catholic officials in Rome, in particular, became his enemies. They were trying to fight the growth of Protestantism, and Bruno got in their way.

Today, Bruno would be considerd an appealing person. His ideas were all-embracing and poetic. They influenced those who came after him. The seventeenth-century philosophers Baruch Spinoza and Gottfried Leibnitz

A young Giordano Bruno.

adopted them. The twentieth-century Irish novelist James Joyce paid Bruno tribute in the essay "The Nolan" and in his novel *Finnegans Wake.* Many of Bruno's contemporaries (people who lived at the same time), however, thought him dangerous for his beliefs.

Bruno was born in Nola, Italy, in 1548. As a youth, he joined the Dominican order of monks. He became a priest in 1572. Four years later he left the Dominicans and fled Italy. He was in danger of being prosecuted for heresy. From then on he felt religion helped authorities to control ignorant people.

Bruno went to Geneva, Switzerland, first, where he joined the Calvinists. They were followers of the French Protestant reformer John Calvin, who believed that man lacked free will. The Calvinists, though, also found Bruno's beliefs intolerable. So Bruno moved on to Paris. Not liking the religious conditions there, he went to London.

Homeward Bound

In England, Bruno came to believe that humans were not the center of the universe. He developed this idea by reading the work of the Polish astronomer Nicholas Copernicus. Bruno also pursued his interest in magic.

Once again, however, Bruno angered authorities. This time his opponents were the philosophers at Oxford University. They opposed the ideas of Copernicus. They drove Bruno out of England in 1585. He first

Giordan Bruno was
found guilty of
heresy on February
8, 1600, and was
burned at the stake
eleven days later.

returned to Paris, then went to Germany. He lived in a number of towns, including Wittenburg. This was the home of the founder of Protestantism, Martin Luther. Bruno even adopted the Lutheran faith for a time. But in the end, Bruno found Luther's version of the Christian religion just as restricting as the pope's. For their part, the Lutherans could not accept Bruno's pantheism (equating God with the universe). Just as the Calvinists had done in Geneva, the Lutherans drove Bruno out of Germany.

"I dislike unanimity [unity in opinion] and I hate commonality," Bruno wrote in an attempt to explain why he was unable to stay out of trouble. "I am suspicious of majorities. It [God] is the One which wins my love; the One that gives me freedom in my bondage, peace in my torment, wealth in my poverty, life in my death."

Bruno next took a job as a tutor in Venice, Italy, in mid-1591. The offices of the Catholic Church in Venice remained independent from Rome. For that reason, Bruno hoped he would be safe in Venice. But he quarreled with his Venetian host and chief pupil, Zuane Mocenigo. Mocenigo told the Inquisition in Rome (the church organization responsible for punishing heretics) that Bruno was a former priest who was now a nonbeliever.

So Bruno, now forty-four years old, began eight years of interrogation, trial, and imprisonment.

The Trials

The hearings opened May 26, 1592. Two booksellers who had known Bruno in Germany testified. The first said that the publishers in the German city of Frankfurt regarded Bruno as "a man of no religion." The second, who had gone to Bruno's lectures, said that he had never heard the defendant say anything that did not conform with church teachings.

The third witness was Jacob Britano, who had known Bruno in Frankfurt, in Venice, and in Zurich, Switzerland. Britano testified: "The Prior [officer of a religious house] of the Convent in Frankfurt told me that Bruno was mainly occupied in writing and devising foolishness and astrology and seeking new things. The Prior said he had a fine talent as a man of letters, was a 'universal' man. The Prior believed that he had no religion, for he said Giordano declares that he knows more than the Apostles knew and that he would have dared, had he so desired, to bring about that the whole world should be of one religion."

The inquisitors cross-examined Bruno about every aspect of his life and thought. They were especially interested in Bruno's ideas about the

Holy Trinity—God, Christ, and the Holy Ghost combined into one being. Bruno admitted that he did not regard the three as entirely separate entities. "But in fact," he insisted, "I never wrote or taught this, but merely doubted." In any case, he said, he had not intended to challenge accepted religion. He wrote only to express his own ideas and test others.

Bruno wanted to be acquitted (found not guilty) of the charge of heresy, of course. He admitted that he had not fasted on certain days, as the Church required. He acknowledged that he had made a mistake in praising England's Queen Elizabeth I, a notorious heretic. And he offered the church an all-purpose confession. He said, "All the errors which I have committed until today, and all heresies which I have believed, and the doubts I have entertained concerning the Catholic Faith and in matters determined by the Holy Church, I now abhor [hate] and detest them all and I repent having done, held, said, believed or doubted concerning anything non-Catholic."

The Venetian judges were lenient, and they might have accepted Bruno's apology. However, the church in Rome was following the case closely. In September, the Vatican called Bruno to Rome to stand trial. The Venetians delayed at first, then agreed to turn Bruno over. On February 27, 1593, the jailers of the Holy Office of the Pope led Bruno down into the dungeons of the Castello Sant'Angelo in Rome.

For years the interrogators hounded Bruno. Periods of intense questioning were followed by long stretches of time during which they ignored him. Bruno complained about the cold, the poor and small amount of food, and the lack of books. But he continued to work on his own defense. On January 14, 1599, the judges finally told him about the evidence they held against him. It consisted of eight passages from his published works. They demanded that he take back everything contained in these passages.

The Verdict

Bruno defended himself well. He tried to show that the beliefs of Copernicus and those of the Catholic Church were compatible. While the church held that only God is infinite (neverending), Bruno had written that the universe is infinite. But, Bruno said now, "It would be unworthy of God to manifest himself in a less than infinite universe." The judges were not convinced. On December 21, 1599, with no arguments left to make, Bruno announced that he had nothing to retract. On February 8, 1600, seven

THE INQUISITION

The word *inquisition* means "interrogation" or "lengthy examination." In the Middle Ages, the Inquisition was the official tribunal (court) of the Roman Catholic Church. It was formed to suppress heresy—ideas that went against church teachings. The Inquisition was first established in 1233 by Pope Gregory IX to combat the heresy of a French group known as the Albigensians. In 1542, Paul III, concerned about the rise of Protestantism, revived the Inquisition, which went on to try Giordano Bruno some fifty years later.

years and four months after his arrest, his accusers reached a verdict. They called him an unrepentant heretic.

The judges gave Bruno eight days to recant or be burned at the stake. "You are more afraid of this than I am," Bruno announced defiantly. On February 19, three days after the deadline, the jailers led him to the Campo di Fiori square, where they stripped him naked, tied him to a stake, and forced a wedge into his mouth to prevent him from voicing other blasphemies (statements against God). A group of priests gathered around Bruno's funeral pyre, chanting and waving crucifixes. A German witness, Gaspar Schopp, watched the condemned man closely: "When the image of our Saviour was shown to him before his death he angrily rejected it with averted face," Schopp reported.

Suggestions for Further Reading

Hale, J. R., ed. *A Concise Encyclopedia of the Italian Renaissance.* New York: Oxford University Press, 1981.

Yates, Frances. *Lull & Bruno.* Boston: K. Paul, 1982.

Galileo Galilei Trial: 1633

Defendant: Galileo Galilei

Crime Charged: Heresy (opinions that defied church authority)

Chief Defense Lawyer: None

Chief Prosecutor: Vincenzo Maculano, Commissary General of the Congregation of the Holy Office

Judges: Vincenzo Maculano and the Holy Office

Place: Rome, Italy

Dates: April 12–June 22, 1633

Verdict: Guilty

Sentence: Abjuration (being forced to reject his former beliefs, under official oath)

SIGNIFICANCE: The trial of Galileo Galilei raised basic questions, still not entirely settled, about the relationship between religion and science. In the short term, it confirmed total authority of the pope over such matters.

Sarcastic, quick-witted, and controversial, Galileo Galilei pushed the limits of science. The controversy he aroused often got him into trouble. Take, for example, the telescope. It was invented in 1608; Galileo later redesigned and improved it. He then used it to make a number of important astronomical discoveries. Some of these discoveries confirmed what he already believed. For instance, he thought that the astronomer Nicholas Copernicus had been correct in 1543 when he wrote that Earth did not stand still, but revolved around the sun.

Galileo was born in Pisa, Italy, in 1564. He studied mathematics and astronomy and eventually taught at the university. His work on the laws of motion challenged accepted wisdom. They drew such hostility from the teachers at the university that Galileo resigned in 1591, moving to Florence. His work between 1592 and 1610 at the University of Padua increased his reputation as a scientist. Students came from all over Europe to hear his lectures.

**G a l i l e o
G a l i l e i
T r i a l : 1 6 3 3**

The 1616 Inquiry

In 1613, Galileo published a powerful defense of Copernicus's ideas. It attracted the attention of the Roman Catholic Church. In 1616, the Congregation of the Holy Office ordered Galileo to come to Rome. It had replaced the Inquisition, a church organization that investigated "nonbelievers" during the Middle Ages. At first investigators cleared Galileo. Then they instructed him to abandon Copernicus's radical views of Earth's motion.

Gossip had it that the Holy Office had condemned Galileo and forced him to disavow his views. To counter this rumor, Galileo asked a sympa-

The Church of Santa Maria Sopra Minerva in Rome, located next to the headquarters of the Inquisition, where Galileo's trial was held.

thetic Vatican administrator, Cardinal Robert Bellarmine, to write a letter for him. The letter would say Galileo had neither been tried nor convicted. Bellarmine did so on May 26, 1616.

Galileo promised the Holy Office that he would drop his support of the ideas they condemned. For some years he occupied himself with other scientific matters. Then, in 1632, he returned to Copernicus's works. He again published a defense of the astronomer and attacked accepted scientific authority.

The Summons

Galileo's villa at Arcetri, just outside Florence, Italy. After he left prison in December 1633, Galileo spent the last nine years of his life at his home, until his death on January 8, 1642.

Galileo's defense appeared at an awkward moment for Pope Urban VII. Other books questioning accepted beliefs had been published recently. Galileo's seemed one more challenge to the pope's authority. In addition, someone told Pope Urban that the book presented him as a dimwit. The pope also had larger problems. The great Catholic-Protestant conflict of the Thirty Years' War (1618–1648) dragged on, with no end in sight. Pope Urban's Habsburg allies (supporters) were members of one of Europe's greatest royal families. They were unhappy with his leadership of the Counter-Reformation, an attempt by the Catholic Church to stop the rise

of Protestantism. Galileo may have been a victim of the pope's need to assert his power. In the autumn of 1632, the Congregation of the Holy Office again ordered Galileo to Rome.

Galileo pleaded advanced age and ill health, the difficulty of traveling in winter, and an outbreak of plague in Florence as reasons not to go to Rome. Still the inquisitors (investigators) in Rome were insistent. Carried on a stretcher, Galileo arrived in Rome in February 1633, on the first Sunday of the church festival of Lent. The Holy Office ignored him for several weeks.

This illustration appeared across from the title page in Galileo's Dialogo *(Florence, Italy, 1632).*

The Trial

The proceedings finally began on April 12, 1633. Vincenzo Maculano, a member of the Dominican order of priests and the commissary general of the Holy Office, was in charge. Galileo could not have a lawyer. At first, Galileo was not even shown the specifics of the case against him.

The Holy Office put the scientific issue plainly: Did Earth revolve around the sun? The inquisitors were curious, too, about several other questions. Must physical truth be observable, or can something be true even though only its effects are seen? Could instruments such as the telescope be properly used in the search for truth? Finally, there were, for the Holy Office, the all-important issues of the scientific authority of the Bible and the worldly authority of the pope.

Maculano and his assistant, Carlo Sinceri, prosecutor of the Holy Office, began by asking Galileo whether he knew or could guess why he had been summoned.

"I imagine," said Galileo, "it is to account for my recently printed book." He went on to identify a copy of his work, to describe its contents in a general way, and to say he had written it in Florence over a period of seven or eight years.

Maculano asked about the 1616 inquiry. Galileo answered clearly, agreeing that Cardinal Bellarmine and others had warned him to stay clear of Copernicus. He then produced a copy of the "certificate" Bellarmine had written for him.

The inquisitors pressed the matter. Had Galileo been given any sort of injunction, a legal document preventing him from taking up Copernican theory again? He said he could recall no such thing. They then produced an injunction, which they said had been read to Galileo in front of witnesses. It stated that he must not "hold, teach or defend in any way whatsoever, verbally or in writing" Copernican views about Earth's motion. Galileo repeated that he did not recall the words.

Finally, Maculano questioned him about his published defense of Copernicus. How and from whom had be obtained permission to print it? Galileo replied that the master of the Sacred Palace, a church administrative organization, had reviewed the book and had licensed it for publication.

Had he told the master anything about his encounter with the Inquisition in 1616?

At this point, Galileo denied the evidence of his own book, declaring that it was intended to counter Copernican theory. With this, Maculano dismissed the accused and put him under house arrest in a room of the Palace of the Holy See in Rome. As far as Galileo knew, that's where matters stood for a full two weeks.

Evidence Mounts

Meanwhile, the inquisitors had received a set of reports from a special commission established to review Galileo's work. One of the commissioners, the Jesuit priest Melchior Inchofer, wrote in his April 17 report:

> I am of the opinion that Galileo not only teaches
> and defends the immobility or rest of the sun or cen-
> ter of the universe, around which both the planets
> and the earth revolve with their own motions, but
> also that he is vehemently suspected of firmly ad-
> hering to this opinion, and indeed that he holds it.

During the last week in April, Maculano went privately to Galileo and advised him to avoid a long trial and a lot of trouble by confessing. Otherwise, he faced solitary confinement (being kept in a prison cell alone) for a long time and possible torture. When Galileo appeared for a second hearing on April 30, he went prepared to admit his mistake in return for what he believed would be a lighter, more symbolic sentence.

Galileo claimed he had been carried away by the glitter of his own arguments to make too strong a case for Copernicus. Maculano dismissed him but allowed him to return a little later to add to his statement. Now Galileo offered to revise his publication to reflect church-authorized scientific opinion.

The Third Session

The third session began on May 10. On that day, Galileo presented his entire defense. He said again that he could not recall the injunction of 1616. Again, he offered to revise the book. He concluded with a plea for leniency (mercy). The shadowy, unreal, and unbearably intense atmosphere of the Inquisition had broken the last of the old man's defenses.

Galileo's appeal to his inquisitors' mercy did not, however, end the matter. The pope had not yet been satisfied and was possibly influenced by a rumor that Galileo had used the forbidden art of astrology to predict the date of his death. On June 16, the Holy Office met to pass sentence. At Pope Urban's insistence, there would be a further interrogation, "even under the threat of torture." Galileo would be forced to renounce his works. He would be condemned to prison at the will of the Holy Office. He would no longer "treat further, in whatever manner, either in words or in writing, of the mobility of the Earth and the stability of the Sun." His defense of Copernicus would be banned. Finally, the inquisitor of Florence would "read the sentence in full assembly and in the presence of most of those who profess the mathematical art." Galileo would be forced to humble himself in front of his scientific peers.

The inquisitors did not carry out their threat of torture. In the final interrogation on June 21, Galileo submitted to all the Holy Office's demands. "I do not hold this opinion of Copernicus," he said, "and I have not held it after being ordered by injunction to abandon it. For the rest, I am here in your hands; do as you please."

Dressed in the white robe of a penitent who asks for forgiveness of his sins, Galileo made his way the next day to the hall of the Dominican convent of Santa Maria Sopra Minerva. He knelt there to hear his sen-

**RELIGION AND
HERESY**

THE DISCOVERIES OF GALILEO

Galileo Galilei made many important scientific discoveries. One of his most famous is his contradiction of Aristotle's teachings about falling bodies. The ancient Greek philosopher and scientist Aristotle said that the speed of an object's fall depended on its weight. Galileo was the first to perform experiments to test Aristotle's theory. He weighed a number of objects. Then, he let them fall. As they fell to the ground, he measured their speed. At the time, it was very controversial to challenge the great Aristotle. It was also controversial to experiment and observe nature, rather than reading and accepting the theories of an authority.

tence read—abjuration. Galileo had to take back all that he had said about his astronomical discoveries. Its harshness surprised even Maculano.

Many years afterward, a tale went around that Galileo had ended his retraction with a defiant whisper: "But it still moves." This never occurred. Galileo turned to new fields of inquiry and never dealt in Copernican theory again. In 1638, four years before his death, he published *Two New Sciences,* a work that became a foundation of modern physics and engineering. His work on Copernicus remained on the Vatican's list of banned (forbidden) books until 1835.

Suggestions for Further Reading

De Santillana, Giorgio. *The Crime of Galileo.* New York: Time Life Books, 1981.

Drake, Stillman. *Galileo.* New York: Hill and Wang, 1980.

Finocchiaro, Maurice A., ed. *The Galileo Affair: A Documentary History.* Berkeley: University of California Press, 1989.

Galilei, Galileo. *Dialogue Concerning the Two Chief World Systems.* Translated by Drake Stillman. Berkeley: University of California Press, 1967.

Ronan, Colin A. *Galileo.* New York: G. P. Putnam's Sons, 1974.

Salem Witchcraft Trials: 1692

Defendants: Two hundred accused, including Sarah Bishop, Sarah Good, Sarah Osburn, and Tituba, a slave

Crime Charged: Witchcraft

Chief Examiners: John Hathorne and Jonathan Corwin

Place: Salem Village (now Danvers, Massachusetts)

Dates of Hearings: March 1, 1692, and throughout the spring

Chief Defense Lawyers: None

Chief Prosecutors: None

Judges for the Court of Oyer and Terminer: Jonathan Corwin and others

Place: Salem Town (now Salem, Massachusetts)

Dates of Trials: June 2–September 1692; a superior court in January 1693 held trials in several cities

Verdicts: Twenty-nine guilty of witchcraft

Sentences: Nineteen hanged; remaining prisoners released over a period of years

SIGNIFICANCE: What prompted these accusations of witchcraft—which were made primarily against women—has been a matter of intense historical debate for over 300 years.

In the seventeenth century many people believed in witchcraft. English courts were especially interested in hurtful acts committed by supposed witches against their neighbors. Yet before the Salem Witchcraft Trials,

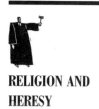

only about 100 people had ever been accused of witchcraft. Of these, only 15 were executed. Yet in 1692, 200 people were accused in only a few months' time.

Hysteria Sets In

Over the centuries, witch-hunts occurred during periods of social unrest. When the Puritans first landed in Massachusetts, they had a great deal of freedom. In 1684, England combined several colonies to create the Dominion of New England. In the upheaval, Massachusetts lost its independence. Its residents lost their land ownership. Then, following England's Glorious Revolution of 1688, King James II was dethroned. Also that year the governor of New England was overthrown. The legal status of Massachusetts became uncertain.

This nineteenth-century drawing depicts the Salem witchcraft trials of the 1690s.

During the winter of 1691–1692, Tituba, an enslaved woman from the Caribbean Islands, worked in the household of Reverend Samuel Parris of Salem, Massachusetts. Tituba looked after the minister's nine-year-old daughter, Betty, and his eleven-year-old niece, Abigail Williams. She

entertained them with magic and fortune-telling. Eventually, the two girls invited eight more girls, ages twelve to twenty, to join the fun.

To the Puritan residents of Salem, playing around with magic was serious business, as it went against their religious beliefs. The girls grew tense with the strain of keeping their games secret. By January 1692, the tension had become hysteria. Betty Parris and Abigail Williams began to demonstrate strange behavior. They fell into trances and, when spoken to, made noises and gestures. Abigail had convulsions and screamed as if in pain. Other girls began to act the same way. Panic seized the village.

In February, Reverend Parris called in Dr. William Griggs, who concluded that the girls were bewitched. Several ministers were called in to pray over the girls. When their efforts failed, they insisted the girls give them the names of those who were bewitching them.

The Puritans believed that the Devil had to work through one person—who became his agent—in order to get to another person. The Devil could then appear to his victims in the shape of his agent. This shape was thought to be visible only to the victims. This "spectral evidence," which some criticized, was accepted by the court.

Salem
Witchcraft
Trials: 1692

Mistress Godman's trial portrays an older woman accused of witchcraft during the 1630s.

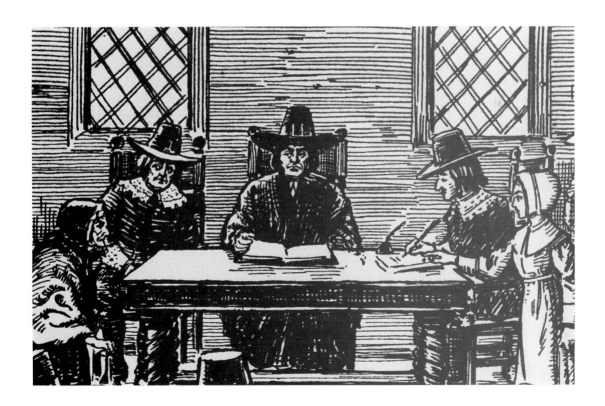

Under pressure, the girls named Tituba, the slave; Sarah Good, a lonely, destitute woman; and the unpopular Sarah Osburn. On February 29, 1692, warrants were issued and the three were arrested.

Magistrates Hold a Hearing

On March 1, two judges, Jonathan Corwin and John Hathorne, opened a public hearing in the packed meeting house of the village of Salem. The examining magistrates behaved more like prosecutors than investigators. Pregnant and dressed in rags, Good stood before them and denied tormenting the children. The girls fell into fits and blamed Good for their pains. Good responded by blaming Osburn.

Osburn, dragged from her sickbed, also denied tormenting the children. The girls again reacted with fits and screaming. Osburn then said she herself was bewitched. She related a dream in which she was visited by something "like an Indian all black, which did pinch her in the neck." Osburn died in jail awaiting trial.

Tituba told the judges what they wanted to hear. After briefly denying she had any "familiarity" with the Devil, she made a strange claim. She said that, "there is four women and one man, they hurt the children, and then they lay all upon me; and they tell me, if I will not hurt the children, they will hurt me." She named Good and Osburn, but claimed she could not identify the other three.

One of the next two accused, Martha Corey, was suspect because she did not believe the girls' stories. Rebecca Nurse, however, had never questioned them. A frail, elderly woman, Nurse had few enemies—except, perhaps, those who been involved in a land dispute with her family. Her sisters were later accused of witchcraft. Both women had to testify while the girls continued their fits and visions, but they held fast to their denial of any involvement.

Jails Fill with Accused

By May, the jails of Salem Town and Boston were filled with people awaiting trial. More women than men were in jail. Those imprisoned ranged from Good's five-year-old daughter, Dorcas, to the Reverend George Burroughs, who was the former pastor of Salem Village. Putnam claimed Burroughs had killed his first two wives, as well as some soldiers who had battled Indians along the border. Reverend Cotton Mather believed Burroughs to be the witches' master.

By May, Massachusetts had a new governor, Sir William Phips. Phips called together the General Court, which appointed a special court to put the witches on trial. Sarah Bishop, a tavern keeper, was the first tried. According to Samuel Gray, a ghostly image of Bishop appeared over his child's cradle, bringing about the child's illness and death. Bishop was convicted and, on June 10, hanged.

The judges recessed the court to consult with several ministers for guidance about evidence of witchcraft. The ministers warned against putting much trust in spectral evidence, saying the "demon may assume the shape of the innocent."

The court re-opened on June 28. Of the five people tried next, Rebecca Nurse was briefly acquitted (found not guilty). The jury was impressed by the way she conducted herself in court and by a petition of support signed by her fellow citizens. After the verdict declaring Rebecca Nurse not a witch was read, the girls in the courtroom fell into howling fits, and Justice William Stoughton addressed the jury:

> I will not impose on the jury, but I must ask you if
> you considered one statement made by the prisoner.
> When Deliverance Hobbs was brought into court to
> testify, the prisoner, turning her head to her said,
> 'What, do you bring her in? She is one of us.' Has
> the jury weighed the implications of this statement?

After reconsidering, the jury declared Rebecca Nurse guilty.

On July 19, the five women were hanged. Urged to confess by Reverend Nicholas Noyes, who said "she knew she was a witch," Good responded: "You're a liar. I am no more a witch than you are a wizard. If you take my life away, God will give you blood to drink." It was later reported that Noyes died bleeding from the mouth.

Six more were convicted in August. The execution of Elizabeth Proctor was delayed because she was pregnant. The delay saved her life. Her husband, John Proctor, was an outspoken critic of the girls' visions, and he was hanged. Although some of the witnesses tried to take back their testimony, on September 15 more people were convicted and eight hanged. These would be the last hangings. Governor Phips suspended the trials and postponed further executions. He soon released those against whom there was only spectral evidence.

Salem
Witchcraft
Trials: 1692

RELIGION AND HERESY

THE CRUCIBLE

In 1953, the playwright Arthur Miller wrote *The Crucible*. It was a dramatic portrayal of the Salem witch trials. Many observers, however, saw in Miller's play a portrait of their own time. In the 1950s there was a "Red Scare," in which the House Committee on Un-American Activities (HUAC) asked Communists and Communist sympathizers to "name names" of others in their group. In Miller's play, alleged witches who said they repented of their "witchcraft" were asked to name the names of other witches. They thus exposed their friends and neighbors to arrest and possible execution. Miller also suggested that the "good citizens" who accused others of witchcraft were often motivated by self-interest, such as wanting to acquire their neighbors' land.

Evidence Questioned

Some independent clergymen from New York criticized almost every type of evidence the Massachusetts court had allowed to be entered. When the court reopened, spectral evidence was no longer used as a basis for conviction. Only three more were actually convicted. Eventually, Phips pardoned all who had been condemned to die.

As the hysteria subsided, doubts about the witch trials grew. In January 1697, the General Court ordered a day of prayer and fasting in memory of those who died. In 1703 and 1710, in response to appeals, the legislature reversed most of the convictions. It also voted to pay compensation to those convicted or their surviving families, who still had to pay prison lodging fees for time spent in jail. The convictions of seven still remain on the record.

Suggestions for Further Reading

Barrow, Anne Llewellyn. *Witchcraze: A New History of the European Witch Hunts.* San Francisco: Pandora, 1994.

Hall, David D. *Witch-Hunting in Seventeenth Century New England: A Documentary History, 1638–1692.* Boston: Northeastern University Press, 1991.

Karlsen, Carol. *The Devil in the Shape of a Woman: Witchcraft in Colonial New England.* New York: W. W. Norton, 1987.

Stanton, Elizabeth Cady, Susan B. Anthony, and Matilda Joslyn Gage. *History of Woman Suffrage,* Vol. 1. Salem, NH: Ayer Company, 1985.

Salem
Witchcraft
Trials: 1692

John Thomas Scopes Trial
(The "Monkey Trial"):
1925

Defendant: John Thomas Scopes

Crime Charged: Teaching evolution

Chief Defense Lawyers: Clarence Darrow, Arthur Garfield Hays, and Dudley Field Malone

Chief Prosecutors: William Jennings Bryan and A. T. Stewart

Judge: John T. Raulston

Place: Dayton, Tennessee

Dates of Trial: July 10–21, 1925

Verdict: Guilty; however, neither side won the case because the decision was reversed on a technicality involving the judge's error in imposing a fine that legally could only be set by the jury

Sentence: $100 fine

SIGNIFICANCE: The John Thomas Scopes trial halted the influence of fundamentalism in public education and stripped William Jennings Bryan of his dignity as a key figure in American political history. The trial also marked the beginning of new American thought: science began to be taken much more seriously.

In the early 1920s, American morality (sense of right and wrong) was deeply divided. In the cities, people discussed sex while drinking the bootleg alcohol outlawed by a constitutional amendment. In rural areas, particularly in the South, religious fundamentalism relying on a literal reading of the Bible set the dominant mood. A showdown between the modern and the traditional seemed certain.

Evolution As Heresy

Fundamentalists especially objected to the teaching of Charles Darwin's theory of evolution in public schools. To them, it seemed that their tax dollars were being spent to turn their children against their religion—and them. Led by former presidential candidate William Jennings Bryan, the fundamentalists tried to get their legislatures to rid schools of Darwin's theory of natural selection. It related man to lower life forms, which they saw as an attempt to relate apes and men.

In the Tennessee legislature, a bill sponsored by John Washington Butler made it unlawful "to teach any theory that denies the story of the divine creation of man as taught in the Bible." It also made it illegal "to teach instead that man has descended from a lower order of animals." The bill became law in February 1925. Afraid that other states would follow Tennessee's lead, the American Civil Liberties Union (ACLU) announced it would defend any teacher charged with violating the new law.

John
Thomas
Scopes
Trial: 1925

The crowded courtroom during the Scopes trial. Clarence Darrow (far right) and his defense team are in the foreground.

A few weeks later, in the little town of Dayton, Tennessee, a former New Yorker who believed in evolution was involved in a debate with two fundamentalist lawyers. Finally, they settled their differences by agreeing that a trial testing the new law would do much good for the local economy. They enlisted John Thomas Scopes, the local high school science teacher, to act as their guinea pig. The ACLU quickly confirmed its willingness to defend Scopes.

Using a textbook that had been approved by the state, Scopes taught a lesson on evolution on April 24 to his high school class. Arrested on May 7, he was quickly indicted by a grand jury. The press was already calling the confrontation the "Monkey Trial."

The Circus in Dayton

The all-male jury from the John Thomas Scopes Trial, 1925.

Both the prosecution and the defense hired famous lawyers. The ACLU sent its chief attorney, Arthur Garfield Hays, and his partner, Dudley Field Malone, as well as the celebrated trial lawyer Clarence Darrow. Darrow, who had gained fame defending controversial clients, became the chief lawyer for the defense. He was an agnostic (a person who doubts that

William Jennings Bryan, one of the chief prosecutors in the Scopes Trial.

there is a God) who had long fought against religious fundamentalism. He saw the Scopes trial as his chance to win that battle. The chief lawyer for the prosecution was William Jennings Bryan himself. No one was more effective in defending the old-fashioned values of rural America than "the Great Commoner," as Bryan liked to call himself.

Both fundamentalists and evolutionists (people who believe in the theory of evolution) regarded the trial as a winner-take-all debate between religion and science, traditional and modern values, and the forces of light and the forces of darkness. Scientists and intellectuals were horrified by the prospect that scientific knowledge would be removed from the classroom. The ACLU and others who believed in individual liberty saw the case as a test of academic freedom. Fundamentalists declared that the trial was a last-ditch effort to save their children's souls.

The editors of city newspapers regarded the trial as a circus and sent their columnists to Dayton to poke fun at the local inhabitants. Dozens of new telegraph lines had to be added in Dayton to handle the increased number of news agencies using them. In addition to lawyers and reporters, the town was overrun by traveling preachers, salesmen, and numerous chimpanzees with their trainers. Monkey dolls, umbrellas with monkey handles, and dozens of other souvenirs with a monkey theme were put up for sale.

Despite the circus-like atmosphere, the trial was no laughing matter to Bryan. Arriving a few days early, he preached to a large audience: "The

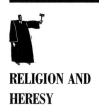

RELIGION AND HERESY

contest between evolution and Christianity is a duel to the death. . . . If evolution wins in Dayton, Christianity goes."

Evolution On Trial

Jury selection began Friday, July 10, 1925, with Judge John T. Raulston presiding. More than 900 spectators filled the sweltering courtroom, while a jury of ten farmers, a schoolteacher, and a clerk was selected.

On the first business day of the trial, the defense team tried to have the indictment thrown out. It was, they said, unconstitutional. It violated the Fourteenth Amendment's guarantee of due process under law and the First Amendment's guarantee of freedom of religion. The attempt failed.

A. T. Stewart, the attorney general of Tennessee, then made the opening statement for the prosecution. Scopes had contradicted the biblical story of creation, thereby violating the Butler Act. Dudley Malone responded for the defense. He said that in order for the state to convict Scopes, it had to prove two things. First, that Scopes had denied the biblical creation story. Second, that he had taught instead that man came from a lower order of animals. Proving both would be difficult for the prosecution. (While Scopes had admitted to teaching evolution, there was no evidence that he had denied the Bible's version of man's origins.) Malone agreed that there were some differences between Darwinism and the Bible, but he added that many people managed to live with both theories of creation. Only the fundamentalists maintained that science and religion were totally incompatible on the subject.

The prosecution then presented its case. The superintendent of the Rhea County school system where Scopes taught, testified that Scopes had admitted teaching evolution in a biology class. Stewart then offered a King James Bible as evidence of what the Butler Act described as the biblical account of creation. Hays objected that this was only one version of the Bible, but the judge accepted it anyway.

Scopes's students testified that he had taught that mammals had evolved from one-celled organisms. From Scopes they learned that men, like monkeys, were mammals. Up next on the witness stand was the owner of the local drugstore where Scopes had purchased the textbook he used to teach evolution. The druggist testified that the state of Tennessee had authorized the sale of the book. Darrow and the drugstore owner read passages from Darwin aloud. Stewart, in turn, read the first two chapters of the Old Testament's Genesis into the court record. With that, the prosecution rested.

The next day, Thursday, July 16, the defense called to the witness stand a zoologist from Johns Hopkins University. The prosecution objected, saying that the jury did not need a lecture on evolution. All that was to be decided was whether Scopes had violated the law by teaching evolution. At this point, Bryan gave his major speech of the trial. He charged that Darwinism weakened moral standards by creating atheists (people who do not believe in God). As evidence, he pointed to the German philosopher Friedrich Nietzsche (NEE-chee). Nietzsche's writings, he said, had inspired the infamous Chicago "thrill-killers," Nathan Leopold and Richard Loeb. Darrow objected that Bryan was wrong about Nietzsche's views and was wrongly influencing the jury. Judge Raulston overruled him. Bryan ended his remarks defiantly, declaring that the Bible would survive attacks from scientists.

Dudley Malone delivered the defense's closing argument. He charged that the fundamentalists were attempting to silence new ideas out of fear. Malone then proclaimed: "The truth always wins. . . . The truth does not need the forces of Government. The truth does not need Mr. Bryan. The truth is imperishable." He concluded triumphantly, "We feel we stand with progress. . . . We feel we stand with the fundamental freedom of America. We are not afraid. Where is the fear? We defy it!"

However, Malone failed to convince the judge, who ruled that scientific evidence was not admissible in the case. All the defense could do to counter this blow was to insist that the opinions of scientific experts be read into the court record, since they could not be delivered in front of the jury.

Darrow Deflates Bryan

The trial seemed to be winding down when Hays dropped a bombshell. He wanted to call Bryan to testify as an expert on the Bible. This was an unheard-of legal tactic, yet Bryan eagerly agreed. Darrow, who was known for trapping witnesses with their own testimony, dropped his gentle manner. First, he got Bryan to state that every word in the Bible was literally true. Then he asked how the Old Testament figure Cain got a wife. If Adam and Eve and their sons Cain and Abel were the only four people on earth, where did the fifth come from? Next, Darrow pointed out that the Book of Genesis says that the serpent that tempted Eve in the Garden of Eden was condemned by God to slither on its belly. Did the snake walk on its tail before that? The more questions Darrow asked, the more tangled Bryan became in contradictions. He and his cause began to look foolish.

Sweating and shaking, Bryan admitted that he did not think the earth had been made in six twenty-four-hour days. This was a startling concession, because belief in the literal meaning of the words of the Bible was the cornerstone of fundamentalism. The personal dislike between Darrow and Bryan grew. Bryan accused Darrow of insulting the Bible. Darrow responded, "I am examining you on your fool ideas that no Christian on earth believes."

Finally, after an hour and a half, Judge Raulston adjourned the court. It was a clear attempt to save Bryan from more embarrassment. When the trial resumed the next morning, the judge declared Bryan's testimony to be irrelevant. It was removed from the trial record. The defense immediately rested.

The End of an Era

In his closing argument, Darrow asked the jury to find Scopes guilty so that the case could be appealed (a legal method for obtaining a new trial). After nine minutes, the jury returned with a guilty verdict. Because of technicality, the verdict was thrown out. On appeal, the Butler Act was upheld, although no new trial was ordered for John Thomas Scopes, who had by then given up teaching.

Although Scopes and the evolutionists had lost the case, they won a larger battle. No attempt was ever made again to enforce the Butler Act. (It ceased to be a law in 1967.) Efforts to enforce similar laws in other states ended. The U.S. Supreme Court ended the debate in 1968 when a similar Arkansas law was struck down because it violated the separation between church and state required by the First Amendment.

Yet the Scopes trial is remembered more for its cultural impact than for its legal significance. Before the trial, religion was the basis for much of America's outlook. Afterward, science dominated. Most saw Bryan's death just a few weeks after the trial as the end of an era.

Suggestions for Further Reading

Blake, Arthur. *The Scopes Trial: Defending the Right To Teach.* Brookfield, CT: Millbrook Press, 1994.

Darrow, Clarence. *The Story of My Life.* New York: Charles Scribner's Sons, 1932.

De Camp, L. Sprague. *The Great Monkey Trial.* Garden City, NY: Doubleday & Co., 1968.

Ginger, Raymond. *Six Days or Forever: Tennessee v. John Thomas Scopes.* Boston: Beacon Press, 1958.

EVOLUTIONARY MYTHS

Other legal attempts to change the teaching of "evolution theories" in U.S. schools surfaced many years after the Scopes trial. Two court battles occurred; one in Arkansas in 1981 and one in Louisiana from 1981 to 1982. In both cases, the courts made their decisions in 1985. Both agreed that creation science (which opposes the scientific content of evolutionary biology) could not replace a scientific explanation or theory. The courts could not agree to the teaching of a biblical story of creation in any state-supported school system as it would violate the First Amendment of the U.S. Constitution (by attempting to establish religion in public schools). Darwin's theory is still taught in public schools throughout the United States.

Hays, Arthur Garfield. *Let Freedom Ring.* New York: Boni & Liveright, 1928.

Koenig, Louis W. *Bryan: A Political Biography of William Jennings Bryan.* New York: G. P. Putnam's Sons, 1971.

McGowen, Tom. *The Great Monkey Trial: Science vs. Fundamentalism in America.* Danbury, CT: Franklin Watts, 1990.

Scopes, John. *Center of the Storm.* New York: Holt, Rinehart & Winston, 1967.

Tierney, Kevin. *Darrow: A Biography.* New York: T. Y. Crowell, 1979.

TREASON

Thomas More Trial: 1535

Defendant: Sir Thomas More

Crime Charged: Treason

Chief Defense Lawyer: Sir Thomas More

Chief Prosecutor: Richard Riche

Judges: Thomas Cromwell and seventeen others

Place: London, England

Date of Trial: July 1, 1535

Verdict: Guilty

Sentence: Death

SIGNIFICANCE: Sir Thomas More, a writer, politician, religious thinker, and lawyer, was a man with many talents. His trial showed, however, that he was above all things a man of great courage.

Sir Thomas More served as Lord Chancellor to the English king Henry VIII and was one of the most powerful men in the country. By 1532, however, his health had begun to fail, and he had begun to distrust the king. More resigned his office, retiring from public life.

More, a devoted Catholic, was distressed about the King's disregard for the laws of the Roman Catholic Church. When Henry grew tired of his wife Catherine of Aragon, he had asked the church, which does not recognize divorce, to declare the marriage invalid. When the church refused, Henry passed a law naming himself as head of the Church of England, thus freeing himself from any obligation to Roman Catholicism. On

May 23, 1533, Thomas Cranmer, Archbishop of Canterbury, dutifully declared Henry and Catherine's marriage invalid. Nine days later, Anne Boleyn, who was already pregnant with Henry's child, the future Queen Elizabeth I, was crowned queen of England. (Henry and Anne had already secretly married four months earlier.)

More's Loyalty to Catholicism

More did not attend the coronation. He was, however, required to appear before a royal commission. There he was asked to approve under oath the Act of Succession (1534), which declared Henry's marriage to Catherine void and the king's marriage to Anne valid. Although he admitted that

Thomas More, a devoted Catholic, was executed in 1535 after he refused to take an oath of supremacy to Henry VIII as head of the Church of England.

Anne was now the true queen, More refused to take the oath because it required him to reject the supremacy of the Catholic Church. For this act of defiance, he was thrown into the Tower of London. When he was questioned on May 7, 1535, about the Act of Supremacy (1534), which declared that Henry was the "supreme head" of the established Church of England, More refused to answer directly. As a result, he was charged with treason.

More's trial began seven weeks later on July 1, 1535, at Westminster Hall. He appeared there before a panel consisting of Thomas Cromwell, the King's secretary, and seventeen other judges, including Anne Boleyn's father and brother. More had no doubt about the outcome of his trial. Still, despite the fact that he had suffered during the time he had been jailed, he managed to defend himself with great skill and a thorough knowledge of the law. He refused to accept the advice offered by members of the panel, who, according to the custom then, served as both prosecutors and counselors to the accused persons who appeared before them.

Multiple Counts of Treason

More faced four counts of treason: first, that when questioned on May 7, he refused to accept that Henry was the head of the Church of England; second, that More had exchanged treasonous communications with Bishop John Fisher (who was executed for treason on June 22, 1535) when they were both imprisoned in the Tower of London; third, that he had referred to the Act of Supremacy as a two-edged sword which, if he accepted it, would save his body but kill his soul, and if he rejected it would save his soul but kill his body; fourth, that he has spoken against the Supremacy Act to Solicitor General Richard Riche, one of Cromwell's allies.

More addressed each of these charges in turn. He reminded the judges that when he was questioned on May 7 he had remained silent and that, under English law, silence is regarded as agreement. Noting that his letters to Bishop Fisher had been burned and that nothing Fisher had said about the their contents could be regarded as treasonous, More argued that these letters could not be used as evidence against him. More went on to say that his remark about the Supremacy Act being a two-edged sword had been made merely for the sake of argument.

More convinced the judges that the first three charges against him should be dropped. That left only the charge growing out of his conversation with Richard Riche. Riche testified against More, and More responded strongly, denying what Riche said and accusing him of lying before the court. More had long been a politician, and he knew how to destroy an opponent's character; now he used all his skill to weaken Riche's testimony. Then More concluded by reminding the judges of his long and loyal service to the king. But he had little hope of saving himself, and he was in fact convicted of treason shortly thereafter.

A Final Strategy

Even as Lord Chancellor Thomas Audley rose to sentence More, the convicted man argued that he should not be sentenced because the law used to convict him was not valid. The Act of Supremacy, More said, went against the higher authority of the Catholic Church, as even the English Parliament must realize. The judges grew impatient, but More continued to speak. He stated that the Supremacy Act contradicted even the Magna Carta, the founding document of English law. This line of argument seemed to shake the confidence of at least some of the judges, but Lord Audley went ahead and passed sentence.

Initially, More's sentence was the same as that given most traitors: hanging, followed by drawing and quartering—that is to say, after he was hanged, his body would be cut up. More, however, managed to have his sentence changed to beheading. On July 6, 1535, he walked steadily to the block on Tower Hill to receive his

SIR THOMAS MOORE'S

VTOPIA:

CONTAINING,

AN EXCELLENT, LEARNED, WITTIE, AND PLEASANT
Difcourfe of the beft ftate of a Publike Weale,
as it is found in the Gouernment of the new
Ile called *Vtopia*.

FIRST WRITTEN IN LATINE,
by the Right Honourable and worthy of all Fame,
Sir THOMAS MOORE, Knight, Lord Chan-
cellour of *England* ; And tranflated into Englifh
by RAPHE ROBINSON, fometime
Fellow of *Corpus Chrifti* Colledge
in *Oxford*.

*And now after many Impreffions, newly Corrected and
purged of all Errors hapned in the
former Editions.*

LONDON,
Printed by *Bernard Alfop*, dwelling in *Diftaffe* lane
at the Signe of the *Dolphin*,
1 6 2 4.

The title page from Thomas More's Utopia, *printed in London in 1624.*

punishment. Up to the end, Henry VIII had feared the power of More's speeches, sending a messenger to More's cell on the morning of his beheading to request that More say little at his execution. More obeyed. He went quietly to his death.

Consequences of More's Death

More's conviction has been criticized because it was obtained through the testimony of a single witness. But there can be no doubt that, as the law stood at the time, it was a legal decision. Opinion in England was changing in favor of requiring two witnesses to testify about any crime punishable by death, but the law was not actually changed until 1547. In fact,

THE DRAMA OF THOMAS MORE

Like Joan of Arc, Thomas More has inspired many playwrights. Robert Bolt wrote *A Man for All Seasons* about More's trial and execution, a play that was later made into a movie starring Paul Scofield. William Shakespeare also depicted More in his play *Henry VIII*. However, since Shakespeare's patron was Elizabeth I, More is portrayed much less sympathetically. Incidentally, More is also known for creating the word *utopia*, which was the title of a work he wrote in 1516, portraying an ideal state founded on reason. More invented the word from Greek language. Literally, it means "no place"; the word has come to mean an ideal place that does not, in fact, exist.

the older common law had always accepted the testimony of a single witness if that person was thought to be of good character.

On May 19, 1935, four centuries after his death, Thomas More was canonized as a saint by the Roman Catholic Church.

Suggestions for Further Reading

Marius, Richard. *Thomas More.* New York: Weidenfeld, 1993.

Rupp, G. *Thomas More.* London: Collins, 1978.

Wegemer, Gerard. *Thomas More On Statesmanship.* Washington, DC: Catholic University of America Press, 1996.

Mary, Queen of Scots Trial: 1586

Defendant: Mary Stuart

Crime Charged: Treason

Chief Prosecutors: Sir Thomas Bromley, Sir Francis Walsingham, and Robert Cecil

Judges: The king's commissioners

Place: Fotheringay, England

Dates of Trial: October 15–16, 1586

Verdict: Guilty

Sentence: Death

SIGNIFICANCE: Trials for treason were nothing new in England, but never before had the defendant been someone of such high rank.

Born Mary Stewart on December 7 or 8, 1542, to King James V of Scotland and Mary of Guise, Mary became queen when she was only a week old, upon the death of her father. Five and one-half years later her mother, related to a powerful French family, arranged for Mary to marry Francis, the young son of King Henry II of France. Mary went to France and, for the next 10 years, was raised in the Catholic French court.

On April 24, 1558, Mary and Francis were married. Over the next two years, events changed her life dramatically. In November of that year, the queen of England, Mary I, died. Her Protestant half-sister Elizabeth I became queen. But many Catholics in Europe did not recognize Elizabeth as the rightful heir to the throne. They thought the marriage of her parents (King Henry VIII and Anne Boleyn) was not legal. They believed the Scottish Mary, as the grandniece of Henry VIII, carried the royal bloodline and should sit on the throne.

In July 1559, Mary's life was further complicated when Henry II died from wounds suffered during a jousting tournament. Francis and Mary were crowned king and queen of France. A year later, though, Mary's happiness ended when she learned of her mother's death. Then just six months later, Francis died. Mary was devastated and her health declined. She finally accepted an invitation to return to Scotland to become its ruler. What she truly desired, though, was the crown of England.

Mary, Queen of Scots, shown here in 1559, was tried and convicted of treason and publicly beheaded on February 8, 1587.

Assumes Rule in Scotland

Scotland was a far different country from the one Mary had left thirteen years before. Previously tied to the French, Scotland now associated itself with Protestant England. Most of the Scottish people turned against Catholics. The Scottish Parliament had even forbidden the celebration of the Catholic Mass. When Mary began her rule she insisted upon having Mass said in her own chapel. But she accepted Protestantism in her country, and even approved certain laws against Catholics. The Scottish people looked up to her. She had shown great courage by defending her own beliefs. But she had shown also good will and sense by accepting policies the majority of people wanted.

In the meantime, Mary tried to secure her right to the English throne by marrying her first cousin Henry Stewart, Lord Darnley, on July 29, 1565. Many Catholics thought Darnley, as grandnephew of Henry VIII, was next in line to the throne after Mary. But Mary soon tired of Darnley, whom she thought stupid and arrogant. She refused to give him the crown matrimonial—a lawful promise that he would have power during her reign.

Darnley, irritated by his wife's neglect, plotted to kill David Rizzio, an Italian musician who had become Mary's most trusted friend. On March 9, 1566, a band of nobles dragged the screaming Rizzio from the queen's chamber and stabbed him fifty-six times. But Mary, who was six months pregnant at the time, regained Darnley's affection. On June 19, 1566, she gave birth to a son, the future King James I of England.

After the birth of their son, Mary's distaste for Darnley only deepened. On February 10, 1567, the house where Darnley had been staying was blown up. His body was found strangled in the garden. Many people believed the murderer was James Hepburn, earl of Bothwell, who was rumored to be Mary's new lover. He was put on trial for the murder, but found not guilty. Then, granted a quick divorce from his wife, he married Mary on May 15, 1567. This last act turned many of Mary's loyal followers against her. A month later, her government was overthrown. On July 24, she was forced to abdicate (give up) the throne in favor of her son.

Investigated for Murder

In May 1568, Mary escaped to England to seek help from her cousin Elizabeth I. Elizabeth did not trust Mary, however, and had the English government investigate Mary's part in Darnley's murder. At the trial, a collection of letters written by Mary to Bothwell (the "Casket Letters") were presented that supposedly proved her guilt. Although, the court did not find her guilty in the murder plot, she was not allowed to return to Scotland. Instead, she was forced to spend the rest of her life in England.

For the next eighteen years, held captive in cold and drafty castles, Mary planned her escape. Many Catholics, both in Scotland and in England, plotted to put Mary on the English throne. In 1586, Sir Francis Walsingham, secretary of state and a Puritan, seized control of the situation. Walsingham, an early spymaster (chief of intelligence), maintained a nationwide network of agents who fed him information about every aspect of public life. Like his close ally, Robert Cecil, Walsingham was willing to interfere with affairs of state. Together, they decided to gather enough evidence to convince Elizabeth that permitting Mary to live was not only unwise but unthinkable.

Through one of his agents—Gilbert Gifford, who acted as a letter carrier for Mary—Walsingham heard of yet another Catholic plot to aid the imprisoned Scottish queen. A northern squire, Sir Anthony Babington, had gathered together a group of six who had developed a plan to replace Elizabeth with Mary on the English throne. When Babington wrote to Mary about the plot, she wrote back, foolishly unaware that Walsingham saw every one of her letters. Even more foolishly, Babington wrote of his plan to kill Elizabeth. Assisted by her secretaries, Claude Nau and Gilbert Curle, Mary wrote a coded response that did not specifically rule out this course of action. Walsingham and the other conspirators interpreted her message to mean that she approved of the assassination plot. However, Walsingham wanted more proof. Accordingly, he forged a postscript to one of Mary's letters, requesting the names of the conspirators and asking to be kept informed of developments concerning their plans.

Conspirators Captured

Babington received the letter with the forged postscript at the end of July. On August 3, he wrote back to the Mary, telling her he had received her message. Then Walsingham gave orders for the conspirators to be rounded up. Under questioning, Babington admitted everything and was forced to reconstruct his harmful letter. On August 11, a messenger from Elizabeth went to Chartley Hall in Staffordshire, where Mary was being held, and told her that her treachery was known. At that time, Nau and Curle were taken into custody. Mary felt betrayed by her secretaries, but she judged them too harshly. Facing the very real possibility of their own deaths, they had merely testified about the contents of the letter. (There is some possibility that Nau was in fact one of Walsingham's agents. He was sent to France and given his freedom after a few months, while Curle remained imprisoned for a year.)

Mary Tried for Treason

Despite pleas from the French ambassador that Mary be permitted the assistance of a lawyer, Elizabeth refused to provide an accused traitor with a counselor.

Mary's examination began on Wednesday, October 15, 1586. She hobbled into the Great Hall at Fotheringay with painful slowness, almost

TREASON

completely crippled with rheumatism. After looking at the faces of the commissioners, she remarked to her attendant, Sir James Melville, "Ah! They are my counselors, but not one is for me." She was visibly upset that she was not seated on the throne that had been placed there. Instead, she had to sit on a smaller chair, a deliberate ploy that Cecil hoped would make the Scottish queen distressed. It did: "I am a Queen by right of birth and my place should be there under the dais [platform]!" she announced. Yet this was the only time she showed her irritation. Throughout the remainder of the trial she was calm, maintaining a quiet attitude that troubled some members of the commission.

The first speech from the Lord Chancellor, Sir Thomas Bromley, declared that Elizabeth, upon learning of Mary's conspiracy against her, had no choice but to call up a commission to question her cousin. The accused, he stated, would have every opportunity to respond to the charges against her.

Mary listened to evidence concerning the capture of Babington and his fellow conspirators, and to other testimony about the written confessions obtained from Nau and Curle. She protested that this evidence was secondhand, stating that she would not admit to anything on the basis of such indirect proof. As evidence of her current lack of ambition, the forty-four-year-old queen pointed to her frail condition: "My advancing age and bodily weakness both prevent me from wishing to resume the reins of government. I have perhaps only two or three years to live in this world, and I do not aspire to any public position. . . ."

Cecil Intervenes

Mary's statements did not sit well with Cecil, the self-appointed chief examiner. He pointed to Mary's refusal to sign the Treaty of Edinburgh (1560), in which she formally gave up any claim to the English throne. Mary denied that she had always desired Elizabeth's position. She did not deny, however, that she felt she had a right to be second in line for the throne, since she was the English queen's cousin and heir. With the same note of acceptance, she indicated that she no longer blamed her secretaries for what had happened to her. However, she did object to the manner in which their evidence emerged at the hearing.

Mary defended herself well against the torrent of charges the commissioners put to her. However, by the end of the first day, she was exhausted. She had learned English late in life, so she didn't have a very good grasp of the language, and she had spent nearly half of her forty-four years in prison with little physical exercise. Even so, she recognized that

Queen Elizabeth I signed the death warrant for the execution of Mary, Queen of Scots on February 1, 1587.

the evidence of Nau and Curle was crucial to the case against her. Just before the proceedings ended for the day, she declared, "If they were in my presence now they would clear me on the spot."

The next morning, a visibly paler Mary entered the hearing room. The mood of the commissioners, however, seemed to have changed overnight. There were to be no more rough exchanges. Nevertheless, the commissioners remained determined that Mary should pay for her crimes with her head. As the group gathered that morning, Mary's aides noticed that every member of the court was wearing riding dress, indicating that none expected the proceedings to last the entire day. Mary herself understood what was about to happen. As she left the courtroom that day, she said, "May God keep me from having to do with you all again."

Treachery Confirmed

Her wish was granted. On October 25, the commissioners met again in the Star Chamber in London to hear evidence from Nau and Curle. Both reaffirmed their earlier testimony. The commission then found that Mary was guilty of conspiring to assassinate Queen Elizabeth I. When they received the verdict, both the House of Lords and the House of Commons in Parliament passed a sentence of death on Mary.

TREASON

THE CONFLICT BETWEEN CATHOLICS AND PROTESTANTS

Queen Elizabeth I ordered Mary, Queen of Scots to be beheaded. She had a huge stake in the triumph of Protestantism and the defeat of Catholicism. Under Catholic doctrine, Elizabeth was not the true ruler of England. Elizabeth was the daughter of Henry VIII and his second wife, Anne Boleyn. Henry married Anne only after divorcing his first wife, Catherine of Aragon, a devout Catholic. At that time, Henry was also Catholic. Since Catholics cannot divorce, Henry had asked Pope Clement VII to grant him an annulment—a way of ending a marriage by declaring it invalid. When the pope refused the annulment, Henry left the Catholic Church and founded the Church of England, with himself—not the pope—at its head. By Catholic law, then, Elizabeth was illegitimate, since Catholics still considered Henry to be married to Catherine. Seven years after Henry's death, in 1544, Parliament declared Elizabeth to be in line for the throne. However, she was imprisoned for a time and gained her freedom only by pretending to be a practicing Catholic. After she finally became queen, in 1558, she established the Protestant Church of England as Britain's official church. Elizabeth's successor was James IV of Scotland, the son of Mary, Queen of Scots, who had allied himself with Elizabeth against his mother and had calmly accepted Mary's death. He ruled England as James I, angering both Catholics and Protestants with his inconsistent attitude toward Catholics.

For months afterward, Elizabeth put off acting on the sentence. In delaying so, she went against the advice of her counselors, one of whom noted, "As long as life is in her [Mary], there is hope. So long as they [Catholics] live in hope, we live in fear." Finally, on February 1, 1587, Elizabeth yielded to pressure and signed the death warrant. One week later, on the morning of February 8, Mary was beheaded in the Great Hall at Fotheringay. It was a gruesome occasion. Twice the headsman failed to complete his task. Only after the third blow was he able to grab a handful of Mary's red hair and hold her severed head upward, crying, "God Save the Queen!" Later that day her body was buried somewhere in the castle, in a spot that remains unknown.

Mary had not feared death by beheading. For years she had worried about being assassinated in some dark dungeon. When she learned she would be publicly beheaded, her physician reported, "Her heart beat faster and she was more cheerful and she was in better health than ever before." If Mary hoped to promote Catholicism with her death, she was mistaken. The most lasting effect of her death was an increasing lack of respect for royalty.

Mary, Queen of Scots Trial: 1586

Suggestions for Further Reading

Cannon, John and Ralph Griffiths. *The Oxford History of the British Monarchy.* Oxford: Oxford University Press, 1988.

Fraser, Antonia. *Mary, Queen of Scots.* New York: Delacorte Press, 1969.

Wormald, Jenny. *Mary, Queen of Scots.* London: Collins & Brown, 1991.

Walter Raleigh Trials: 1603 and 1618

Defendant: Sir Walter Raleigh

Crimes Charged: Conspiracy and treason

Chief Defense Lawyer: None (Raleigh acted as his own lawyer at both trials)

Chief Prosecutors: First trial: Edward Coke; second trial: Sir Henry Yelverton and Sir Thomas Coventry

Judges: First trial: Panel of eleven commissioners led by Lord Chief Justice John Popham; second trial: panel of commissioners led by Lord Chief Justice Henry Montague

Places: First trial: Winchester, England; second trial: London, England

Dates of Trials: November 17, 1603; October 22, 1618

Verdicts: Guilty

Sentences: Death (lifted by King James I after the first trial)

SIGNIFICANCE: For centuries, history has viewed Sir Walter Raleigh's fate as a failure of justice. Did history get it wrong?

Sir Walter Raleigh planned the colonization of Virginia and Carolina, introduced tobacco and the potato to Britain, and led an English battleship against the Spanish Armada. He was a hero and a favorite of Queen Elizabeth I. However, in 1592, his status changed abruptly. News that he had seduced and secretly married one of the queen's ladies-in-waiting led to his being thrown into the Tower of London. Although he was quickly released, he never regained his earlier prominence. When James I came to power in

A portrait of Sir Walter Raleigh, English explorer.

1603, Raleigh lost still more power and influence. The new king disliked him and ordered that his belongings be taken from him. When rumors of a Spanish plot to seize the English throne arose, Raleigh was suspected of being involved. Within months, he found himself facing charges of treason.

Raleigh Tried for Treason

Because an outbreak of plague in London was claiming 2,000 lives a week, Raleigh's trial was transferred to Winchester, about 60 miles southwest of London. Raleigh's journey there, during which he was battered with stones and tobacco pipes by people who gathered along the route, gave some indication of what was to come. On November 11, 1603, a panel of eleven commissioners gathered to hear charges of treason issued by Attorney General Edward Coke. Raleigh acted as his own attorney, maintaining a breezy manner throughout the trial, while Coke hurled bitter accusations at him. The commissioners seemed to be won over by Raleigh's calm insistence of his own innocence.

Raleigh's Legal Blunder

Raleigh gained confidence as the trial proceeded. Then, however, he made a grave error, asserting that "by the law and statutes of this realm in cases of treason, a man ought to be convicted by the testimony of two witnesses if they be living." Lord Chief Justice John Popham then

TREASON

This Victorian engraving shows Sir Walter Raleigh's birthplace, Hayes Barton, located near East Budleigh in Devon.

pointed out that a recent change in the treason laws had done away with this requirement.

The single witness to testify about Raleigh's alleged treason was a sailor named Dyer, who was only able to quote the words of others as to Raleigh's supposed offenses. Raleigh objected to the admission of such remote evidence. He cited his military service, which had pitted him against the Spanish three times. Clearly, he was not on the payroll of a nation he had fought against. However, Coke then produced a letter from Raleigh's close friend and alleged fellow conspirator, Lord Henry Brooke Cobham, in which Cobham claimed he had contacted agents in Spain only at Raleigh's urging. Raleigh could not counter such direct evidence, and he was sentenced to death.

Just days before he was to executed, Raleigh watched from his cell window at Winchester Castle as Cobham and two others were led to the executioner. After waiting for thirty minutes, each was led to the block, but before the axe could be raised to behead them, each execution was stopped. Hoping to obtain the same mercy, Raleigh quickly wrote a letter to the king, begging for his mercy.

Saved

The king granted Raleigh's request, but only after he had let everyone know about the convicted man's groveling plea. At a time when honor was valued more highly that life itself, the once heroic explorer became a figure of contempt. Although he spent the next twelve years of his life in the Tower of London, Raleigh was confined there rather than actually jailed. His wife visited him regularly, and he fathered a son during that period. In a small garden, he grew plants and herbs which he used to make medicines. He also wrote at great length, producing his *History of the World,* a monumental work that confirmed his literary reputation.

Sir John Popham, one of the judges in Sir Walter Raleigh's trial.

Throughout his detention, he appealed for freedom, trying to convince James I that gold mines in Guiana, run by the Spaniards, should be raided and that he should lead the raid. In 1616, his request was granted. Just fifteen months later, Raleigh set sail. It was a catastrophe. There was no gold, and he lost 250 men in combat with the Spanish. Despite these developments, Raleigh returned to England, only to be sent to the Tower for the third and last time in August 1618.

Retrial

On October 22, 1618, Raleigh faced yet another panel of judges. The attorney general, Sir Henry Yelverton, recited the charges against him. Much

TREASON

THE LOST COLONY

In the United States, Sir Walter Raleigh is probably best known for having founded the earliest English colony in North America: Roanoke Island. This island is only twelve miles long and three miles wide, located off the northeast coast of North Carolina, between the Albemarle and Pimlico sounds. Raleigh sent out a group of colonists who landed on Roanoke in August 1585. The following year, they returned to England, unable to make a success of life in this new and difficult world. A second group of colonists arrived in 1587. When a third boat from England landed in 1591, bearing fresh supplies, none of the colonists were to be found. Historians still do not know exactly what happened to them. Artifacts from the lost colony are on display on the island, at the Fort Raleigh National Historic Site.

of the evidence consisted of testimony from Raleigh's previous trial, and it led to Raleigh's earlier sentence being reaffirmed. On October 28, he made his final presentation at the Palace of Westminster. Lord Chief Justice Henry Montague told him that, by law, he had been a dead man for the past fifteen years and "might at any minute be cut off." The next morning Raleigh was beheaded in Old Palace Yard, next to Westminster Hall.

Was Raleigh an Innocent Man or a Traitor?

British history has long held that Raleigh's conviction for treason was unjust. However, evidence discovered at Oxford University's Bodleian Library and released in November 1995 shows this assumption to be open to question. Researchers at the Bodleian had accidentally discovered the first complete account of the prosecution's case against Raleigh. This evidence included statements written in Raleigh's own hand. They indicated that he had indeed spoken of a desire for Spain to invade England and had offered to act as a spy in exchange for what amounted to $6,000 a year.

These disclosures indicate that Raleigh's reputation as an innocent victim owed more to Coke's courtroom manner during Raleigh's trial than to the facts of the case. By assuming the manner of an innocent man in the face of Coke's verbal assault, Raleigh was converted in the public's eyes from an admitted traitor to a sacred martyr.

Suggestions for Further Reading

Cannon, John and Ralph Griffiths. *The Oxford History of the British Monarchy.* Oxford: Oxford University Press, 1988.

Lacey, Robert. *Sir Walter Raleigh.* New York: Atheneum, 1973.

Sinclair, Andrew. *Sir Walter Raleigh and the Age of Discovery.* New York: Penguin, 1984.

Walter
Raleigh
Trials: 1603
and 1618

Gunpowder Plot Trial: 1606

Defendants: Thomas Bates, Sir Everard Digby, Guy Fawkes, John Grant, Robert Keyes, Ambrose Rookwood, Robert Winter, and Thomas Winter

Crime Charged: Treason

Chief Defense Lawyer: None

Chief Prosecutor: Sir Edward Coke

Judges: Panel of five judges headed by Sir John Popham

Place: London, England

Date of Trial: January 27, 1606

Verdicts: Guilty

Sentences: Death

SIGNIFICANCE: In 1534 the Act of Supremacy declared that King Henry VIII, rather than the pope, was the head of the Church in England. Afterward, the country underwent religious turmoil. Protestants, who had been the target of public outrage, soon became the tormenters of a shrinking Catholic minority. Catholic resentment toward the Protestant majority was powerfully expressed in the conspiracy that became known as the Gunpowder Plot.

Toward the end of the sixteenth century, the Catholic religion was dying out in England. Under Queen Elizabeth I, the state tried to end it forever. Laws made it a crime punishable by death to attempt to convert anyone to Catholicism. Because of heavy taxes imposed on Catholic churches, simply worshipping as a Catholic became an expensive and

GunPowder Treafon.

In this contemporary drawing, the illustrator shows God keeping an eye on the Gunpowder Plot conspirators.

difficult task. Catholics at first looked to James I, the newly crowned English king who was the son of the Catholic Mary Stuart. They hoped he would make their lives easier. It was not to be. Following the advice of his chief counselor, Sir Robert Cecil, James enforced the punishing laws to their fullest extent.

Catholic Plot

Robert Catesby, a wealthy landowner from the English Midlands, was also a Catholic. He had given up hope of any improvement in the lives of British Catholics. Toward the end of 1603, he approached John Wright, Thomas Percy, and Thomas Winter. These were three men with whom he had much in common, including Catholicism. The group discussed ways of easing their difficulties and, according to a confession later forced from Winter, Catesby was the first to suggest that the group plot to assassinate both James I and Robert Cecil. The next person to join the conspiracy was Guy Fawkes, a shadowy figure about whom we still know very little. His name, however, has always symbolized the "Gunpowder Plot."

In December 1904, after Robert Keyes, another prominent Catholic, had joined their number, the plotters rented a property next to the houses of Parliament in London. Then they began digging a tunnel between the two buildings. After Christmas, they began to bring gunpowder across the Thames River to their tunnel. Their plan was to set off the explosives on the day James was present for the annual ceremony marking the opening of a new parliamentary session. They hoped to blow up the king, his son (the Prince of Wales), Robert Cecil, and most of the king's highest ranking advisers (the Privy Council). As a consequence, the country would be left without a central government.

The Conspiracy Widens

Around this time, Catesby poured out his worries to a Jesuit priest named Father Henry Garnet. Catesby was concerned about killing unsuspecting Catholic members of Parliament, and wondered if such a sacrifice was justified. Although Garnet later said that Catesby had discussed the issue only vaguely, it was enough for Garnet. He counseled against it. However, he was but bound by his oath not to reveal anything learned in the confessional. So he could take no active role in trying to stop the conspirators from carrying out their plan. Garnet's inability to act on what he knew would later cost him dearly.

Gradually, the conspiracy widened to include Sir Everard Digby, Ambrose Rookwood, and John Grant—all wealthy Catholics. Thomas Bates and Thomas Winter's brother, Robert, also joined the group, as did Francis Tresham, who was later suspected of betraying the conspirators by revealing their plot to government authorities.

Betrayal?

Although the Gunpowder Plot remains mysterious, we do know that Robert Cecil was aware of the tunnel even as it was being dug. Cecil even knew what the plotters intended to do. Still for a long while he did nothing to stop them, preferring to wait until he could gain political advantage in exposing the conspiracy. By turning a blind eye on the criminal activities taking place nearly next door, Cecil enabled the plotters to dispose of the earth they displaced. They obtained gunpowder, which was scarce.

At around midnight on November 4, 1605, with James I due at Parliament the next day, Cecil finally acted. Guy Fawkes was arrested in the cellar of the houses of Parliament where he was guarding three dozen barrels of gunpowder, enough to cause a massive explosion. When they

An anonymous engraving of the Gunpowder Plot conspirators.

TREASON

learned of Fawkes's arrest, his co-conspirators panicked. Many of them fled north. On November 8, a sheriff's posse killed Catesby and Percy. They rounded up other plotters and took them to the Tower of London, where they were questioned.

Fawkes had already undergone questioning, which in his case included two days of torture on a rack. He nevertheless remained silent until, on November 17, he finally gave a statement. By that time, however, Fawkes was too weak to sign it. Cecil could make no use of Fawkes's "confession." Nowhere did it mention Jesuit involvement with the plot. After days of torture, Thomas Bates finally gave Cecil a confession he could use, but it vanished under mysterious circumstances. On December 23, the public learned that Tresham had suddenly died in custody and had been quickly buried. Speculation grew that he had been murdered in order to ensure his silence.

Show Trial

As in most prominent seventeenth-century trials, the government had established the guilt of the conspirators before the trial began. The trial of the Gunpowder Plot defendants was a show trial staged for the general public. The trial opened in Westminster Hall in London on January 27, 1606, before a panel of five judges headed by Sir John Popham. The attorney general, Sir Edward Coke, had a reputation for savage prosecution. He had gained it during the trials of Sir Walter Raleigh and the Earl of Essex. Coke began mildly. He said that the defendants were decent men who had been led astray. Soon, however, Coke reverted to form, declaring the scheme one of "the greatest treasons that ever were plotted in England and concerning the greatest king that ever was in England." Above all, he blamed the Jesuits, attacking the absent Father Garnet for his alleged part in the conspiracy. Some said that James and his family witnessed Coke's prosecution from a private room overlooking the court.

The defense consisted only of statements given by the conspirators. All the defendants were humble and begged for forgiveness. The genuineness of at least one confession, that of Thomas Winter, is doubtful. Not only was it obtained under force, but it was signed "Winter," when the defendant always spelled his own name "Wintour."

After a brief recess, the jury returned with the expected guilty verdict. It sentenced all but one of the conspirators to death. Digby, the only one to plead not guilty, was tried separately. He too received the death sentence. The defendants returned to the Tower of London, where they spent their final days alone.

KING JAMES I

The rule of King James I was stormy and controversial, but it did produce one of the world's most enduring works of literature: the King James version of the Bible, also known as the "Authorized" version. This Bible was commissioned by King James at the Hampton Court Conference in 1604. The translation took seven years to complete and finally appeared in 1611.

Guy Fawkes Day

On January 30 and 31, 1606, they were all publicly hanged. Rookwood's dying wish was that the Lord would "make the King a Catholic." Fawkes, broken by torture and sickness, literally crawled to his death. The same day, the man whom Cecil suspected to be one of the major conspirators, Father Garnet, was taken into custody. He, too, was executed.

Although it was the work of just a handful of religious extremists, the Gunpowder Plot dealt a dreadful blow to all English Catholics. The laws that punished them for their beliefs were tightened. They could not live in or near London. They could not practice medicine or law. Finally, they had to attend Protestant churches or submit to having two-thirds of their property taken away. One other effect of the plot was that James declared a day of thanksgiving, which has ever since been known as Guy Fawkes Day. To this day in Britain, every November 5 bonfires are lighted and "guys"—likenesses of Guy Fawkes—are burned, usually accompanied by a fireworks display.

Suggestions for Further Reading

Cannon, John and Ralph Griffiths. *The Oxford History of the British Monarchy.* Oxford, England: Oxford University Press, 1988.

Haynes, Alan. *The Gunpowder Plot.* Dover, England: Alan Sutton, 1994.

Winstock, Lewis. *Gunpowder, Treason and Plot.* New York: Putnam, 1973.

Charles I Trial: 1649

Defendant: Charles Stuart
Crime Charged: Treason
Chief Defense Lawyer: None
Chief Prosecutor: John Cook
Judge: John Bradshaw
Place: London, England
Dates of Trial: January 20–27, 1649
Verdict: Guilty
Sentence: Death

SIGNIFICANCE: Until the mid-seventeenth century, those who wanted to challenge a British king or queen's right to rule did so out of the public eye. A prime example of this was the murder of Edward II in 1327. This changed with the trial of King Charles I. For the first time a reigning British monarch was judged by a law passed by commoners. Although the strict legality of that statute might be open to question, its effects are being felt to this day.

W hen he ascended the British throne in 1625, Charles I was liked for his appreciation of the arts and for his shy manner. This was a sharp contrast with his coarse father, James I. Unfortunately, Charles's desire for war overshadowed these admirable qualities. Wars with France and Spain made impossible demands on the treasury. Furthermore, they placed the king at odds with Parliament. The long-running feud between Charles and Parliament came to a head on January 4, 1642. On that day the king forced his way into the House of Commons in a foolish attempt to arrest five members who had refused to do his bidding. This event sparked a civil war in England between the royalists (those who supported the King) and those who supported Parliament.

The King Charged with Treason

It was a bloody dispute. In February 1647, aware that he could not hold out, Charles surrendered into custody. His greatest fear was giving up the throne. He prepared for the worst, however, by working to make sure his son, Charles II, the Prince of Wales, would succeed him. Confined to Hampton Court just outside London on the Thames River, Charles began to suspect that public sentiment had turned against him. He began to hatch plots and once managed to escape briefly to Carisbrooke Castle on the Isle of Wight. However, all of his hopes crashed when the royalist forces lost in battle at Preston in 1648. The hero of that battle, Oliver Cromwell, was now the most powerful man in England. He aimed to end the monarchy.

On January 1, 1649, the House of Commons passed a law demanding that the king be tried for treason. The grounds were that he had waged war on Parliament and on the country. When the House of Lords examined the new law, the noble members of that body rejected it. The House of Commons responded by again passing the bill requiring Charles to stand trial. This time it added another law establishing a High Court of Justice with 135 commissioners taken from the military and from Parliament.

Reluctant Commission

On January 19, 1649, guards brought Charles from Windsor Castle in south-central England to London. The next day, he faced a commission headed by the chief justice of Chester, John Bradshaw. He was a minor figure in the world of English law, but one of the few persons willing to take charge of what was sure to be a difficult matter. People were unwilling to participate, and Cromwell struggled to keep enough individuals involved so that the hearing could go forward. Of the original 135 commissioners called, less than half attended when the trial began in Westminster Hall, across the road from Westminster Abbey. Self-preservation was clearly one reason that so many were absent; people on both sides were angry and some thought that soldiers loyal to Charles could violently try to free the king. Bradshaw, for his part, had his hat reinforced with metal plates.

TREASON

John Glover's
engraving of the
House of Commons,
circa 1648.

The King's Trial

Charles entered the hall clothed entirely in black, except for his collar and cuffs. Deliberately, he walked toward the prisoner's dock away from public view. He listened as solicitor general John Cook read the charge against him. As evidence of Charles's treason, Cook recited a list of battles from the civil war and pointed to Charles's attempts to use foreign troops to fight the royalist cause.

At the charge's conclusion, Charles openly laughed in the faces of his accusers, demanding to know on what authority they tried him: "I am your King. I have a trust committed to me by God, by old and lawful descent. I will not betray that trust to a new unlawful authority." These were themes he would return to repeatedly. The trial was illegal. An outdated and unrepresentative House of Commons, elected eight years earlier, was trying him.

The hearing ended for the sabbath. As Charles returned to his quarters, crowds both jeered and cheered him. All of Charles's guards hated him. All through that weekend they insulted and taunted him. They blew tobacco smoke, which he hated, into his face. They did everything they could to wear him down before court resumed on Monday morning.

At that time, Bradshaw took up where he had left off Saturday. He instructed Charles that he must either confess his guilt or deny the charge. Charles refused to answer or to recognize the authority of the commission. When he insisted that he was not an ordinary prisoner, one of the commissioners, Colonel John Hewson, rushed forward, crying "Justice!" and spat in the king's face. The next day, Bradshaw again attempted to get Charles to respond to the charge of treason. When Charles began once again to attempt to delay the proceedings, Bradshaw instructed Cook to read the charge one final time. Charles, however, still refused to acknowledge the tribunal's legitimacy.

Ordered from Court

Bradshaw's patience finally broke. Over Charles's protests, he demanded that the prisoner be taken away. For the remainder of that week, the commission heard evidence in the Painted Chamber adjoining Westminster Hall. Meanwhile, Charles remained under guard at his quarters. Cromwell took charge at this point. Although he spoke very little, by Friday he had persuaded the court to pass the sentence the next day.

TREASON

A Continuation of the

NARRATIVE

BEING

The last and final dayes Proceedings

OF THE

High Court of Iustice

Sitting in Westminster Hall on Saturday, *Jan.* 27.

Concerning the Tryal of the King;

With the severall Speeches of the
King, Lord President, & Solicitor General.

Together with a Copy of the

Sentence of Death

upon CHARLS STUART King of England.

Published by Authority to prevent false and
impertinent Relations.

To these Proceedings of the Tryall of the King, I say,
Imprimatur, GILBERT MABBOT.

London, Printed for *John Playford,* and are to be sold at his
shop in the *Inner Temple, Jan.* 29. 1648.

Shown here is a portion of the third installment of Mabbot's licensed account of Charles I's trial, published on January 29, 1648.

On January 27, Charles came back to Westminster Hall to learn his fate. As Bradshaw read aloud the verdict of the commissioners, two masked women, one of whom was thought to be the wife of one of the absent commissioners, protested aloud. In the furor that followed, the two managed to escape. Bradshaw allowed Charles one final statement, providing he did not again challenge the court's authority. Shrewdly, Charles requested an opportunity to address the House of Lords and House of Commons, going over the heads of the commission.

Bradshaw hastily adjourned the court. Several of the commissioners did not see how they could refuse what seemed like a fair request. Cromwell, however, ruled the day. A short while later, the court met to hear the judgment: Charles was to be beheaded.

Execution

Three days later, Charles stepped from a window at the Banqueting Hall in the district of Westminster onto a scaffold draped in black. Earlier he had asked his attendant to give him an extra shirt, saying, "The season is so sharp as shall probably make me shake, which some observers may imagine proceeds from fear." In the few moments he had left, he restated his belief in the right of the monarchy. He then laid his head on the wooden block. A single blow of the executioner's axe ended his life.

Vengeance

Britain did not then become a republic. On Cromwell's death in 1658, his son, Richard, assumed the role of lord protector, but he lacked his father's strong personality and lasted only one year in office. After Richard left for the continent, Charles II ascended to the throne. A popular monarch, Charles immediately set about taking vengeance on the men who had destroyed his father. Forty-one of those who had signed Charles I's death warrant still lived. Many of these fled abroad, but guards captured several. Of these, nine went to trial and were executed. Few, it seemed, had any regrets about what they had done.

Even Cromwell, dead since 1658, did not escape Charles II's vengeance. He had men dig up his body, which had been buried with great ceremony, and dragged through the streets of London. They hung it publicly at Tyburn. Later, it was reburied in a common grave. For the next several years, until a gale blew it down, Cromwell's severed head stood on a pole outside Westminster Hall.

TREASON

OLIVER CROMWELL AND THE PURITANS

Oliver Cromwell was a Puritan, a member of a religious and political movement for reform in the Church of England. Since the king or queen headed the Church of England, many thought the Puritans were enemies of the throne. The group was founded under the rule of Queen Elizabeth I with the purpose of *purifying* the church—which is how they got their name. From 1640 to 1660, those Puritans who stood with Cromwell and the Parliamentary Party had a great deal of power in England. After the *Restoration*—when the king was restored to the throne—the Puritans were expelled from the Church of England. As a result of the persecution that followed, a group of Puritans left England to come to America, where they intended to create the ideal religious community they had failed to establish in England.

The consequences of Charles I's execution were long-lasting. Never again would a king or queen of England rule with the kind of absolute power previous generations had taken for granted. At one stroke, the "divine right" of the monarchy was undone, ranking the trial of Charles I among the most significant in British history.

Suggestion for Further Reading

Ashley, Maurice. *The Battle of Naseby and the fall of King Charles I.* New York: St. Martin's Press, 1992.

Cannon, John and Ralph Griffiths. *The Oxford History of the British Monarchy.* Oxford: Oxford University Press, 1988.

Daniels, C. W. and J. Morrill. *Charles I.* Cambridge: Cambridge University Press, 1988.

Gregg, Pauline. *King Charles I.* Berkeley, CA: University of California Press, 1984.

Louis XVI and Marie Antoinette Trials: 1792 and 1793

Defendants: Louis XVI and Marie Antoinette, king and queen of France

Crimes Charged: Various acts of treason

Chief Defense Lawyers: Louis: Chrètien de L. de Malesherbes, François-Denis Tronchet, and Romain de Sèze; Marie: Claude Chauveau-Lagarde

Chief Prosecutors: Louis: National Convention; Marie: Revolutionary Tribunal

Judges: Louis: National Convention; Marie: Revolutionary Tribunal

Place: Paris, France

Dates of Trials: Louis: December 26, 1792; Marie: October 14–15, 1793

Verdicts: Guilty

Sentences: Execution by guillotine

SIGNIFICANCE: The trials of Louis XVI and Marie Antoinette brought France's old royal line to an end. The proceedings, with their political aims and mockery of legal form, foretold of the show trials that were part of the oppressive political tactics of the twentieth century.

TREASON

Louis XVI was king of France until the French Revolution ended his reign and his life in 1793. When violence first erupted in 1789, Louis tried to end the uprising with military force, but failed. His troops provoked uprisings in Paris. The uprisings, in turn, led to the attack on the city's Bastille prison on July 14, which freed the prisoners. Afterward, Louis and his ministers tried to change the constitution to permit the revolutionaries and monarchy to co-exist. However, this attempt failed, since by definition a republic is a government ruled by a head of state who is *not* a monarch. Finally, in June 1791, Louis and his queen, Marie Antoinette, escaped house arrest (confinement often under guard to one's house or quarters instead of in prison) at the Tuileries Palace in Paris and fled to Varennes near the Belgian border. There the revolutionaries caught up with them and returned them to Paris.

The final blow to the monarchy came in April 1792, when France went to war with Austria. A political group had pushed Louis into the conflict. Most people, however, blamed the king alone. On August 10, armed crowds attacked the Tuileries Palace. The king, Marie Antoinette, and their two children escaped, although hundreds of Swiss palace guards and rebels died. A day or two later, at the urging of a republican group called the Commune of Paris, the National Assembly "suspended" the king and jailed

Louis XVI was convicted of treason and sentenced to die on January 21, 1793.

the royal family in the medieval stronghold known as the Temple. (The National Assembly was made up of reformers from the nobility and clergy, who swore never to dissolve until France had a constitution.)

It was a comfortable sort of prison, at least at first. A domestic staff of thirteen looked after the family, and Louis's captors allowed him to send out for books. He was not allowed, however, to wear his honorary decorations on his afternoon walk, and the authorities, perhaps fearing he would kill himself, refused to give him a razor. Louis protested by refusing to allow himself to be shaved. He and his wife spent their mornings tutoring Louis Charles, their son and heir, and his sister, Marie Thérese.

The Indictment

The National Convention, a governing body that sat in judgement of Louis, called the king on December 11. They referred to him as "Louis Capet," his common family name instead of "King" or "Majesty." "It was the surname of my ancestors," Louis protested, meaning that it was a common name, and therefore a put-down. The king stood before a full house for the reading of the charges against him. The charges included, among other acts of treason, having three times ordered troops to fire on the people. The revolutionary authorities also charged Louis with having gained complete control of the coffee and sugar markets. Finally, they claimed he had tried to buy off the French people with money, although Louis protested that he had simply been giving to the poor. "I always took pleasure in relieving the needy, but never had any treacherous purpose," he said.

The National Convention ordered Louis back to the Temple and held in solitary confinement to await trial. His lawyers had less than two weeks to prepare their case. They advised Louis to challenge the authority of the National Convention, which would act as both his judge and his jury. Instead, Louis chose to contradict the accusations against him. He argued that, as the legitimate ruler of France, he had broken no laws.

A number of radical members of the National Convention insisted that Louis should not be tried at all, simply sentenced. In any case, argued Maximilien Robespierre, one of their leaders, the trial had already taken place; the armed uprising of August 10 had settled the question of the king's guilt. Nevertheless, the convention chose to bring the king into court.

The Trial of Louis XVI

The trial opened the morning of December 26, 1792. One of the king's lawyers, Romain de Sèze, argued that the king had not been a dictator, merely a victim of circumstances. Clean-shaven now (the guards had finally given him back his razor), Louis spoke briefly. Those who saw him noted his calm, quiet dignity. He referred to his attempts to compromise with the revolutionaries, and he strongly denied ever having caused the death of a single French person.

But the court had already made its decision. When the convention met again on January 15, 1793, all 693 members present voted to find Louis guilty. They could not, however, agree on a sentence. A roll call lasted throughout the night of January 16–17, during which each member called out his vote. Some also gave speeches. Finally, in a surprisingly close vote, the members approved the death sentence. Several pleas for delay followed. The American revolutionary Thomas Paine, speaking through an interpreter, proposed that Louis come to the United States, where he could be made into a new man in the purer air of the New World.

The convention, however, confirmed the death sentence on January 20. That evening the jailers allowed Louis to see his family for the first time since December 11. Marie Antoinette and the children had not known about the outcome of Louis's trial, but he told them where matters stood.

The Execution

Louis arose early on January 21 and heard mass, and at 8 A.M. the guards came for him. He and an escort of 1,200 soldiers made their way from the Temple to the Place de la Concorde in a journey that lasted two hours. At around 10 A.M., Louis mounted the scaffold.

A large crowd had gathered to watch. Louis spoke to them, declaring his innocence. A drum roll drowned out his words as the guillotine blade fell. One of the men plucked the king's severed head out of the basket into which it had fallen and held it up for the crowd to see.

The Case against the Widow Capet

Marie Antoinette, the daughter of Austrian Emperor Francis I and Maria Théresa, had been a strong-willed, big-spending queen. She was a highly conservative advisor to her husband. On the night of August 2, 1793, the guards carried her off to the worst of Paris's prisons, the Conciergerie on the Ile de la Cité in the middle of the Seine River. She remained alone, in an eleven-by-six-foot room, with two guards assigned to watch over her day and night.

Popular sentiment ran strongly against the queen. Marie Antoinette's captors referred to her as "the Austrian she-wolf." She was only thirty-seven, but prison had aged her. Her hair had thinned, and she had lost weight; she looked very old and very ill.

The Revolutionary Tribunal sent for the queen on the evening of October 12. In a shadowy room lit by only two flickering candles, her enemies set out the case against her. To begin with, she was guilty simply for having ruled as queen. The examiners went on to question her about sending money and information to Austria to be used in the war against France. They asked her about influencing her husband against liberal political

A young Marie Antoinette, in a painting done by Le Maitre.

ideas, and about her role in the 1791 flight to Varennes. There were thirty-five questions altogether, although some of these were accusations rather than questions. That night, after the prisoner had been returned to her cell, the prosecutor, Fouquier-Tinville, drew up an eight-page indictment listing the charges against her.

The Queen's Trial

The tribunal ordered the trial to begin on October 14. Marie Antoinette's lawyer asked for a delay, protesting that he had not had sufficient time to prepare her defense. The revolutionaries denied the request, and the trial began. Nicolas Hermann presided. Witnesses testified that the queen had

TREASON

In prison, Marie Antoinette bids a sad farewell to her children before her execution in October 1793.

MAXIMILIEN ROBESPIERRE: REVOLUTIONARY LEADER

Maximilien Marie Isidore Robespierre was known as "the incorruptible" because of his rigid leadership of the French Revolution. Robespierre was a lawyer. He first became interested in the ideals of democracy when he read the works of French philosopher Jean-Jacques Rousseau. During the revolution, two main groups emerged: the Girondists and the Jacobins. The Girondists were moderates. They represented the educated middle class of the French countryside. Although they opposed the king, they did not want him dead. The Jacobins, representing the poor and working people of Paris, were more extreme. Robespierre became a leader of the radical Jacobin Club (1791–1792) and later of the Montagnards, another popular radical party. He demanded the deaths of the French king and queen in 1792 and 1793. Robespierre was responsible for much of the Reign of Terror, sending his friends Georges Jacques Danton and Camille Desmoulins to the guillotine in 1794. On July 27, his Reign of Terror ended when a more moderate group (the "Revolution of Ninth Thermidor") overthrew him. The next day Robespierre was arrested, tried, and executed.

conspired with Austria against France, had organized a movement to resist the revolutionaries, and had somehow brought about the famine of 1789. The prosecution continued its assault on her character. On the second day, one of her accusers returned to the charge that the queen had been a faithless and controlling wife.

Late at night, near the end of the trial, Marie Antoinette rose to make a final statement. She stated that as the wife of Louis XVI, she had to obey him. This plea had no effect on her jurors. They met for barely an hour before returning with a guilty verdict and a death sentence. They based this on the charge that Marie Antoinette had aided Austria with money and information and that she had plotted to touch off a civil war in France.

TREASON

The Execution

Louis's widow awoke at dawn the next day, rose, and changed into a white dress. At 11 A.M., the executioners came. They tied her hands and cut her hair and led her out to an open cart, where the queen of France sat facing backward as she was driven slowly to the Place de la Concorde. Her strength failed her in the end, and she had to be helped out of the cart and onto the scaffold. The guillotine fell, and her body was buried in an unmarked grave.

Suggestions for Further Reading

Cronin, Vincent. *Louis and Antoinette.* New York: William Morrow and Co., 1975.

Doyle, William. *The Oxford History of the French Revolution.* Oxford, England: Clarendon Press, 1989.

Jordan, David. *The King's Trial.* Berkeley: University of California Press, 1979.

Schama, Simon. *Citizens: A Chronicle of the French Revolution.* New York: Alfred A. Knopf, 1989.

Aaron Burr Trial: 1807

Defendant: Former Vice President Aaron Burr

Crime Charged: Treason

Chief Defense Lawyers: Benjamin Botts, Luther Martin, Edmund Randolph, and John Wickham

Chief Prosecutors: George Hay, Gordon MacRae, and William Wirt

Judges: Cyrus Griffin and John Marshall

Place: Richmond, Virginia

Dates of Trial: August 3–September 1, 1807

Verdict: Not guilty

SIGNIFICANCE: The Aaron Burr trial marked the first time in American history that a court tried a high-level government official for treason. Although a court found Burr innocent of the charge, the trial ruined his career in politics.

In the early 1800s the states wanted more independence from the federal government. The major political parties, the Federalists and the Democratic-Republicans, fought about what policies to follow. In particular, they quarreled about the attitude of the United States toward other nations. Despite the Revolutionary War, the Federalists believed that the United States should trade with Great Britain. The Democratic-Republicans, on the other hand, believed that the United States should ally itself with France, then warring with England. France, they reasoned, had helped the colonies in their war against England. Also, the French Revolution had created a

TREASON

democracy in France that had more in common with the government of the United States than did the British monarchy. Aaron Burr's ideas and ambition landed him in the center of this controversy.

Born in Newark, New Jersey, Burr attended Princeton University. He served as an officer in the American Army during the Revolutionary War. After the war, he became a lawyer in New York. Perhaps tiring of the law, he joined the Democratic-Republican Party. In the election of 1800, Burr tied with Democratic-Republican presidential candidate Thomas Jefferson for the presidency. The House of Representatives chose Jefferson as president and Burr as vice president. However, Jefferson never trusted his old rival. In the election of 1804, he persuaded the Democratic-Republicans not to nominate Burr as vice president a second time.

Although former vice president Aaron Burr was found not guilty of treason on September 1, 1807, people across the United States believed that he was guilty. From that time on, Burr's political career collapsed.

Burr had made additional enemies, including Alexander Hamilton, a prominent Federalist. Alexander Hamilton had helped secure Thomas Jefferson's victory over Burr in the presidential election of 1800. In 1804, Hamilton also opposed Burr's bid to become governor of New York State. Burr challenged Hamilton to a duel after Hamilton made comments about Burr's character during that election. On July 11, 1804, at Weehawken, New Jersey, Burr shot Hamilton in the chest. Hamilton died shortly afterward, dealing his opponent's reputation a mortal blow.

Officials in New York and neighboring New Jersey decided to bring criminal charges against Burr for killing Hamilton. Wisely, Burr decided to go west into the frontier. He planned, with help from Britain, to lead a revolt against the federal government. After this uprising had succeeded, he would establish a "Western Empire," over which he would rule. Burr found supporters among the British and some American officials. However, the conspirators did not act on their plan for over a year. In the fall of 1806, they finally set up operations on a private island owned by a wealthy supporter from Ohio, Harman Blennerhassett. By then they had lost the support of the British. President Jefferson, who had learned about the threat from one of the former conspirators, crushed the rebellion.

Aaron Burr
Trial:
1807

Burr Tried before Chief Justice Marshall

Burr's treason trial began on March 26, 1807, in federal court in Richmond, Virginia. Normally Judge Cyrus Griffin would have heard the case. However, he yielded that role to John Marshall, chief justice of the United States Supreme Court. Marshall happened to be in Richmond at the time.

After challenging Alexander Hamilton to a duel on July 11, 1804, Aaron Burr shot Hamilton in the chest. Hamilton died soon after.

TREASON

A QUESTIONABLE DUEL

What happened at the famous duel between Alexander Hamilton and Aaron Burr? Historians agree that Hamilton opposed the idea of dueling, especially since his own son had been killed in a duel. Nevertheless, Hamilton felt he had to defend his honor as well as that of the declining Federalist Party. No one knows what happened at the duel itself. Some say that Hamilton, who fired first, missed Burr on purpose. Others say that he just missed. Novelist Gore Vidal offered a fictional version of the conflict in his novel, *Burr*, in which Burr says, "At the crucial moment his hand shook and mine never does." In any case, Burr shot Hamilton, who suffered for some thirty hours before he finally died.

As a Federalist and opponent of Thomas Jefferson, he eagerly took charge of the widely publicized trial.

The government hired a team of lawyers that included two members with strong political connections. These were George Hay, who was the son-in-law of future president James Monroe, and Gordon MacRae, an attorney and the lieutenant governor of Virginia. Burr's defense team also featured a lawyer with important political ties, Edmund Randolph. He had served as George Washington's secretary of state. A former attorney general for the federal government, he had also served as governor of Virginia. Of the two sides, the defense had the easier job. The Constitution required the government lawyers to produce two witnesses who could testify about an "overt act," plainly equivalent to warfare, that Burr had committed against the United States. However, Burr had not been present on Blennerhassett's island while preparations were underway to launch the rebellion, and Jefferson had stepped in to end the conspirators' plot before it took place. So it seemed that such proof would be impossible to find.

Finally a grand jury found that there was enough evidence to try Burr, and the trial started on August 3, 1807. The government failed to produce eyewitnesses who could testify that Burr had done more than make plans to attack the federal government. Therefore, Marshall ruled that the government's evidence could not come into court and ordered the jury to ignore it. The jury then found Burr not guilty.

Despite this verdict, Burr could not regain his reputation, The public thought him a traitor to his country, and there was no chance that he could revive his political career. Pursued by money lenders, who had helped him to maintain a good lifestyle during the years he was politically active, Burr fled to France, where he lived for several years. In 1812, he returned to the United States, but he never regained a place in American society. When he died in 1836, he was a broken man.

Suggestions for Further Reading

Burr, Aaron. *Reports of the Trials of Colonel Aaron Burr.* (Reprint.) New York: Da Capo, 1969.

Lomask, Milton. *Aaron Burr.* Vols. 1 & 2. New York: Farrar, Straus & Giroux, 1979 and 1982.

Nolan, Charles J. Jr. *Aaron Burr and the American Literary Imagination.* Westport: Greenwood Press, 1980.

Parton, James. *The Life and Times of Aaron Burr.* Broomall, PA: Chelsea House, 1983.

Wilson, R. J. "The Founding Father." *New Republic* (June 1983): 25–31.

John Brown Trial: 1859

Defendant: John Brown

Crime Charged: Insurrection (rebellion) and murder

Chief Defense Lawyers: Lawson Botts, Thomas C. Green, Samuel Chilton, and Hiram Griswold

Chief Prosecutor: Andrew Hunter

Judge: Richard Parker

Place: Charles Town, Virginia

Dates of Trial: October 27–November 2, 1859

Verdict: Guilty

Sentence: Death by hanging

SIGNIFICANCE: In an effort to aid Southern slaves, John Brown led a notorious but unsuccessful raid on the federal arms warehouse in Harpers Ferry, Virginia. The court found him guilty and executed him. Later he became a martyr to some people who were determined to abolish slavery.

The condition of the United States in the years leading up to the Civil War was a desperate one. Tension between the Northern states, where slavery had been banned, and the Southern slave-holding states had existed since the birth of the nation. When the founding fathers wrote the United States Constitution, they did little to address the issue of slavery. Over time the North and South grew further apart because of slavery.

In the first half of the nineteenth century, many western territories in the United States applied for statehood. The North insisted that these new states be free of slavery. The South wished them to enter the Union as slave states. Both North and South wanted to have the votes of the representatives and senators that a new state would send to Washington. Pro-slavery and anti-slavery forces struggled for control of these territories. When other means failed to settle their differences, they turned to violence.

Brown Raises Sword of Abolition

John Brown became a part of this conflict. He was born on a farm in Torrington, Connecticut, in 1800. Brown went to school to become a minister. However, he was a poor student, and soon returned to the family farm. Brown also failed to earn a living as a farmer, a surveyor, a real-estate investor, a postmaster, a teacher, a racehorse breeder, a tanner, and a wool merchant.

Brown was in his fifties when he became involved with the antislavery cause. With money from East Coast abolitionists, he set up a farm

The Tragic Prelude,
a mural of John
Brown by John
Steuart Curry.

in North Elba, New York. On this farm, runaway slaves learned to become farmers. Brown soon lost interest in this project, but kept his focus on freeing slaves. He headed west to the new territories, where the struggle between abolitionists and slave holders was most intense.

Brown in "Bleeding Kansas"

In the mid-1850s, Brown moved with his wife and several of his sons to the small village of Osawatomie, Kansas. Kansas was not yet a state in the Union. People called it "Bleeding Kansas" because it was the site of bloody conflicts between free and slave state forces. Brown and his sons joined the battle. He led several men on a raid into the pro-slavery town of Potawatomie. Brown and his followers killed five people there. They then went on to conduct attacks against more pro-slavery settlements in Kansas and other states.

Brown continued to receive money from wealthy eastern abolitionists. The most important of these called themselves the "Secret Six." They were a group of men that included the famous poet Ralph Waldo Emerson. In 1859, Brown received financial backing from the Secret Six for a raid on Harpers Ferry, Virginia, where the federal arsenal was located. Brown planned to take guns there and arm the slaves he expected to join him when they heard about the success of his raid. Then he would lead this army to destroy Southern state capitals and end slavery forever.

The Attack On Harpers Ferry

On October 16, 1859, Brown and twenty-one followers seized the arsenal at Harpers Ferry. Enslaved Africans never joined Brown's cause. Instead, local white residents surrounded them. Federal troops led by Colonel Robert E. Lee arrived and stormed the arsenal. Brown and his followers who had survived were captured. Lawmen took them to nearby Charles Town, Virginia.

Henry A. Wise, the governor of Virginia, feared that whites would lynch Brown. The governor also wanted a speedy trial. Federal law allowed the governor to decide the location of Brown's trial. Wise's options were either a federal court or a state court. Since a grand jury was already in session in Charles Town, Wise decided to try Brown in a Virginia state court.

Andrew Hunter, the district attorney for Charles Town, served as the prosecutor. Like Governor Wise, he wished for a speedy trial. Lawson

John Brown, shortly before his death on December 2, 1859.

Botts, a local Virginia attorney, and Thomas C. Green, an attorney who was also the mayor of Charles Town, represented Brown. Brown, trapped inside a Virginia prison cell and facing a trial dominated by Southerners, wrote to his abolitionist allies. He asked them to help him obtain an attorney who shared his opinions.

Judge Richard Parker, who presided over the court then in session in Charles Town, also wanted a speedy trial. The grand jury took only twenty-four hours to find that there was enough evidence to proceed against Brown. Judge Parker refused a request from Brown's attorneys that the trial be delayed until Brown recovered from injuries suffered during the storming of the arsenal. When the trial began on October 27, Brown attended the proceedings lying on a cot.

Brown's Lawyers Search for a Defense

Brown's attorneys decided to use the insanity defense to save Brown from being hanged. As evidence, they cited a telegram from someone who had known Brown many years earlier when the Brown family had lived in Akron, Ohio. The telegram read in part: "Insanity is hereditary in that family. . . . These facts can be conclusively proven by witnesses residing here, who will doubtless attend the trial if desired." Brown, however, refused to permit his lawyers to use this defense. He replaced them with Hiram Griswold, an attorney from Cleveland, Ohio, and Samuel Chilton,

A STIRRING SPEECH

John Brown's final statement in court on November 2, 1859, has gone down in history as a famous anti-slavery speech: "The court acknowledges, as I suppose, the validity of the law of God. I see a book kissed here which I suppose to be the Bible, or at least the New Testament. That teaches me that all things whatsoever I would that men should do to me, I should do even so to them. It teaches me, further, to 'remember them that are in bonds, as bound with them.' I endeavored to act up to that instruction. I say, I am yet too young to understand that God is any respecter of persons. I believe that to have interfered as I have done—in behalf of His despised poor, was not wrong, but right. Now, if it is deemed necessary that I should forfeit my life for the furtherance of the ends of justice, and mingle my blood further with the blood of my children and with the blood of millions in this slave country whose rights are disregarded by wicked, cruel, and unjust enactments, I submit, so let it be done."

an attorney from Washington, D.C. Judge Parker, however, refused to give Griswold and Chilton extra time to prepare their defense strategy.

Numerous witnesses testified about Brown's rebellion and the murders that accompanied it. Griswold maintained in his closing argument that as a non-Virginian Brown owed no loyalty to the state. However, after only a one-hour conference, the jury declared Brown to be guilty of both of the charges Virginia had filed against him. On November 2, Judge Parker sentenced Brown to hang one month later.

Brown's Martyrdom

At his sentence Brown delivered a stirring speech before the court that further inflamed public opinion against slavery and the South. During the following month, Judge Parker received thousands of letters pleading for mercy in Brown's case. Some of these letters even came from Southerners who realized that Brown's execution would only strengthen the forces who opposed them. Brown was nevertheless hanged on December 2, 1859, but not before delivering a final message predicting the outbreak of civil war.

John Brown Trial: 1859

Suggestions for Further Reading

Emerson, Ralph Waldo. "John Brown." *Emerson's Complete Works.* Boston and New York: Houghton Mifflin Company, 1878 and 1883.

Finkelman, Paul. *His Soul Goes Marching On: Responses to John Brown and the Harpers Ferry Raid.* Virginia: University of Virginia Press, 1995.

"The Ghost at Harpers Ferry." *American Heritage* (November 1988): 30–31.

McGlone, Robert E. "Rescripting a Troubled Past: John Brown's Family and the Harpers Ferry Conspiracy." *Journal of American History* (March 1989): 1179–1200.

Potter, Robert R. *John Brown: Militant Abolitionist.* Austin, TX: Raintree Steck-Vaughn, 1995.

Scott, John Anthony. *John Brown of Harper's Ferry.* New York: Facts on File, 1993.

Alfred Dreyfus Trials: 1894 and 1899

Defendant: Alfred Dreyfus

Crime Charged: Treason

Chief Defense Lawyers: Maitre Edgar Demange and Fernand Labori

Chief Prosecutors: André Brisset and Major Carriere

Judges: E. Maurel and Albert Jouaust

Places: Paris and Rennes, France

Dates of Trials: December 19–22, 1894; August 7–September 9, 1899

Verdicts: Guilty

Sentence: Deportation to the Devil's Island penal colony, French Guiana

Final Outcome: Verdicts invalidated; Dreyfus declared innocent

SIGNIFICANCE: The Dreyfus case made it clear that France in the late nineteenth century was full of anti-Jewish feeling.

In September 1894, a letter listing secret French military papers turned up in the French War Office. Officials thought it proved that a French traitor had delivered the papers to the Germans.

They suspected that the spy probably worked in the branch of the army handling artillery (weapons). Or perhaps he worked with the General Staff part-time. Only a few men fit this description. One was Alfred Dreyfus, a thirty-five-year-old artillery captain on staff duty. "The name of Dreyfus was the only one we could think of," recalled General Pierre-Elie Fabre. Dreyfus was the son of a wealthy manufacturer. He was a Jew in a largely Catholic army. He made a poor impression on some of his senior officers, who found him standoffish. "A bit too sure of himself," one said. Fabre compared Dreyfus's handwriting to that on the suspicious letter. They seemed to match.

Dreyfus Arrested

The order came down for Dreyfus's arrest, and he entered Cherche-Midi Prison. There Major Armand du Paty de Clam, of the War Office, questioned Dreyfus night after night for more than two weeks. Du Paty did not specify the charges against Dreyfus, and his questions confused the prisoner. Meanwhile, the Statistical Section began to produce a file that would frame Dreyfus.

Dreyfus seemed baffled and dazed. His jailer studied him closely. He looked, prison commandant Ferdinand Forzinetti thought, like a madman. His eyes were bloodshot. The things in his cell had been thrown about. Still, Forzinetti believed Dreyfus was innocent. "You are off the track," Forzinetti told a senior general. "This officer is not guilty." Nevertheless, on December 4, a military lawyer prepared a document accusing Dreyfus of treason and ordering a court martial.

The Case against Dreyfus

Most of the evidence against Dreyfus was insignificant. Handwriting experts concluded that Dreyfus had not written the letter sent to the War Office. What remained? Dreyfus spoke German. He expressed curiosity about military matters. He questioned his fellow officers about professional issues. He had a habit of loitering in offices. "Wherever he passed," the military lawyer said, "documents disappeared." Most damning, Dreyfus was a Jew. Du Paty, who built the case against Dreyfus, was strongly anti-Jewish. Someone had stolen the documents and sold them to France's enemies; in Du Paty's view, the thief could not possibly have been a Frenchman.

These were the origins of "the Affair," as the twelve-year ordeal of Dreyfus and of France came to be called. There were deeper causes, however. One was the history of defeat of France by Prussia and the loss of the provinces of Alsace and Lorraine in eastern France in 1870–1871. Another was government corruption. Still another was challenges from the

Courtroom Drama

political groups to the conservative authority of the army and church. Finally, there was spreading anti-Jewish feeling. Alfred Dreyfus was both the main victim and the chief symbol of the troubled atmosphere of late nineteenth-century France.

The First Trial

The court-martial of Dreyfus began at noon on December 19, 1894, in a small room in the Cherche-Midi. The military commander, Andre Brisset, demanded a closed trial. Dreyfus's lawyer, Edgar Demange, argued that the trial should be open to the public. The judge ruled for Brisset.

Witnesses testified on December 19, 20, and 21. Du Paty said that he had realized Dreyfus was guilty when he saw the prisoner's foot move slightly during questioning. Major Hubert Henry, the officer who had forged the documents, insisted that an informer had named Dreyfus as the traitor.

Several defense witnesses testified to Dreyfus's honesty, loyalty, and excellent record of service in the army. Dreyfus himself had little to add, beyond saying he was innocent. On December 22, Demange delivered his long final argument.

During the conference that followed, Du Paty delivered to the judges a package of "evidence"—more forgeries—supposedly proving Dreyfus's guilt. At 7:30 P.M., the court announced a unanimous verdict of guilty. The sentence was the loss of military rank and exile to the penal colony at Devil's Island in French Guiana.

A few days later, the authorities rejected Dreyfus's request for an appeal of his sentence. On the cold, gray morning of January 5, 1895, he arrived under guard at the courtyard of the Ecole Militaire. Several thousand Parisians stood outside the walls, shouting "Death to the Jew!" and "Death to Judas!" The clerk of the court-martial read out the verdict. Military decorations, symbols of rank, and even the red stripes on Dreyfus's trousers were torn off. An officer broke Dreyfus's sword over his knee.

The Affair

Interestingly, documents continued to disappear from the War Office even though Dreyfus was imprisoned. In March 1896, Major Georges Picquart, the new chief of military intelligence, discovered new evidence. It was a message card that seemed to point to a new suspect. Picquart began to suspect an officer named Charles Esterhazy.

OPPOSITE PAGE

French soldier Alfred Dreyfus was accused and convicted of revealing military secrets to the Germans in 1894. In 1895, he was forced to march around the courtyard of the Ecole Militaire in front of the troops.

TREASON

This illustration, from the January 13, 1895 edition of Le Petit Journal, *depicts Dreyfus's humiliation as his sword is broken by a member of the troops.*

ZOLA ACCUSES

One of the most famous phrases in history is *"J'accuse"* (JACK-cues), French for "I accuse," the title of the 1898 article that Emile Zola wrote to defend Alfred Dreyfus. Zola was a novelist who had helped to develop the style of naturalism, in which social life is portrayed in minute detail. Two of his most famous books are *Nana* (1880) and *Germinal* (1885).

Picquart learned that Esterhazy had written the message card. He had also received money from a German diplomat. Lastly, he had passed French military secrets to the Germans. Picquart turned this evidence over to the chief of the General Staff, and Dreyfus's supporters began to work for a retrial. However, in October, the army banished Picquart to Algeria. Meanwhile, Major Henry added new forgeries to Dreyfus's file.

The high commander refused to admit that the military had made a mistake. However, the matter now exploded into a national crisis. Those opposed to Dreyfus accused his supporters of trying to destroy France. His friends responded that the conviction was a shameful injustice. The politician Georges Clemenceau and the author Emile Zola were especially supportive of the former officer.

Meanwhile, risking his military career, Picquart passed on all that he knew of the case to certain politicians. They in turn pressured the army to arrest Esterhazy. On January 10, 1898, Esterhazy appeared before a court-martial in Paris. To cries of "Long live the army!" and "Down with the Jews!" the court cleared him of all charges the next day. Zola responded with the famous essay *J'accuse!* which resulted in the author's trial and conviction for libel. A few weeks after the court cleared Esterhazy, the German foreign minister informed his government that there had never been any connection between Dreyfus and any German agency.

Nothing happened for eight months. Then, in August, Major Henry admitted that he had forged evidence against Dreyfus. He then committed suicide. Esterhazy, who had fled France, admitted publicly that he had written the original letter to the War Office. He had done so, he claimed, on orders from a superior military officer, who wanted to catch the spy.

TREASON

The Second Trial

After a two-month review of Dreyfus's case, on June 3, the court canceled the earlier verdict against him and ordered a new court-martial at Rennes, in the Brittany region of France. Six days later, a warship carried Dreyfus away from Devil's Island.

The second trial began on August 7. Colonel Albert Jouaust, the court president, questioned Dreyfus harshly. Dreyfus, who was a near wreck of a man, gave short answers. Devil's Island had ruined his health and aged him beyond his years.

During three days of closed sessions, the court reviewed Dreyfus's secret file. On August 12, General Auguste Mercier, the war minister in 1894–1895, testified. He said that he remained convinced of Dreyfus's guilt. At this Dreyfus showed strong emotion for the first time. Much of the time, he seemed detached from the trial. He paid close attention, however, to the testimony of Picquart, whose activities had caused the military to fire Dreyfus. Speaking strongly and forcefully, Picquart left little room for doubt that the defendant had been wrongly accused. Still, to some, Dreyfus's guilt or innocence was beside the point. He still was guilty of casting "the Army and the Nation into turmoil." When the judges returned their verdict on September 9, they seemed to agree. "In the name of the French people, by a majority of five votes to two, yes, the accused is guilty," Jouaust said. "By a majority there are extenuating [partly excusing] circumstances." Ten days later, the French government pardoned Dreyfus.

The End of the Affair

In the end, Dreyfus went free. Still, he and his supporters pressed for a reversal of the verdict against him. By 1906, when the High Court of Appeals took up the case again, anti-Jewish feeling had lessened and the Dreyfus Affair was no longer so hotly debated. Dreyfus was declared innocent, and he returned to the army in July 1906. He retired a year later, but was called back to service to fight at Chemin des Dames and Verdun in World War I. He remained on active service until the end of the war.

Until the end of his life in 1935, Dreyfus did not accept the larger meaning of his case. To him, the army had simply accused the wrong man. To others, however, the conspiracy against Dreyfus helped set the stage for the anti-Semitism and dictatorship that resulted in the next world war.

Suggestion for Further Reading

Bredin, Jean-Denis. *The Affair: The Case of Alfred Dreyfus.* New York: George Braziller, 1986.

Chapman, Guy. *The Dreyfus Case: A Reassessment.* Westport, CT: Greenwood Press, 1979.

Hoffman, Robert L. *More Than a Trial: The Struggle over Captain Dreyfus.* New York: The Free Press, 1980.

Snyder, Louis L. *The Dreyfus Case: A Documentary History.* New Brunswick, NJ: Rutgers University Press, 1973.

Alfred
Dreyfus
Trials:
1894 and
1899

Roger Casement Trial: 1916

Defendant: Sir Roger Casement

Crime Charged: High treason

Chief Defense Lawyers: Arthur M. Sullivan, Thomas Artemus Jones, and John H. Morgan

Chief Prosecutors: Sir F. E. Smith, Archibald Bodkin, and Travers Humphreys

Judges: Lord Chief Justice Reading, Sir Horace Avory, and Sir Thomas Horridge

Place: London, England

Dates of Trial: June 26–29, 1916

Verdict: Guilty

Sentence: Death

SIGNIFICANCE: Sir Roger Casement's was the most hotly debated treason trial of the twentieth century, and there are still just as many people who consider him a patriot as those who consider him a traitor.

At daybreak on April 21, 1916, three men waded ashore on a deserted stretch of coastline in southwest Ireland. They had climbed out of a German submarine before the light dawned, then rowed for hours over rough seas to reach shore. The leader of the group was Sir Roger Casement, a fifty-one-year-old former British diplomat and a passionate Irish nationalist. After World War I had broken out in 1914, Casement had traveled in Germany to recruit Irish soldiers to return to their homeland and fight for independence from Britain. He arrived in Ireland with fellow nationalist Robert Monteith and Daniel Bailey, a private in the Royal Irish Rifles, who followed him to escape from a German prisoner of war camp.

Discovery

The three headed inland, and even though it was still only about 5:00 A.M., several people in County Kerry watched them find their way to the ruin known as McKenna's Fort. Here they split up. Monteith and Bailey left to meet up with the Irish Volunteers, while Casement stayed on to rest and regain his strength. Before he left, Monteith handed Casement a communication code from the German General Staff that was meant for the Irish Republican headquarters in Dublin.

Irish Nationalist Roger Casement, in an 1890s portrait. Casement was convicted of high treason in 1916 and condemned to death by hanging.

Casement Captured

Meanwhile, a farmer named John McCarthy had found the boat on the beach. Later that morning, his eight-year-old daughter uncovered several guns. McCarthy contacted the police. At around 1:00 P.M., lawmen arrested Casement. (Monteith later escaped to America. Bailey was arrested and charged, but later cleared.) He was carrying a pair of binoculars, ammunition, and various maps. In addition, a young man handed over to po-

TREASON

lice two scraps of paper. Casement had hurriedly thrown them on the road at the time of his arrest. Pieced together, they spelled out the German code.

Casement was taken to London and charged with high treason, a crime punishable by death. A search of his lodgings in London turned up his diaries—even more damaging evidence.

Casement's Diaries

Although they never came into court, Casement's diaries had an effect on the court proceedings. The diaries contained detailed accounts of homosexual activity, but to this day there is doubt about their genuineness. Some have found them to be forgeries, created by some in the British government to support their case against Casement. Others have no doubt that they are genuine. (The British even offered the diaries to the defense to use as evidence of insanity. The defense refused.)

The Trial Opens

Leaks to newspapers concerning the diary's contents helped inflame public feeling against Casement. When Casement's trial opened on June 26, 1916, however, the government spoke only of Casement's attempts to recruit prisoners of war in Germany for the Irish Brigade. If the German Navy were to succeed, Casement had to land a brigade in Ireland. Should Germany lose the war, each brigade member would receive a bonus of up to 20 pounds sterling (equivalent to $80) and free passage to America.

Several former prisoners of war in Germany told how Casement had stood on a table in their barracks to address them. "He spoke of how much the Germans liked the Irish, and how much the Irish liked the Germans," said one. Others testified about Casement's movements on the Irish coast on April 20. Lawman Bernard Riley described Casement's arrest at McKenna's Fort. It was Riley who had met the young man who had found the scraps of paper Casement discarded. They contained details of future arms shipments and how to make contact with foreign agents. Noticing that the number seven was written in the German style—with a dash across the downstroke—Riley returned to McKenna's Fort. There he conducted a search that turned up three overcoats. In the pocket of one was a first-class sleeping railway ticket from Berlin to Wilhelmshaven, dated April 12, 1916. This was powerful evidence that pointed strongly to Casement's guilt.

THE EASTER REBELLION

The Easter Rebellion was an uprising that took place the Monday after Easter in 1916. After years of trying to separate from England, some Irish independence groups took extreme measures, planning an armed uprising. Germany, at war with England, hinted it would support an Irish rebellion in order to weaken England. Casement went to Germany to try to find weapons, as well as to organize Irish soldiers who had been taken prisoner while fighting for England. He met with little success in either effort. By the time Casement died, many of the leaders of the rebellion had also been executed.

Defiant Speech

Casement's defense lawyer, Arthur Sullivan, K.C. (King's Counsel), could do little in the face of such evidence. He decided to call no witnesses, relying instead on the power of his own speechmaking. However, there was one final ploy: a request for his client to read a statement from the prisoner's dock. Lord Chief Justice Reading granted this request. However, he cautioned the jury to remember that because Casement had declined to give any evidence, his statement was not sworn testimony.

Casement made little attempt to deny the main charges against him. Instead he concentrated on denying charges that he had accepted money from enemy powers. When Sullivan took over again, he declared that Casement had acted for Ireland, not Germany. The lawyer argued hard and at great personal cost. With the strain plainly visible on his face, he began addressing things not testified about in court. As the judges began to grow restless, Sullivan suddenly swayed and whispered, "My Lords, I regret to say I have completely broken down." Court ended for the day.

The Willing Martyr

The next morning, with Sullivan ill and confined to his bed, Thomas Artemus Jones took up Casement's defense. Smith's response was to ask why, in the cause of Irish independence, Casement had gone to Germany? It

TREASON

The Casement funeral procession as it crossed O'Connell Street by the Dublin General Post Office.

was a point that was difficult to answer. The jury retired at 2:53 P.M. on the fourth day of the trial to consider the evidence. At 3:48, they came back with a guilty verdict. Before he heard his sentence of death, Casement addressed the court. He had clearly expected this outcome. He concluded his speech by remarking scornfully, "I am prouder to stand here today in the traitor's dock to answer this impeachment than to fill the place of my right honorable accusers."

The next day, June 30, officials announced that Casement had been stripped of his knighthood. As his supporters began a campaign to save him from the death penalty, rumors about the diaries began to circulate. No one knows what part they played in the British government's decision not to lift the death penalty. For Casement, this question was unimportant: he could not wait to assume his role as a martyr. Like other freedom fighters before and since, he was of more use dead than alive. He was executed on the morning of August 3, 1916.

Suggestions for Further Reading

Inglis, Brian. *Roger Casement.* New York: Harcourt Brace Jovanovich, 1973.

Montgomery Hyde, H. *Trial of Sir Roger Casement.* London: Hodge, 1960.

Reid, B. L. *Lives of Roger Casement.* New Haven, CT: Yale University Press, 1976.

Sawyer, Roger. *Casement: The Flawed Hero.* London: Routledge, 1984.

The Reichstag Fire Trial: 1933

Defendants: Marinus van der Lubbe, Ernst Torgler, Georgi Dimitrov, Blagoi Popov, and Wassil Tanev

Crimes Charged: High treason and arson, by setting fire to the Reichstag (the German parliament building)

Chief Defense Lawyers: Philipp Seuffert, Alfons Sack, and Paul Teichert

Chief Prosecutor: Karl Werner

Judge: Wilhelm Buenger

Place: Leipzig, Germany

Dates of Trial: September 21–December 23, 1933

Verdicts: Van der Lubbe: guilty; all others: acquitted

Sentence: Execution by beheading

SIGNIFICANCE: By using this show trial to demonstrate that there was a conspiracy by the International Communist movement that threatened Germany, Hitler and his National Socialist Party gained an excuse for seizing power and holding on to it.

In 1923, Adolf Hitler attempted to overthrow the Bavarian state government in southwestern Germany. The coup failed, and a court found Hitler guilty of treason. After he was released from prison in 1924, Hitler went on to lead his National Socialist German Workers' Party (the Nazis). In the election of 1932, the Nazi Party held the largest number of seats in the German parliament, or Reichstag (RIKE-shtahg). Hitler also ma-

A show trial found Marinus van der Lubbe guilty on charges of high treason and arson on December 23, 1933. He was beheaded on January 9, 1934.

nipulated the aging president of Germany, the war hero Paul von Hindenburg, who on January 30, 1933, named Hitler as chancellor.

This was only the beginning of Hitler's plan to take total control of Germany. He needed elections that would give his Nazi Party a full majority. However, there were many parties fighting for votes. One such party was the Communist Party, which held the third largest group of seats in the Reichstag. With the Communists already in control of the Soviet Union, many Europeans were fearful that the Communist movement would seize power in their own countries. Hitler and his Nazis saw themselves not just as an alternative to the Communists, but as a means of doing away with them.

The Fire

At about 9 P.M. on February 27, 1933, with the election campaign well under away, a flame burst out. A policemen stationed outside the Reichstag, the enormous fifty-year-old stone building where the German legislature sat, heard the sound of glass breaking. Peering into the ground floor of the building, he saw flames and a shadowy figure who seemed to be rushing through the building. More police came, and alarms brought the fire department. By about 9:20, just as the first fire ladders went up, the huge glass dome over the chamber of the building began to crack. A few minutes later it shattered.

At about the same time, a search party inside the Reichstag came across a man crouching in a small side room. He was Marinus van der Lubbe, a Dutchman, and he gave himself up at once. At the police station, officials began calling him a Communist. In fact, for some years he had been involved with the Dutch Communists, but he was not a revolutionary. He was really a rather confused, unbalanced person, somewhere between a tramp and a mental patient. The twenty-four-year-old van der Lubbe, a poorly educated worker, had lost much of his eyesight in an industrial accident. With his allowance from the Dutch government, he had set off in 1931 to travel around Europe. By 1933, he had shown up in Berlin, where he drifted about and attended at least one Nazi rally. He had, apparently, already attempted to set fire to two other buildings.

Wild Charges

The Nazi leaders did not wait to learn all this. Even before they knew much about van der Lubbe, they called the Reichstag fire a Communist plot. Hermann Goering was the first Nazi leader on the scene. Even as the fires were raging, he blamed them on the Communists. Hitler arrived on the scene a few minutes later, proclaiming, "A sign from heaven!" He then ordered mass arrests of Communists. Within twenty-four hours, police rounded up roughly four thousand Communists, Socialists, pacifists (people who advocate non-violence), and others. While this was going on during the day of February 28, Hitler persuaded President Hindenburg to discontinue all guarantees of civil liberties, giving Hitler and his Nazis the freedom to do as they pleased.

A Communist Conspiracy?

Hitler wanted to strengthen the notion that only the Nazis stood between the German people and a Communist conspiracy. So he made a major production of the Reichstag fire investigation and trial. It would not be enough to have only the pathetic van der Lubbe to blame. During the night of the fire, various individuals reported that Ernst Torgler, a Communist parliamentary leader, had been seen in the Reichstag as late as 8:15 P.M. When he read in the newspapers that he was a suspect, Torgler turned himself in to show that he had nothing to hide. He, too, would face trial. Meanwhile, a waiter in a Berlin restaurant claimed he had seen van der

Lubbe dining with some foreigners the afternoon before the fire. These foreigners turned out to be three Communists from the nearby country of Bulgaria. They also came to trial.

The Nazis Concentrate their Power

On March 5, national elections took place. Again, although they won the largest group of seats in the parliament, the Nazis still did not have a clear majority. However, because all the Communist members were either in jail or in hiding, the Nazis could exercise a voting majority. In the weeks that followed, they passed laws allowing Hitler to govern.

Meanwhile, as Hitler's government organized its case against the Communists, the world at large took notice. The international Communist network launched a campaign to blame the Nazis and sabotage the trial. They organized a committee of celebrated international lawyers and lawmakers who held a "countertrial" in London in September. As a result of these hearings, the committee decided that while only van der Lubbe could possibly be guilty, there was a chance that the Nazis might also be involved.

The Trial

The trial began in the city of Leipzig on September 21, 1933. There was no jury. A panel of judges, headed by Dr. Wilhelm Buenger, would decide the case. When the five accused men entered the courtroom, everyone noticed how terrible they looked after having been held in chains for four months. Van der Lubbe looked not only weak and spiritless, but devastated. His eyes appeared drowsy, mucus dripped from his nose and saliva from his mouth, his head drooped, and his arms hung at his sides. Not surprisingly, many people decided he had been drugged.

Ernst Torgler, the Communist deputy, had hired a respected trial lawyer, who made sure that his client's defense was separate from the others' defense. Torgler argued simply that there was no real evidence to convict him. The Bulgarians were assigned a lawyer, Paul Teichert. However, Georgi Dimitrov, one of the Bulgarian defendants, actually conducted the defense during the weeks of the trial. Dimitrov did an expert job of exposing the shallowness of the prosecutors' case and the depth of their bigotry.

The only real case was against van der Lubbe, but his conduct in court undercut the prosecution's charge that he had set the fire. He seemed

TREASON

THE PARLIAMENTARY SYSTEM

The German parliamentary system worked differently than the U.S. system of electing people to Congress. In the United States, particular individuals run for particular seats in Congress. Whoever gets the most votes in an election wins. In a parliamentary system, however, voters cast their ballots for parties, not individuals. If a party gets, say, 30 percent of the votes, its reward is 30 percent of the seats in parliament. Moreover, in a parliamentary system, there are usually several parties, rather than only two dominant parties, as in the United States. So a minority party like the National Socialists can still have the largest number of seats in parliament. Historians looking back at the rise of National Socialism often point out that if two other parties had joined in coalition, they could have defeated the Nazis, who never had majority support in Germany.

barely able to speak German, and when he did, he gave contradictory answers. He claimed that he had set the fire at the Reichstag by himself, using fire starters and his own clothes as torches. Yet questions remained. How could one individual have set so many fires in so little time? (Also, van der Lubbe was half blind, not bright, and had never been in the place before.) How did whoever set the fire gain entrance to the Reichstag? (An underground tunnel from the residence of the president of the Reichstag—none other than Goering—was said to have been the route.) There was no follow-up on these issues. Instead, the government continued to hammer away on the charge that the fire was part of a broad Communist plot.

The whole world followed these proceeding as they moved from Leipzig to Berlin, where van der Lubbe reenacted his version of what he had done. Then the trial moved back to Leipzig. The longer it went on, the less convincing the government's case appeared to be. It called some 250 witnesses, made around 7,000 recordings of testimony, and filed more than fifty 10,000-page volumes of evidence. In the end, the chief prosecutor himself recommended that the court clear the three Bulgarians, and it did. He asked that Torgler be found guilty of involvement "in some manner or another," but he, too, was acquitted. Only van der Lubbe was found guilty, but it was not clear whether anyone believed he had done it on his own, or with some aid.

Aftermath

On January 9, 1934, Marinus van der Lubbe was beheaded by guillotine. Torgler was held in "protective custody" until November 1936. The three Bulgarians were sent to Moscow in February 1934; Dimitrov emerged after World War II as the leader of Bulgaria.

The question of who set the Reichstag fire has never been entirely resolved. Some think that it was the result of a Nazi plot, and that van der Lubbe was entirely innocent. Others believe that van der Lubbe set the fires as part of a Communist conspiracy. There is the possibility that the fire involved both the Nazis and van der Lubbe. Whoever set the fire, Hitler turned the burning of the Reichstag into a holocaust that destroyed much of Europe and many of its people.

Suggestions for Further Reading

Bullock, Alan. *Hitler—A Study in Tyranny.* Revised Edition. New York: Harper & Row, 1962.

Reed, Douglas. *The Burning of the Reichstag.* London: Victor Gollancz, 1934.

Shirer, William. *The Rise and Fall of the Third Reich.* New York: Simon & Schuster, 1960.

Tobias, Fritz. *The Reichstag Fire.* Translated by Arnold Pomerans. New York: Putnam, 1964.

The Moscow Purge Trials: 1936 and 1937–1938

Defendants: Three groups of approximately seventy "Old Bolsheviks" (radical Communists) former political opponents of dictator Joseph Stalin

Crimes Charged: Murder, terrorism, espionage, and political deviation

Chief Defense Lawyers: In most cases, none

Chief Prosecutor: Andrei Vyshinsky

Chief Judge: Vasily Ulrikh

Place: Moscow, Soviet Union

Dates of Trials: August 1936; January 1937; March 1938

Verdicts: Guilty, in every case

Sentences: Death, in all but a few cases

SIGNIFICANCE: At these so-called "confessional" trials, the critics of dictator Joseph Stalin publicly withdrew their objections to his rule. This exercise left a tradition of state-sponsored terror in the Soviet Union. It also created a permanent system of labor camps, called the Gulag, to which the government could send any citizen.

By 1934, Joseph Stalin had won out over his rivals for supreme power in the Soviet Union. A calm fell over the country. For many ordinary people, living conditions were finally beginning to improve. Soviet borders were secure. Despite this relative peace, or perhaps because of it, Stalin began a campaign of terror that affected not only his political opponents, but hundreds of thousands of ordinary Soviet citizens as well.

The Great Terror

The murder of Leningrad party chief Sergei Kirov on December 1, 1934, touched off "the Great Terror." Stalin may have arranged the murder himself, in order to settle a political dispute. In any event, he used it as an excuse to impose cruelty on his people. Over the next four years, he framed and had executed thousands of Communist Party officials. Stalin's conspiracy spread from the Kirov murder to all sorts of other murderous plots. In the end, more than five million people were arrested from 1936 to 1938 alone. In 1937 and the three years that followed, the "purge" destroyed 70 percent of the officers in the Red Army.

A nationwide system of informers resulted in an endless stream of victims. Children turned on their parents; friends turned on their friends. According to one authority, one of every five people in every factory or office acted as a spy for the Soviet secret police. Stalin's henchmen carried out mass executions and sent hundreds of thousands of political prisoners to camps where they worked like slaves. It is estimated that as many as twenty million people may have died as the result of execution, from illness or overwork in the prison camps, or simply from starvation due to Stalin's failed economic policies.

The Moscow Purge Trials: 1936 and 1937–1938

Show Trials

The three Moscow show trials of 1936 to 1938 were also part of the Great Terror. Some seventy "conspirators" faced public trial, most of them "Old Bolsheviks." Some had credentials dating from the times of the czars. These men, the prosecutors claimed, made it possible for such an astonishing number of terrorists, spies, and other enemies of the people to remain at large. Stalin blamed them for the massive crop failures that led to starvation and for the poor industrial planning that created shortages of nearly every type of product and service.

All three trials had this in common: coerced confessions. Guards obtained them by torture, blackmail, threats to wives and children, and false promises. Such activities were justified by the argument that the Communist Party's concerns came first; as a service to the party, many of the defendants agreed to confess to imaginary crimes.

The First Trial

A wave of arrests followed the killing of Sergei Kirov. The secret police captured and immediately killed the assassin, Leonid Nikolayev. Within

TREASON

a month, police arrested 30,000 to 40,000 people in Leningrad alone, charging them with aiding in Kirov's murder. What happened to one woman helps to explain the twisted logic of the party. She worked at a Young Communist library that Nikolayev had used. On the basis of this slim connection, police arrested her, her sister, her sister's husband, and the secretary of her local party group.

Stalin's real targets were the Old Bolsheviks Lev Kamenev and Grigori Zinoviev. Their trial took place in secret in Leningrad in mid-January 1935. They admitted (through force) to sharing moral responsibility for Kirov's killing, but they denied any actual involvement. Then, as an excuse for even more purges, Stalin decided to hold a second trial of the two men, this time with another Old Bolshevik, Ivan Smirnov, and thirteen others.

The trial opened on August 19 in the October Hall of the Trade Union House in Moscow. Nearly everything had been arranged in advance. To encourage the accused to confess, guards beat them and would not allow them to sleep. One by one, the defendants agreed to admit their guilt in open court in return for Stalin's guarantee that their lives and those of their families would be spared. The "conspirators" faced charges of plotting to kill Stalin and other party leaders. Most of the approximately two hundred spectators were carefully chosen members of the secret police. About thirty hand-picked diplomats and foreign journalists sat in so that they could carry a report of the conspiracy to the world.

The presiding judge, Vasily Ulrikh, opened the proceedings by asking if any of the defendants wanted a lawyer. All said they did not. The court clerk then read out the charges: direct involvement in the Kirov assassination, plots to murder the chief party leaders, and connections to the exiled former Communist leader Leon Trotsky. The accused pleaded guilty on all counts, except for the stubborn old revolutionary Smirnov and one other. Zinoviev, Stalin's chief target, confirmed he had acted under Trotsky's instructions. He and the others provided evidence against Smirnov, who continued to accept general responsibility while denying the specific charges. The next day, August 20, Kamenev confessed.

On August 24 the court delivered its verdict: all were guilty and all were to be shot. Smirnov remained defiant to the end, but the others went meekly, perhaps believing that Stalin would live up to his promise to spare their lives. But there were no pardons. Zinoviev, Kamenev, Smirnov, and the others were taken to the execution cellars and shot, each with a bullet to the back of the head, probably within a week after the trial ended.

A few days later, Stalin ordered the head of the secret police, Genrikh Yagoda, to execute 5,000 political prisoners in the labor camps.

Yagoda was in turn replaced with a rising star in the party, Nikolai Yezhov. Under Yezhov, the terror worsened. He gave his name to its most ferocious phase: *Yezhovshchina*.

The Second Trial

The second show trial opened on January 23, 1937. The seventeen defendants were mostly Old Bolsheviks, once important and respected party members. Now the government called them "the Anti-Soviet Trotskyite Center." The four chief targets were Grigori Pyatakov, Grigori Sokolnikov, Leonid Serebryakov, and Karl Radek. They were accused of plotting to destroy the Soviet economy and of spying for Germany and Japan. The government claimed that former Communist leader Trotsky had directed them from abroad.

The defendants "confessed" that they had been poor planners and had organized terrorist acts, such as factory explosions and train wrecks. No evidence other than these forced confessions came into court. On January 30, the court handed down a guilty verdict. It also imposed a death sentence on all but Sokolnikov, Radek (who would later die in the Arctic labor camps), and a few defendants of lesser importance. Stalin had again permitted a few western journalists to watch the trial. It seems hard to understand now, but a few of these reporters actually believed that the trials were legitimate, the charges real, and the confessions true.

The Third Trial

Now the terror took on a life of its own. No one was safe. The secret police came in the middle of the night, knocking on people's doors. People jumped to accuse someone else before they themselves were accused. By March 1938, Stalin could not have believed that the Old Bolsheviks any longer threatened his power. Still, the third show trial provided a grand finale, tying together every sort of opposition to Stalin in one great conspiracy.

The chief defendants were Nikolai Bukharin, Alexei Rykov, and Nikolai Krestinsky. All had been members of former Soviet leader Vladimir Lenin's cabinet. Also accused was Yagoda, the former chief of the secret police. The charges were familiar: spying for Germany and Japan, plotting to bring back capitalism, and conspiring to assassinate Stalin. As in the earlier trials, the accused accepted formal responsibility

STALIN'S ENEMY, LEON TROTSKY

Many of those sentenced in the Moscow Purge Trials were accused of conspiring with Leon Trotsky, the Russian revolutionary who, along with Vladimir Lenin, had helped to lead the original October Revolution. When Lenin died in 1924, Trotsky and Stalin were the chief rivals to succeed him. At that time, Stalin was the general secretary of the Communist Party, while Trotsky was head of the Red Army. Trotsky believed that unless the entire world adopted Socialism, the revolution could not succeed in the Soviet Union. He advocated always trying to convert other countries to Communism, a doctrine known as "permanent revolution." Stalin, on the other hand, said that the Soviets had to face facts. Since revolution was unlikely to occur elsewhere in the world, at least in the near future, the Soviets should follow the doctrine of "socialism in one country." Gradually, Stalin's ideas came to be accepted while Trotsky's were condemned. In 1925, Trotsky lost his post as commissar of war. In 1927, he was expelled from the Communist Party, and in 1929 he was sent into exile, where he continued to write criticisms of Stalinism and the Soviet Union, although he remained a committed Socialist. In 1940, two years after the last purge trial, Trotsky was assassinated in Mexico, in what many believe was a death ordered by Stalin.

for the general failures of Soviet industry and agriculture. All twenty-two defendants plead guilty, except for Krestinsky, who withdrew his "confession" without warning. However, on the evening of the second day, he rose, looking weakened by what had probably been a night of torture, and confessed.

The trial ended on March 12. At four o'clock the next morning, the judges returned their verdicts. As before, the court found each guilty of all charges. Nineteen of the twenty-two defendants received death sentences. Bukharin and Rykov remained defiant to the end, but the end came quickly. Guards shot them, together with some of the others, in the cellars of Moscow's Lubyanka prison.

Suggestions for Further Reading

Conquest, Robert. *The Great Terror: Stalin's Purge of the Thirties.* New York: Macmillan, 1968.

Medvedev, Roy. *Let History Judge: The Origins and Consequences of Stalinism.* Translated by George Shriver. New York: Columbia University Press, 1989.

Vaksberg, Arkadii. *Stalin's Prosecutor: The Life of Andrei Vyshinsky.* New York: Grove Weidenfeld, 1991.

The Moscow Purge Trials: 1936 and 1937–1938

Henri Philippe Pétain and Pierre Laval Trials: 1945

Defendants: Henri Philippe Pétain and Pierre Laval

Crimes Charged: Pétain: treason; Laval: plotting against the state, (trading) intelligence with the enemy

Defense Lawyers: Pétain: Fernand Payen, Jean Lemaire, and Jacques Isorni; Laval: Pierre Laval, Albert Naud, and Jacques Baraduc

Chief Prosecutor: André Mornet

Judge: Paul Mongibeaux

Place: Paris, France

Dates of Trials: Pétain: July 23–August 13, 1945; Laval: October 4–8, 1945

Verdicts: Guilty

Sentences: Execution (Pétain's sentence changed to life imprisonment)

SIGNIFICANCE: The trials of Pétain and Laval gave the French people, and the world, the first deep understanding of the treachery of France's Vichy government, which had cooperated with the Nazis during World War II.

In August 1945, French politician Henri Philippe Pétain was eighty-nine years old. He was a brigadier general when World War I began in 1914. In 1916, his brilliant victory over the Germans at Verdun-sur-Meuse had made him a national hero. Following World War I, he had served as France's minister of war and as its ambassador to Spain.

During World War II, as Paris fell to the invading Germans and the French government fled to Bordeaux in southwestern France, Pétain became premier. He began his service on June 17, 1940. Pétain then tried to make peace with Adolf Hitler. On July 11, he assumed absolute power over the French state, establishing his headquarters in Vichy, a health resort in central France.

Pierre Laval was sixty-two in 1945. A Socialist politician since 1914, he was a senator in the French parliament. He also served as an under secretary of state, as minister of justice, and as minister of labor. In 1931, he also served for one year as premier. In 1935, while serving again as the French premier, he had signed a treaty with Italian dictator Benito Mussolini that helped Italy to invade and conquer Ethiopia. In 1940, Laval joined Pétain's Vichy government as vice premier.

Henri Philippe Pétain and Pierre Laval Trials: 1945

The Vichy Government

As World War II dragged on, the Allies opposed the Vichy government. U.S. president Franklin D. Roosevelt, British prime minister Winston Churchill, Soviet dictator Joseph Stalin, and General Charles de Gaulle, head of the Free French forces in London, led the Allies. They knew that Pétain's Vichy government was cooperating with the Germans. However, they did not know how close they were. The French people knew even less until Pétain and Laval came to trial soon after the Germans surrendered in the spring of 1945, ending the war in Europe. They knew so little because in the confusion that resulted from the fall of France in 1940, little dependable news reached them. (Newspaper staffs had joined the millions who fled south from Paris when the Germans entered the city.) What is more, Pétain had been so beloved that he was able to seize power at Vichy without challenge.

Five Judges, Two Juries

The Pétain trial opened on Thursday, July 23. It was housed in a cramped, hot, and shabby courtroom in the Palais de Justice in Paris. Five judges and two separate twelve-man juries heard the evidence against Pétain and Laval. One jury was chosen from members of the French Resistance (those who had fought underground against the Nazi occupation). The other came from "the Bordeaux parliament" (those who had maintained a French government in the south and who had voted against putting Pétain in charge of the wartime administration).

The judges and juries saw before them Pétain, elderly but still handsome in his marshall's uniform and medals. The prosecutor began by reciting from memory the details of the June 22, 1940, peace treaty Pétain had signed with Germany. It permitted the Nazis to occupy two-thirds of French soil. Pétain jumped from his seat. "That's unfair!" he cried. "You have no right to begin with the worst part." He said he had done what he had for the good of France. "If I treated [negotiated] with the enemy, it was to spare France. I prepared the road to liberation." The crowd of people in the courtroom responded with catcalls.

Afterward, Pétain sat silent, refusing to speak for the next five days, as witnesses presented their evidence. Others, however, interrupted the proceedings. A deputy juror broke in on testimony by former premier Paul Reynaud with comments of his own. Two jurors who had served with the resistance protested Pétain's insults to their noble cause. The judges, who had shown clear prejudice against the defendant, allowed prominent witnesses to bring hearsay evidence (a statement made by someone other than the witness testifying) into the testimony.

Extent of Collaboration Revealed

On the sixth day, however, the facts began to come out. Germany had illegally grabbed the French region of Alsace-Lorraine in August 1940, just after Pétain had made peace with the Nazis. Few had known about this betrayal. Further testimony revealed that the Vichy government had allowed Germany to occupy airfields France controlled in the Middle East and Tunisia. These airfields were then used to ship supplies to German general Erwin Rommel in North Africa.

It turned out that Pétain had ended the authority of parliament. He had tried French politicians who refused to accept the Nazi "new order." His military courts had imposed death sentences on those working in the "underground" resistance movement. Vichy condemned about 15,000 resistance fighters as traitors. He had forced French people to work in Germany. Some testified that he had severed diplomatic relations with the United States after the United States and Great Britain invaded North Africa in 1942. He had not resisted when Germany had invaded the unoccupied section of France on November 11, 1942. In addition to the 150,000 French who had died in German concentration camps, in the last days of the occupation Germany had executed 60,000 French citizens. All this was done without interference from the Vichy government. Finally,

Henri
Philippe
Pétain and
Pierre Laval
Trials:
1945

Henri Philippe Pétain listens solemnly to testimony presented at his 1945 trial. He would later be found guilty and sentenced to life in prison.

Vichy cooperation with anti-Jewish laws permitted the deportation of 120,000 Jews, of whom only 1,500 lived to return home.

On August 13, in response to the prosecution's summation, the judges reduced the charge against Pétain from treason to (trading) "intelligence with the enemy." The juries then found Pétain guilty, and he was sentenced to death. Two days later, General de Gaulle, then president of the temporary French government, reduced this sentence to life in prison.

Trial of Laval

Pierre Laval came to trial on October 4, 1945, as the most hated man in France. The crowd in the courtroom shouted angrily at him, and he screamed back. The French knew that in December 1942 he had released a treasonous statement to the press from Vichy. It read, "Germany's victory will prevent our civilization from foundering in the communistic chaos," and "an American victory would bring in its train the triumph of Jews and Communists." They also knew that in June 1943 he had announced over Paris radio that 200,000 Frenchmen must go to work in Germany.

Laval had been a defiant witness at the Pétain trial. Now he was equally defiant acting in his own defense. When his lawyers refused to appear at the opening of his trial (to protest the investigation of Laval's case), Laval delivered an angry three-hour statement. Responding to his fury, the judge had him removed from the courtroom. When Laval came back, he spoke for another three hours. For three days, Laval dominated the courtroom, sure that he knew the law better than the judge.

"Twelve Balls In the Skin"

Laval proved to be the most capable person in the courtroom. Jurors arrived late. The judge answered his own questions before allowing the defendant to respond. On the third day of the trial, several of the parliamentary jurors attacked Laval verbally, pledging to give him "twelve balls in the skin"—that is, the firing squad. Laval responded with a violent outburst that caused the judge to expel him from the courtroom again. This time, Laval protested by sending a formal letter to the judge from his cell, refusing to return to the courtroom. The trial proceeded anyway.

The jury declared Laval guilty and sentenced him to death. When Laval demanded a retrial, De Gaulle refused the request. On October 14, just before his scheduled execution, Laval swallowed a cyanide pill. He was rushed to the hospital, where his stomach was pumped before the

Henri
Philippe
Pétain and
Pierre Laval
Trials:
1945

COLLABORATION AT VICHY

From 1940 to 1942, the Vichy government controlled only part of France, the portion that the Germans occupied. The southern part of France remained outside of German control; it was known as "Free France." Then, in 1942, the Allies invaded Africa, and in retaliation, German dictator Adolf Hitler seized all of France. The Vichy regime continued to rule German-occupied France, but in such a way as to collaborate closely with German war goals as well as with German plans to deport and destroy the entire Jewish population of Europe. The Vichy regime finally fell when the Allies invaded Normandy, in northern France, in 1944, and advanced throughout France to help bring World War II to an end in 1945.

poison could take effect. In pain, he was returned to the prison to face the firing squad. Shouting "Vive la France!" Laval was executed.

Pétain died at age ninety-six in a fortress prison on the island of Yeu, on July 23, 1951.

Suggestions for Further Reading

Aron, Robert. *The Vichy Regime, 1940–44.* London: Macmillan, 1958.

Chapman, Guy. *Why France Fell.* New York: Holt, Rinehart and Winston, 1968.

Ouston, Philip. *France in the Twentieth Century.* New York: Praeger, 1972.

Shirer, William L. *The Collapse of the Third Republic.* New York: Simon and Schuster, 1969.

Smith, Gene. *The Ends of Greatness.* New York: Crown, 1990.

Williams, Charles. *The Last Great Frenchman: A Life of General de Gaulle.* New York: Wiley, 1995.

Vidkun Quisling Trial: 1945

Defendant: Vidkun Abraham Lauritz Jonsson Quisling

Crimes Charged: High treason, persecution of Jews, execution of Norwegian citizens, and plotting to bring about the invasion of Norway by Germany

Chief Defense Lawyer: Henrik Bergh

Chief Prosecutor: Annaeus Schjodt

Judge: Erik Solem

Place: Oslo, Norway

Dates of Trial: August 20–September 10, 1945

Verdict: Guilty

Sentence: Execution

SIGNIFICANCE: Soon after Germany invaded Norway on April 9, 1940, during World War II, the word *quisling* became another word for traitor. The trial of Norway's former premier in 1945 permanently confirmed the word as a synonym for traitor in any language.

Vidkun Quisling was born to a family that had been respected in Norway for more than six hundred years. Young Quisling was a bright student who read widely. He showed a gift for mathematics, and seemed born to the outdoor Norwegian way of life, hiking miles at a time and hunting bear. When he reached manhood, Quisling was taller than the average Nordic male. His athletic build pointed him toward a military career. He entered Krigskola, the West Point of Norway, in 1905. When he graduated, he had the highest grade-point average ever achieved in the more than one-hundred-year history of the school.

Captain Quisling was sent to Petrograd (now St. Petersburg) in Russia as a diplomat just after the Russian Revolution in November 1917. There, he became an expert on Russia. He learned its language and every aspect of its capacity for war, as he witnessed the vast changes brought about by the Communists. Back in Norway in 1931, Quisling became minister of defense. He resigned the post in 1933 to found the Nasjonal Samling (National Unity Party). Its goal was to do away with Communism and labor unions. Meanwhile, the Labor Party, which Quisling bitterly opposed, gained control of the government.

Quisling's Proposals

In October 1939, Quisling proposed to British prime minister Neville Chamberlain that a commonwealth of European nations be formed. He received only polite thanks for his suggestion. A few days later, he sent German authorities a proposal for disarming European nations and uniting them in a federation. The federation would cooperate in areas such as foreign exchange and freedom of the seas. His proposal came too late. Within weeks, the Red Army marched into Finland. Quisling responded by gaining an appointment with German dictator Adolf Hitler in December 1939.

On April 8, 1940, British destroyers laid minefields in Norway's West Fjord. The British minister warned the Norwegian government not to remove the mines. Norway demanded that Britain remove them or face war. Germany demanded that Norway remove them or face war. The next morning, Norway's military chief of staff proposed that the military be mobilized. The defense minister did nothing. By the afternoon of April 9, German ships were landing troops in Norway. The entire government and general military staff, 146 of 150 members of parliament, and the royal family all fled to Sweden.

The Nazis took over, appointing Quisling as the political leader of Norway. On February 1, 1942, he became minister-president, a position he held until the Germans were thrown out of Norway in May 1945. Quisling's compatriots then arrested him.

Treason and other Charges

An investigation of the activities of Quisling and the Nasjonal Samling during the previous five years began. Many questioned whether the government-in-exile, now returning to Norway, had constitutional authority.

TREASON

No one knew what charge to level at Quisling. Finally the government charged him with treasonable activities on April 9, 1940; treason in declaring a government on February 1, 1942; persecution of Jews; execution of Norwegian citizens; and conspiring with the Germans to bring about the invasion of Norway in 1940.

World attention focused on Oslo on August 20, 1945, for the trial of a man whose name had become synonymous with traitor. The presiding judge was Erik Solem, who had spent several years in a concentration camp. The lawyer for the defense, appointed by the court, was Henrik Bergh, who had long supported the government-in-exile. Bergh made the unusualness of the circumstances clear with his opening remarks:

> The indictment is based upon sections of the penal code, and the case is to that extent a criminal case. The background, however, and the counts of the indictment, show that the case concerns the political viewpoint of the defendant. In this assembly, no one belongs to the political movement of which he was the leader. Neither in the court nor at the bar is there anyone who shares his views, not even his own coun-

Norwegian politician Vidkun Quisling at his trial in Oslo. Convicted on treason charges, Quisling was executed on October 24, 1945.

sel, for all lawyers of his party are barred from pleading if they are not, as most of them are, in prison.

Prosecutor Annaeus Schjodt produced evidence that Quisling's government had introduced, in October 1942, a law taking away all Jewish property. Witnesses testified to Quisling's November 1942 announcement that all Jews must register with the authorities within two weeks. Other testimony indicated that Quisling had put the state police under military law, and that when the Germans had ordered the death of a policeman who had failed to make an arrest they demanded him to make, Quisling failed to save the man. A letter from Quisling to one of Hitler's cabinet members proposing that Norwegian volunteers be recruited to fight alongside German troops was entered as evidence. The defense tried to make the point that Quisling wanted the Norwegians to fight the Bolsheviks, for he knew that Germany was about to turn against its Soviet ally, but had not intended for the Norwegians to fight the British.

The Hitler Visit

In his defense, Quisling explained that he had gone to see Hitler in December 1939 because he knew that Germany would soon occupy Norway in an attempt to stop Soviet expansion into Scandinavia. He told Hitler the Nasjonal Samling was not strong enough to take over the government. Hitler, according to Quisling, said that he hoped Norway would remain neutral, but that he would invade if Great Britain tried to establish itself there. When he went home, Quisling said, he did not report on his meeting with Hitler because he knew the ruling Labor Party did not trust him and thought he exaggerated the threat of Nazi invasion. Quisling insisted he had had no further dealings with Hitler.

It was clear, however, that Quisling had met with Alfred Rosenberg, head of the Nazi Party's Office of Foreign Affairs, as early as 1934, to discuss the supremacy of the Nordic and German peoples. Quisling's defense was that he had intended to influence the Nazis in favor of Norway. He also maintained that his goal during the Nazi occupation was to preserve Norway's independence within the larger Germanic community rather than see his country become subject to total Nazi domination.

The Rosenberg Memo

The most damaging evidence against Quisling was a long memo written by Rosenberg on June 15, 1940, which was discovered just as the

FASCISM IN EUROPE AND AMERICA

In 1931, Vidkun Quisling founded the Nasjonal Samling (National Unity Party)—a Norwegian version of the German National Socialist Party. Both parties were known as *fascist* organizations, after the term first developed by Italian dictator Benito Mussolini, who with his fascist party ruled Italy from 1922 until the end of World War II. Likewise, the falangist party of General Francisco Franco in Spain, which took power in 1939 and held it until Franco's death in 1975, was considered a fascist regime. Most other European countries had fascist movements, as did the United States, although most never came to political power. Fascist political parties continue to exist under a variety of names in Europe, the United States, and Latin America. Generally, fascist movements are characterized by their opposition to democratic, socialist, and workers movements, such as unions; their racist ideologies, including anti-Semitism; their aggressive military policies; and their connection to a strong leader who promises to return the nation to an earlier time when it seemed to fulfill its national ideals.

trial opened. The memo said that Quisling "requested, anticipating the intentions of greater Germany, backing for his party and press in Norway. . . . Quisling saw it was his duty to bind Norway's fate with that of Germany."

The defense tried to prop up its case with witnesses who testified about Quisling's good character. As the trial ended, an exhausted Quisling himself spoke for eight hours without notes, attempting to explain his wartime actions and detailing his political career. He denied having committed treason and suggested that others should be tried in his place; he should be honored for his patriotism, he declared.

On September 10, the court found Vidkun Quisling guilty of all charges and sentenced him to death. An appeal to the supreme court of Norway was rejected. At 2 A.M. on October 24, Quisling was blindfolded against his wishes. His request to shake hands with the ten-man firing squad was granted. Then he was shot. Quisling's body was displayed to the public. Norwegian citizens prodded it to make sure that the man who had betrayed them was really dead.

Suggestions for Further Reading

Hayes, Paul M. *Quisling.* Bloomington: Indiana University Press, 1972.

Hewins, Ralph. *Quisling: Prophet Without Honor.* New York: John Day, 1966.

Hoidal, Oddvar K. *Quisling: A Study in Treason.* Oxford: Oxford University Press, 1989.

Unstad, L. I. *Vidkun Quisling: The Norwegian Enigma.* Selinsgrove, PA: Susquehanna University Press, 1964.

Vidkun
Quisling
Trial:
1945

Ezra Pound Trial:
1946

Defendant: Ezra Pound

Crime Charged: Treason

Chief Defense Lawyers: Thurman Arnold, Julien Cornell, and Robert W. Furniss Jr.

Chief Prosecutors: Isaiah Matlack and Oliver Gasch

Judge: Bolitha J. Laws

Place: Washington, D.C.

Date of Trial: February 13, 1946

Verdict: Unsound mind; charges dismissed in 1958

SIGNIFICANCE: This case involved a unique situation: a well-known and respected poet, charged with treason but suspected of insanity, whose supporters included famous writers such as T. S. Eliot, Robert Frost, Ernest Hemingway, and Archibald MacLeish.

Ezra Pound was born in 1885 in the small town of Hailey, Idaho. At the time it was made up of one street, one hotel, and forty-seven places to drink liquor. Raised near Philadelphia, Pound graduated from the University of Pennsylvania in 1906. He then took a teaching job at Wabash College in Indiana, but he was unhappy there and left for Europe after only four months.

Working as secretary to the Irish poet William Butler Yeats while publishing his own poetry, Pound helped to establish the reputations of literary giants. He launched the careers of poets T. S. Eliot and Robert Frost and that of novelist James Joyce. Living in Paris in the 1920s, Pound ap-

peared completely confi-
dent of his own talent to
the other foreigners who
made their homes there. In
the 1930s, he settled in
Rapallo, Italy, where he
continued to work on the
long series of poems he
called *Cantos*.

*Attorney General Francis Biddle, who brought
charges against Ezra Pound for treason.*

"Europe Calling! Pound Speaking!"

In Europe in the 1930s,
World War II was loom-
ing. Pound had strong
opinions on world poli-
tics, and he favored the
Italian brand of fascism,
an authoritarian, militaris-
tic form of government.
He suggested to the Ital-
ians that they sponsor
publications aimed at pro-
moting American sympa-
thy for Italian fascism, but
they turned him down.

Pound next suggested a series of short-wave radio broadcasts directed at Americans. By January 1941, his voice, declaring "Europe calling! Pound speaking! Ezra Pound speaking!" was regularly on the air. The
fascists paid Pound for his services, and he urged America to stay out of
the war. His broadcasts began to promote anti-Jewish propaganda. After
the Japanese bombed the American naval base at Pearl Harbor, Hawaii,
causing the United States to enter the war in 1942, he declared:

> America COULD have stayed out of the war. . . .
> IF America had stayed neutral the war would now
> be over. . . . For the United States to be makin' war
> on Italy AND on Europe is just plain damn non-

TREASON

sense. . . . And for this state of things Franklin Roosevelt is more than any other one man responsible.

Americans, including President Roosevelt, heard Pound. Attorney General Francis Biddle had Pound charged with treason. It is the only crime actually defined in the Constitution, which says that treason consists only of making war on the United States, or providing the nation's enemies with aid and comfort. Pound, for his part, said that he was "completely surprised."

> I do not believe that the simple fact of speaking over the radio . . . can in itself constitute treason. I think that must depend on what is said. . . .

> I obtained the concession to speak over Rome radio with the following proviso: Namely that nothing should be asked of me contrary to my conscience or contrary to my duties as an American citizen. . . .

> I have not spoken with regard to THIS war, but in protest against a system which creates one war after another. . . . I have not spoken to the troops, and have not suggested that the troops should mutiny or revolt. . . .

After learning that Pound had been charged with treason, poet and Librarian of Congress Archibald MacLeish questioned both the government's wisdom in making the charge and Pound's sanity.

In Rome, even after the Italian government had fallen and the city was occupied by the German army, Pound continued to make his broadcasts. But the day after Italy surrendered to the Allies, Pound was seized by Italian militiamen who had opposed the fascist government. He was imprisoned in Italy for six months, after which he returned to America.

"Poor Old Ezra Is Quite, Quite Balmy"

Novelist Ernest Hemingway said that Pound "ought to go to the loony bin, which he rates and you can pick out the parts in his cantos at which he starts to rate it." MacLeish added, "It is pretty clear that poor old Ezra is quite, quite balmy." Pound's lawyer, Julien Cornell, decided that proving Pound was clinically insane was the best way to save his client from being executed.

After examining him, four different doctors all declared that Pound was not sane enough to stand trial. One doctor even went so far as to say that Pound suffered from delusions that he had valuable connections "in a half dozen countries" and should be "an adviser to the state department." Nevertheless, prosecutor Isaiah Matlack asked that Pound be tried before a jury in a "public insanity hearing."

Pound of "Unsound Mind"

On February 13, 1946, the jury heard testimony supporting claims that Pound suffered from delusions. After deliberating for only three minutes, the jury announced that Pound was of "unsound mind." He was then confined to St. Elizabeth's Federal Hospital for the Insane in Washington, D.C., until such time as he was found fit to stand trial.

Pound himself accepted his situation, spending the next twelve years in his room reading and writing while his supporters made unsuccessful attempts to have him released. In 1948, he was awarded the distinguished

Ezra Pound. Judge Bolitha J. Laws dismissed charges against the author in 1958 because Pound was found to be unfit for trial.

EZRA POUND

Many people are unaware that Ezra Pound was considered a "poor" person. Yet Pound was known for his generosity. He paid for the publication of T. S. Eliot's first book of poetry, *The Love Song of J. Alfred Prufrock and Other Observations*. He worked as an unpaid literary agent for several authors including James Joyce and Ernest Hemingway. Pound also helped the careers of others such as Robert Frost and e. e. cummings.

Bollingen Prize for Poetry, which carried an award of $10,000. Congress then ordered the prize's sponsor, the Library of Congress, to give no more awards. A Presidential pardon was proposed in 1954, but the proposal was dismissed when opponents argued that a pardon cannot be granted to someone who has not yet been found guilty.

In 1955, MacLeish tried to convince the attorney general to cancel the treason charges against Pound. Hemingway, Eliot, and Frost joined the effort. In April 1958, Judge Bolitha Laws, who had presided over the original insanity hearing in 1945, dismissed the charges. The judge based the decision on an official declaration by the superintendent of St. Elizabeth's Hospital that Pound was still unfit for trial.

Ezra Pound was released from St. Elizabeth's and immediately sailed for Italy. He died in Venice in 1972.

Suggestions for Further Reading

Ackroyd, Peter. *Ezra Pound and His World.* New York: Charles Scribner's Sons, 1980.

Carpenter, Humphrey. *A Serious Character: The Life of Ezra Pound.* Boston: Houghton Mifflin, Co. 1988.

Tytell, John. *Ezra Pound: The Solitary Volcano.* New York: Doubleday-Anchor Press, 1987.

József Cardinal Mindszenty Trial: 1949

Defendant: József Mindszenty

Crime Charged: Conspiracy to overthrow the Hungarian government

Chief Defense Lawyer: Koloman Kiczkó

Chief Prosecutor: Julius Alapi

Judge: William Olti

Place: Budapest, Hungary

Dates of Trial: February 3–8, 1949

Verdict: Guilty

Sentence: Life imprisonment

SIGNIFICANCE: József Cardinal Mindszenty became one of the world's best-known victims of the Soviet Union's domination of Eastern Europe after World War II. Mindszenty was a symbol of resistance to oppression in a world dominated by the cold war (the term used to describe the struggle for power and prestige between the Western powers and the Communist bloc from 1945—the end of World War II—until 1989).

József Mindszenty (1892–1975) was a Hungarian archbishop, cardinal, and freedom-fighter. As a freedom-fighter, however, he ran into trouble with Hungarian authorities. In 1919, Hungarian Communist revolutionaries jailed the twenty-seven-year-old priest for his writings. In 1944, Adolf Hitler's allies—the Hungarian Nazis—jailed Mindszenty, then bishop of Veszprém, for trying to make peace with the Soviets.

TREASON

Each time Mindszenty was released from prison he gained stature. In October 1945, Pope Pius XII appointed him archbishop of Esztergom, Prince Primate of Hungary. Two years later, the Communists rose to power. Their leaders were among the most ruthless Hungary had ever known.

Mindszenty's authority as head of the Roman Catholic Church in Hungary was lessening. Nevertheless, he challenged the new political leaders. He protested the state's interference with religion, seizure of church property, and harassment of parish priests. He asked the Americans and the British to protest such acts. He met with the last empress of the Habsburg family and her son. (The Hapsburgs were a family—the Austrian royal house from which came the leaders of Austria, Germany, the Holy Roman Empire, Hungary, Bohemia, and Spain until World War I ended in 1918.)

Shortly after taking power, the Hungarian Communists began terrorizing their political opponents. They had little fear of going after Mindszenty, since he did not have widespread support. Late in 1948, a group of senior Communist officials decided to "liquidate the Mindszenty problem."

Interrogation and Torture

After sunset on Sunday, December 26, 1948, police arrested Mindszenty. In a nationwide sweep, the police also arrested hundreds of priests, opposition politicians, and others for involvement with the cardinal. By the end of January, more than 3,300 people were in jail.

Mindszenty found himself in the interrogation room at police headquarters in the capital city of Budapest. There police charged him with conspiracy against the Hungarian people's republic, spying, and abuses of laws governing foreign currency. They took away his priest's robes and beat him unconscious. When he came to, the questioning began. On December 28, the police released a statement saying that the cardinal had confessed to the charges against him. The next day, they pressed Mindszenty for details that would convince Hungarian Catholics that he had attempted to betray his country. After sixty-six hours of questioning, robbed of food and sleep, Mindszenty asked the police to kill him. After eighty-four hours, he signed a confession, admitting he had been part of a plot to overthrow the republic with American and British aid. Police gave him a few days to recover, then ordered him to write his confession out in his own hand, to make it more believable.

Convicted At a Show Trial

The arrest and jailing turned the cardinal into a martyr (a person who chooses to suffer or die rather than give up their faith or principles) overnight. Pope Pius XII issued a proclamation excommunicating (banning) from the church all those who were guilty of victimizing Mindszenty. Hungarian churches were crowded not only with believers but with political activists. The Communist authorities allowed the churches to remain open, but they spied on masses and censored sermons. They soon realized that it was essential to destroy the cardinal or at least ruin his reputation.

The trial opened on February 3, 1949. William Olti, a former Nazi turned Communist, read out the charges against the cardinal. Mindszenty had met in the United States with Zita, the widow of the Emperor Charles, the last reigning Habsburg, and with her son, Otto von Habsburg. They supposedly plotted the return of royal rule. He had asked United States officials to use force to rid Hungary of the Communists. He had appealed directly to President Harry Truman for help.

Mindszenty admitted that some of the charges read against him were true, but he denied that he had been planning to overthrow the nation. Testimony against him continued for two more days. On the third day, Mindszenty's lawyer, Koloman Kiczkó, admitted that some of the evidence against his client was true. What is more, the cardinal had confessed. He pled for a merciful judgment. On February 8, the court handed down Mindszenty's sentence: life in prison.

Cold War Martyr

The arrest, show trial, and imprisonment of Mindszenty became a cold war cause in the West. It served as one reason that Hungary's admission to the United Nations was delayed. During the anti-Communist uprising in Hungary in October 1956, soldiers freed Mindszenty. A squadron of tanks made sure he arrived safely at his Budapest residence. The shaken Communist government attempted to save face by declaring that the cardinal had been unfairly prosecuted. They then ordered his release.

During the first days of November 1956, Soviet troops positioned themselves to crush the uprising in Hungary. Mindszenty went on the radio and pleaded with the Soviets to give the Hungarians their independence. He also called for free elections, the return of private property, and an end to the Communist oppression of the Catholic Church.

Courtroom Drama

THE 1956 HUNGARIAN UPRISING

József Cardinal Mindszenty was freed during the 1956 Hungarian uprising—an anti-Communist uprising led by former Hungarian premier Imre Nagy. Eventually, Soviet troops suppressed the uprising and restored Communist rule to Hungary. The new government was led by Janos Kadar, who had been one of Nagy's ministers and who was also supported by the Soviet Union. Under Kadar, Hungary's system became more tolerant and more flexible in decision-making. It was in this more liberal climate that Pope Paul VI believed that church-state relations could be improved in Hungary.

At daybreak on November 4, Soviet tanks rolled into Budapest. In only a few days, they crushed resistance to Communist rule. Mindszenty took refuge in the American diplomatic compound in Budapest. He remained there for the next fifteen years, a martyr and a symbol of the conflict between Communism and Catholicism. Several times the embarrassed Hungarian regime offered to let Mindszenty leave the country, but he refused. Perhaps he did not trust the Communists, but he also wanted to stay because he believed that by being there he gave hope to Catholic anti-Communists. Finally, in September 1971, Pope Paul VI persuaded Mindszenty to come to Rome as part of an attempt to heal the relationship between the church and the Hungarian state. Mindszenty died in Vienna in 1975.

Suggestions for Further Reading

Lomax, Bill. *Hungary 1956.* New York; St. Martin's Press, 1976.

Mindszenty, József Cardinal. *Memoirs.* New York: Macmillan Publishing Co., 1974.

OPPOSITE PAGE

On September 23, 1971, after almost twenty-three years of confinement, Cardinal Mindszenty (left) joins Pope Paul VI for mass in the Sistine Chapel.

Tokyo Rose Trial: 1949

Defendant: Iva Ikuko Toguri ("Tokyo Rose")

Crime Charged: Treason

Chief Defense Lawyers: Wayne M. Collins, George Olshausen, and Theodore Tamba

Chief Prosecutors: Thomas DeWolfe, Frank J. Hennessy, John Hogan, and James Knapp

Judge: Michael J. Roche

Place: San Francisco, California

Dates of Trial: July 5–September 29, 1949

Verdict: Guilty

Sentence: Ten years in prison and a $10,000 fine

SIGNIFICANCE: The Tokyo Rose trial was the most famous of seven American treason trials following World War II.

Iva Ikuko Toguri, the woman who would be called "Tokyo Rose," was born on July 4, 1916, in Los Angeles, California. Her parents had come to California from Japan. In July 1941, when she was twenty-five years old, Toguri went to Japan for the first time to visit a sick aunt. While she was there, on December 7, 1941, the United States declared war on Japan. Toguri could not get out of the country.

Toguri had a hard time earning a living in wartime Japan. Food and shelter were expensive and hard to find. Her only skill was her ability to speak and write English. At first, she worked as a typist for news agencies and foreign missions. Then Radio Tokyo hired her. In November 1943, the government forced her to become one of several female radio announcers. Radio Tokyo broadcasts originated from many locations throughout the Japanese Empire, which included much of eastern Asia. American soldiers called all of these Japanese female broadcasters "Tokyo Rose." Toguri never actually used that name. Her broadcasts consisted of popular American music, with a few pro-Japanese messages written for her by her supervisors.

Toguri Tried for Treason

Toguri was only one of 10,000 Japanese Americans trapped in Japan during World War II. However, she was one of the few singled out for punishment for her activities by the American government. The American military arrested her on October 17, 1945, after it had occupied Japan. They released her a few days later when the Justice Department expressed doubts about the charge of treason that had been leveled against her. On August 28, 1948, she was arrested again in Tokyo. She was then brought back to the United States to stand trial in San Francisco.

Toguri had a hard time finding lawyers who were willing to represent her. Finally Wayne M. Collins, George Olshausen, and Theodore Tamba agreed to take her case for free. The prosecutors were Thomas De-Wolfe, Frank J. Hennessy, John Hogan, and James Knapp. The trial began on July 5, 1949, with Judge Michael J. Roche presiding.

Before a jury with no Asian Americans, Toguri pleaded innocent to the eight treason charges filed against her. Despite Roche's prejudice in favor of the prosecution and the strong public sentiment against Toguri, the trial lasted for nearly three months. Afterward the jury deadlocked.

When the jury reported that it was unable to reach a verdict, Roche ordered the jurors to continue to discuss the case until they were willing to vote for a guilty verdict. Nine of the twelve jurors were willing to vote that Toguri was guilty, and after some time, the three holdout jurors were coaxed into agreement. One of the three who reluctantly agreed to convict Toguri was the jury foreman, John Mann:

> She was such an inoffensive little thing . . . . I think
> I knew how she felt because I felt the same way when
> I was cut off from everybody. You ask the judge a
> question and he reprimands you. He definitely tells
> you you're out of order. The count is nine to three
> against you. I couldn't help feeling the isolation she
> must have felt in Japan.

INTERNMENT CAMPS FOR JAPANESE AMERICANS

The anti-Japanese prejudice that affected the Tokyo Rose trial had reached the very highest levels of the U.S. government during the war against Japan. On February 20, 1942, President Franklin D. Roosevelt approved a plan to remove Japanese Americans from their homes and concentrate them in internment camps located in Arkansas, Utah, Colorado, and other states that were away from the Pacific Ocean. The reasoning for this was that it was believed that Japanese Americans were more loyal to Japan than to America, and that if they had contact with Japan via the Pacific Ocean, they could sabotage the U.S. war effort. German Americans and Italian Americans, however, were never given the same treatment. Japanese Americans and their supporters claimed that it was anti-Japanese prejudice rather than any realistic danger that led to these harsh measures. Eventually, some 100,000 Japanese Americans languished in the camps. Ironically, the sons of the interned families often served in the U.S. Armed Forces, frequently in special army units that performed with high honor.

On September 29, 1949, the jury delivered a guilty verdict against Iva Ikuko Toguri. She was sentenced to ten years in prison and a $10,000 fine. After serving six years in a federal women's prison in West Virginia, Toguri was released early for good behavior. On January 18, 1977, after decades of debate about the fairness of her trial, President Gerald Ford pardoned Toguri. The government cleared her of any charges of treason, and restored her U.S. citizenship. Since 1977 she has lived in Chicago, Illinois, where she works for her parents' business.

Suggestion for Further Reading

Arbus, Diane. "The Victimization of Tokyo Rose." *Esquire* (June 1983): 88–89.

Duus, Masayo. *Tokyo Rose, Orphan of the Pacific.* New York: Harper & Row, 1983.

OPPOSITE PAGE

Iva Ikuko Toguri ("Tokyo Rose") is led down a corridor in the Federal Building in San Francisco by U.S. Deputy Marshal Herbert Cole, just before the court found her guilty of treason on September 29, 1945. The court fined Toguri $10,000 and sentenced her to ten years in prison.

TREASON

Gunn, Rex B. *They Called Her Tokyo Rose.* Santa Monica, CA: Gunn, 1977.

Howe, Russell Warren. *The Hunt For Tokyo Rose.* Lanham, MD: Madison Books, 1990.

Milovan Djilas Trial: 1956

Defendant: Milovan Djilas

Crime Charged: Slandering Yugoslavia

Chief Defense Lawyer: Veljko Kovacevic

Chief Prosecutor: Aleksandar Atanackovic

Judges: Five-judge panel presided over by Vojislav Jankovic

Place: Belgrade, Yugoslavia

Date of Trial: First trial: December 12, 1956; second trial: May 14, 1962

Verdict: Guilty

Sentence: First trial: Three years' imprisonment plus one more year from a formerly suspended sentence; second trial: five years' imprisonment

SIGNIFICANCE: Milovan Djilas's 1956 slander trial resulted in his imprisonment by Yugoslavia's Communist government, in which he had once played a major role.

Milovan Djilas was a writer and politician, born in the former Yugoslavia, which was located in southeast Europe largely in the Balkan peninsula. As a young man, Djilas was a Communist, opposed to the monarchy. The Communists, in fact, wanted to overthrow the royal government. After their takeover, they planned to control all the country's railroads, factories, mines and other so-called "means of production." In 1933, police arrested him for his beliefs and activities. Years later, he would become a leading voice against the Communist state he was trying to create in his youth.

Djilas As Communist

After Djilas left prison, he rose quickly through the ranks of the illegal Communist Party. In 1937, he met Josip Broz, known as "Tito." When Tito took control of the Communist Party two years later, Djilas became a member of its governing body (the "Politburo").

In 1941, Adolf Hitler invaded Yugoslavia. The Communists joined other groups to fight the Nazis. When World War II ended in 1945, Tito took control of the country, making it into a Communist state. However, he refused to link the nation's economy with that of the Soviet Union and its allies (East Germany, Rumania, Bulgaria, and Hungary, among others). In taking this position, Tito angered Soviet dictator Joseph Stalin. In 1948, the two countries ended their relationship.

Djilas proved to be a good leader in the underground resistance army during the war. He became one of Tito's closest aides after the war. Eventually, he served as vice president of Yugoslavia. Over the next twenty years, however, Djilas began to reject his earlier Communist beliefs.

Djilas Challenges Party

In late 1953, Djilas wrote a series of articles for a Sunday newspaper. He objected to the undemocratic acts of the party and to its rigid demands. He also criticized the party's leaders for acting like a pampered group. He believed in doing so that his essays had Tito's approval. However, in January 1954, outraged party leaders kicked him out of the Communist Party. They did not like his suggestions for democratic reforms.

In a December 1954 interview that appeared in *The New York Times,* Djilas called for democracy in his county. Officials immediately arrested him. Tito's biographer, Vladimir Dedijer, spoke up for Djilas. Police arrested him as well. The government charged both men under the same law, which prohibited antigovernment actions or beliefs. After a secret trial, both men received prison sentences. These were later suspended.

Djilas continued to write. He also continued to get in trouble with the authorities. After Stalin's death in 1953, relations between his homeland and the Soviet Union improved. This change affected Djilas, in that Yugoslavia was now less intimidated by the Soviet Union.

A Secret Trial

In 1956, Hungarian freedom-fighters rose up against their government. The Russians sent in troops to crush them. Djilas criticized Tito's refusal to join the United Nations debate on the invasion. He saw Tito's unspoken support for the Soviet action as a retreat from his independent position. He wrote that Yugoslavia was no less threatened by the Soviet Union than Hungary had been.

Newspapers in France and America reported all this. When Djilas wrote an article for an American magazine, officials became furious. They arrested him on November 19, 1956.

In an attempt to keep the proceedings against Djilas secret, government lawyer Aleksandar Atanackovic requested a closed trial. He argued that Yugoslavia's foreign policy might be harmed if courtroom testimony became public knowledge. Djilas and his lawyer protested, saying that his statements had merely been those of a private citizen. However, the court ruled in favor of the government.

The December 12, 1956, trial lasted twelve hours. Five judges who had heard the case convicted Djilas after less than ten minutes of deliberation. The court sentenced him to three years in prison. He would spend two years in jail for the slander charge, plus one year added from his 1955 suspended sentence.

Djilas Jailed

While Djilas was serving his sentence, Western publishers received the manuscripts of three new books he had written. One was *The New Class,* which argued that the Communist leaders had become a privileged class whose hunger for power made them just like the leaders they had replaced. The Yugoslav government banned the book. However, when publishers issued it in the United States, the imprisoned Djilas again faced charges for expressing antigovernment sentiments. He faced trial again on October 4, 1957.

When the court read the charges against Djilas, the foreign press had to leave the courtroom. Djilas protested the secrecy of his trial by refusing to answer the prosection's and the judge's questions. After one day of testimony, the court added seven years to his sentence and returned him to his cell. He continued to protest by refusing to appeal the new ruling against him.

Djilas was paroled in January 1961. He quickly finished three more books, including *Conversations with Stalin.* As Tito's deputy, Djilas had met the Soviet dictator four times, one of which was during the 1948 conference held just before Yugoslavia and the Soviet Union severed relations. Djilas's negative portrait of the Soviet leadership—with which Tito

TREASON

was now on good terms—was scheduled for publication in the West in the spring of 1962.

Jailed Again for Revelations on Talks with Stalin

Police arrested Djilas on April 7, 1962. This was only a few weeks after the government passed a new law stopping officials from releasing information to the public. When Djilas stood trial on May 14, the government charged him under this new law. He replied that everything in his book had appeared earlier, yet the government had taken no action against him. The court, however, accepted the prosecution's argument that Djilas's book contained secret information.

The government lawyer again asked for a secret trial. In protest, Djilas refused to hire an attorney. After six and a half hours of testimony, the court convicted Djilas, sentencing him to five years in prison. The three years and eight months remaining from his previous sentence, which he had not served because he had won parole, were added to the new punishment. Djilas concluded that officials intended this imprisonment to improve Yugoslav-Soviet relations and to act as a warning to other Eastern European anti-Communist dissenters (those expressing a difference of opinion).

After Djilas left jail in 1966, he continued to write about his life and his relationship with Tito. He died in Belgrade on April 20, 1995.

Courtroom Drama

Suggestions for Further Reading

Milovan Djilas Trial: 1956

Abel, Elie. "A Defiant Djilas Is Tried In Secret." *The New York Times* (October 5, 1957): 15.

Djilas, Milovan. *Of Prisons And Ideas.* New York: Harcourt Brace Jovanovich, 1986.

Djilas, Milovan. *Tito: The Story From Inside.* New York: Harcourt Brace Jovanovich, 1980.

Underwood, Paul. "Djilas Is Convicted Over Book." *The New York Times* (May 15, 1962): 1.

Cuban Revolutionary Tribunals: 1959

Defendants: First trial: Jesús Sosa Blanco, Ricardo Luis Grau, Pedro Morejon; second trial: forty-four members of the Cuban air force

Crimes Charged: First trial: Murder, arson, looting, theft; second trial: genocide

Chief Defense Lawyer: Both trials: Aristedes de Acosta, accompanied in second trial by five additional attorneys

Chief Prosecutors: First trial: Jorge Zerquera and Mario Colon Davila; second trial: Antonio Cejas and Augusto Martínez Sánchez

Judges: First trial: Humberto Sorí Morín, Universo Sánchez, and Raúl Chibás; second trial: presiding judge Félix Lugerio Peña, replaced by Manuel Piñeiro Losada

Places: First trial: Havana, Cuba; second trial: Santiago de Cuba, Cuba

Dates of Trials: First trial: January 22, 1959, retrial on February 16, 1959; second trial: February 14–March 2, 1959

Verdicts: First trial: guilty; second trial: not guilty

Sentences: First trial: death; second trial: none, although lengthy prison sentences resulted from subsequent retrials

SIGNIFICANCE: The questionable methods employed by Fidel Castro's 26th of July Movement at its war crimes tribunals replaced Cuba's traditional legal system. These methods shook the faith of many of Castro's foreign supporters, who had believed he was a liberal reformer.

The Cuban dictator Fulgencio Batista fled his country January 1, 1959, after a revolution removed him from power. The world waited to see how the rebel leader Fidel Castro would keep law and order while heading up a new government. How would Castro's rebels treat the forces they had recently defeated?

Castro's Trial

Castro himself had faced trial in 1953, after he led a first, failed attempt to overthrow Batista. In July of that year, Castro's fighters had attacked the army barracks at Moncada in Santiago de Cuba. Government soldiers captured several of his men and tortured and killed them. Castro escaped, but fell into their hands a few days later. He used his trial, during which he acted as his own lawyer, to advance his revolutionary cause and his personal popularity.

The court convicted him of trying to topple the government. He had served less than two years of his prison sentence when Batista ordered his release. Fearing for his life, Castro fled to Mexico in 1955, where he planned the revolution that permitted him to return in triumph to Havana in January 1959.

Castro's Justice

Most of Batista's soldiers returned home safely when the fighting ended. However, the new rulers arrested informers, police officers, and soldiers who stood accused of especially horrible crimes. Before Castro's revolt, Cuba had abolished the death penalty. Still, "revolutionary courts" imposed the death penalty for torture, murder, blackmail, treason, spying, rape, and other serious offenses.

Castro's critics in the United States grew alarmed when the dictator put off holding free elections. They saw the revolutionary courts as proof that the new government would not fulfill its promise to reform Cuban justice. Executions climbed, soon numbering nearly 300. Judge Advocate Dr. Humberto Sorí Morín announced that he would bring charges against 1,000 more "war criminals." Americans became deeply disturbed by Castro's failure to protect the rights of the accused, who had to prove their own innocence.

Castro responded by staging a mass demonstration in Havana, the capital of Cuba. During this he criticized the United States for supporting dictators in Nicaragua, the Dominican Republic, and Cuba. Still, the

TREASON

new Cuban regime wanted to win international support. Castro announced that a public trial of three war criminals would take place in Havana's sports stadium. Three rebel officers would act as both judges and jury. Castro promised seats to 400 Cubans and international journalists at the trial. The new government intended the trial to be a worldwide public relations triumph. Its name was Operation Truth.

Show Trial

When the trial opened on January 22, 1959, chaos erupted. Over 18,000 Cubans filled the stands. The first defendant was Major Jesús Sosa Blanco. The government charged the army officer with committing 108 crimes, including murder and arson (setting fires). The first witness against him was a young woman who accused the major of killing members of her family. The elderly widow of a peasant swore that he had shot her husband. Other witnesses stumbled over their words. This led court-watchers to suspect the government had coached them.

Rebel soldiers court-martialed by military judges in Cuba.

Thousands left the stadium as the trial dragged on through the night. Just after 6:00 A.M., after thirteen hours of trial proceedings, the court found the major guilty and sentenced him to death.

Castro intended Operation Truth to give the world a positive image of how the revolutionary tribunals provided justice. Instead, massive television and press coverage produced widespread agreement that the trial had been a farce. To avoid repeating this disaster, the next two defendants had speedier trials. Although the press observed these trials, the public could not. These trials, together with an appeal from Major Blanco, ended with executions.

Trial of the Airmen

On February 14, forty-four pilots, gunners, and mechanics from Batista's air force stood trial for genocide (the willful killing of a whole nation or ethnic group). Resentment of the air force was widespread. It had inspired fear in the Cuban population by carrying out bombing raids against civilians in an attempt to end popular support for Castro and his rebels. Still, the provisional government's case against the forty-four airmen Castro had hand-picked for the trial ran into trouble immediately. While the government lawyers quarreled about whether the accused deserved execution, the defense lawyer claimed that those responsible for the raids had already fled Cuba. Some of the evidence offered against the defendants turned out to be false. Also, the lawyers discovered that the mass-killing charge was not among the crimes listed in the Code of Sierra Maestra, the government's criminal laws. Despite heckling from spectators and an attempt by the government lawyer to bully the judges behind closed doors, the government dropped the charges against the airmen.

The men remained in jail, however. Castro announced on television that his government would conduct "a review" of the trial. Cuban lawyers and international critics objected, saying that a second trial would violate the basic legal principle of double jeopardy, which holds that a defendant cannot stand trial twice for the same offense. Nevertheless, Castro selected a second tribunal to retry the airmen.

Politics Replaces the Rule of Law

No new evidence emerged during the new trial. Officials released two of the mechanics, but suspicions grew that the trial was staged. These suspicions strengthened late in the retrial, when word leaked out that the court had already agreed to sentence eight of the defendants to death. The resulting embarrassment stopped the court from announcing its verdict until several days after the proceedings ended. Eventually, the court found the airmen guilty but sentenced them to terms ranging from two to thirty years in prison.

TREASON

THE BAY OF PIGS

In 1961, President John F. Kennedy's administration launched the Bay of Pigs invasion in Cuba. On April 17, some 1,500 Cuban exiles landed in Cuba's Bay of Pigs (*Bahia de Cochinos*) with the intention of overthrowing Fidel Castro's Communist government. The Central Intelligence Agency (CIA) had trained the exiles in Guatemala and given them U.S. arms. The Cuban Army killed or imprisoned most of them. Finally, in December 1962, Cuba traded 1,113 rebels for $53 million in food and medicine raised privately in the United States.

Castro was pleased with this verdict. "Revolutionary justice is based not on legal precepts, but on moral conviction," he announced. The Revolutionary Air Force's appointed defense lawyer found Castro's moral certainty ironic: Castro had himself pardoned the same forty-four airmen shortly after Batista's defeat. Then he had turned around and used them as scapegoats to satisfy public demand for vengeance against those air force officers who had escaped into exile.

The airmen were not the only ones the government punished. The government dismissed the defense lawyers, condemning them. Major Pena, the judge in the first trial of the airmen, was found in his car, shot dead.

The fate of the airmen and others associated with their trials destroyed any hope that the Castro regime would reform the justice system. The temporary tribunals increasingly became a fact of life in Cuba. By the time of the botched American attempt to invade Cuba at the Bay of Pigs in 1961, trained attorneys and judges had been replaced by militia members in the revolutionary courts. Politics had taken over the entire legal system.

Suggestions for Further Reading

Quirk, Robert. *Fidel Castro.* New York: W. W. Norton & Co., 1993.

Smith, Wayne S. *Portrait of Cuba.* New York: Turner Publications, 1991.

Szulc, Tad. *Fidel: A Critical Portrait.* New York: William Morrow & Co., 1986.

Thomas, Hugh. *Cuba: The Pursuit of Freedom.* New York: Harper & Row, 1971.

Nelson Mandela Trial: 1963–1964

Defendants: Nelson Mandela, Walter Sisulu, Dennis Goldberg, Govan Mbeki, Raymond Mhlaba, Elias Motsoaledi, Andrew Mlangeni, Ahmed Kathrada, and Lionel Bernstein

Crimes Charged: (1) The commission of acts of sabotage together with the Communist Party; (2) conspiracy to aid or procure wrongful acts concerning the recruitment of persons for training in the preparation and use of explosives for committing acts of violence, conspiracy to commit acts of guerilla warfare, acts of assistance to military units of foreign countries invading South Africa, and acts of participation in violent revolution; (3) the execution of the common purpose of committing the acts set out above; (4) soliciting money in South Africa and abroad, and distributing those funds in the interest of their campaign

Chief Defense Lawyers: Bram Fischer, Arthur Chaskalson, Joel Joffe, Vernon Berrange, and George Bizos

Chief Prosecutors: Percy Yutar, deputy attorney general of the Transvaal, assisted by A. B. Krog and others

Judge: Quartus de Wet, judge-president of the Transvaal

Place: Pretoria, South Africa

Dates of Trial: October 9, 1963–June 12, 1964

Verdicts: Mandela, Sisulu, Goldberg, Mbeki, Mhlaba, Motsoaledi, and Mlangeni—guilty on all four counts; Kathrada—guilty on one count; Bernstein—acquitted

Sentences: Life imprisonment for the eight found guilty

SIGNIFICANCE: In this trial, the white South African government tried to ruin the African National Congress. However, Nelson Mandela showed the world that apartheid (the separation of the races) was an immoral policy.

TREASON

On May 10, 1994, Nelson Mandela took his oath of office as South Africa's first black African president. He looked back on the old South Africa as "a valley of darkness." Rich with natural resources, including gold and diamonds, the country was first settled by the Dutch, then the English. It became independent in 1910, but the white minority population ran things. In 1948, this government made apartheid (a-PART-haid) government policy. This policy denied blacks the right to vote, made them live apart from whites, and greatly limited their opportunities to work and gain an education.

Mandela's Activities

Mandela, who had been raised to become a tribal chief, once worked as a policeman in a gold mine. There he saw first-hand how badly blacks were treated. Determined to do something, Mandela completed law school. Then, with Oliver Tambo, he set up the nation's first black law firm in 1952.

At the same time, Mandela and Tambo, led by Walter Sisulu, became active in the African National Congress (ANC). The ANC was a national political group seeking full rights as citizens for South African blacks. After joining the ANC board in 1949, Mandela proposed that blacks join with (Asian) Indians living in South Africa and whites to defeat the country's racist policies. In 1952, he directed the Defiance Campaign, which was a series of acts of civil disobedience and nonviolent practices learned from Indian leader Mohandas Gandhi. The goal was to swamp the South African justice system with mass arrests. The government reacted with increasing violence, and in 1960 killed 69 and injured 180 when police opened fire on a crowd of protesters in Sharpeville.

State of Emergency

After the Sharpeville massacre, the government declared an emergency. It banned the ANC and arrested thousands. In 1961, Mandela and others organized the Umkhonto we Sizwe (MK). In English, the name means "Spear of the Nation." Unlike the banned ANC, MK decided to use violent means—directed at establishments, not individuals—if they were necessary to change government policy.

Pursued by the police, Mandela went "underground." While in hiding, he set up outposts of the MK. He also traveled to England to raise funds and arrange for military training. On his return from one such trip in 1962, police arrested him. A court found him guilty of strike organizing and of leaving the country without a passport. Mandela was sentenced to five years' imprisonment on Robben Island.

Acts of sabotage continued. The government arrested hundreds more under a new ninety-day detention law. This law permitted the police to jail anyone without a trial. Often police kept people in solitary confinement, alone and unable to communicate with the outside world. When the first ninety-day period had ended, police could arrest them over and over again. Police also physically tortured the inmates.

On July 12, 1963, the police raided the MK headquarters at Rivonia, outside Johannesburg, arresting Sisulu and seven others. Officials moved Mandela to prison in Pretoria.

Nelson Mandela in 1961.

The Rivonia Trial

The Rivonia trial opened on October 9, 1963, in Pretoria. It had moved from Johannesburg for security reasons. Not until the trial opened would the government give defense lawyers a copy of the charges against their clients. The lawyers requested a six-week adjournment in order to prepare their case, but the judge granted them only three weeks.

At that point, the government's attempt to put on a show trial began to fall apart. Bram Fischer, the lead defense lawyer, publicly attacked the indictment that listed the government's charges, saying that the document was incomplete. It failed to provide times or places of the offenses it claimed Mandela and others had committed. At Fischer's request, the judge dismissed the indictment.

When the trial started up again, the prosecution still engaged in inferior legal work. It relied on gossip and publicity stunts to make a case against the MK leaders. All plead not guilty to the charges filed against them. The made-up charges meant that the verdict would almost certainly go against them, however, and the main job of the defense team was to prevent their clients from being sentenced to death. The highlight of the defense case came on April 23 when Mandela gave a five-hour speech in court. He ended with the following statement:

> During my lifetime I have dedicated myself to this struggle of the African people. I have fought against white domination and I have fought against black domination. I have cherished the ideal of a democratic and free society in which all persons live together in harmony and with equal opportunities. It is an ideal which I hope to live for and achieve. However, if need be, it is an ideal for which I am prepared to die.

Censorship regulations had been lifted during this trial, so Mandela's talk received wide publicity.

Long-Term Justice

For the defense, the trial was a partial victory. The judge accepted the defendants' claim that they had not decided to begin an underground war against the state. He then sentenced seven of them to prison instead of death. Mandela, who had decided not to appeal his sentence, went back to Robben Island. Sisulu, Mbeki, Mhlaba, Motsoaledi, Mlangeni, and Kathrada went to prison with him. It would be a quarter of a century before all of them saw freedom.

During that time, Mandela's wife, Winnie, acted on her husband's behalf. She constantly protested the government's policies. Officials repeatedly arrested, tried, and imprisoned her. Eventually, her activities grew violent. Shortly after Mandela was released from prison, a court found

N e l s o n
M a n d e l a
T r i a l:
1 9 6 3 – 1 9 6 4

APARTHEID

Nelson Mandela and his colleagues faced trial because they opposed the system of *apartheid,* an Afrikaans word meaning "apartness." (Afrikaans is a language that resembles Dutch, developed by the Boers, Dutch settlers who occupied South Africa in the nineteenth century.) Apartheid was an elaborate system of racial segregation and white supremacy that was first established in 1948, when the Afrikaner Nationalist party came to power in South Africa. Apartheid created both legal and actual separation of whites from nonwhites, as well as separating Africans (called "Bantu") from "Coloureds" (people of mixed ancestry) and both groups from "Asiatics" (people of Indian ancestry). In addition, different African ethnic groups were also separated. Apartheid was the official system of South Africa until Nelson Mandela became president in 1994.

her guilty of kidnapping and assaulting a young boy. Ms. Mandela appealed to a higher court, which upheld the conviction but reduced her sentence to a fine. Her headstrong attitude and behavior continued to embarrass Mandela, however, and they separated in 1992. They finally divorced in 1996.

Only four years after he left prison in 1990, Nelson Mandela was elected president by the people of South Africa. The country had finally abandoned the policy of segregation he had devoted his life to ending.

Suggestions for Further Reading

Benson, Mary. *Nelson Mandela: The Man and The Movement.* New York: W. W. Norton, 1986.

Bernstein, Hilda. *The World That Was Ours: The Story of the Rivonia Trial.* London: SAWriters, 1989.

Gilbey, Emma. *The Lady: The Life and Times of Winnie Mandela.* London: Vintage, Random House, 1994.

Mandela, Nelson. *Long Walk to Freedom: The Autobiography of Nelson Mandela.* Boston: Little, Brown, 1994.

TREASON

Mandela, Nelson. *The Struggle Is My Life: His Speeches and Writings.* New York: Pathfinder, 1990.

Mandela, Winnie. *Part of My Soul Went with Him.* New York: W. W. Norton, 1985.

Meer, Fatima. *Higher Than Hope: The Authorized Biography of Nelson Mandela.* New York: HarperCollins, 1990.

Václav Havel Trials: 1977–1989

Defendant: Václav Havel

Crimes Charged: Subversive activities, helping foreigners produce antistate propaganda, inciting participation at a demonstration, impeding the execution of safety measures

Chief Defense Lawyer: Dr. Josef Lžičař

Chief Prosecutor: Karel Florian

Place: Prague, Czechoslovakia

Dates of Trials: October 18, 1977; October 22, 1979; February 21, 1989

Verdict: Guilty

Sentence: Nine months' imprisonment

SIGNIFICANCE: The final trial of playwright and human rights activist Václav Havel helped to focus public attention on Czechoslovakia's totalitarian (dictatorial) regime, which fell shortly afterwards.

Late in 1976, a group of dissident Czech citizens drafted a statement that they hoped would end a decade of repressive government. The secretly written document was called Charter 77.

Charter 77

Charter 77 listed freedoms the Communist regime of President Gustáv Husák denied its people. It also asked Husak to guarantee basic human

TREASON

rights that already appeared in several documents. The first was Czechoslovakia's constitution. The second was the United Nations human rights agreements. The third was the 1975 Helsinki Accords.

The 242 people who signed Charter 77 declared themselves to be "a loose, informal association of people of various shades of opinion." They did not represent an organized political movement with a plan for creating political change. The charter named three representatives: Dr. Jirí Hájek had been a diplomat; Jan Patoèka was a philosopher; Václav Havel was a famous playwright whose plays were banned by the government.

Charter 77 organizers planned to mail copies of the document to each signer and to deliver copies to President Husak and the Czech Federal Assembly. On January 6, 1977, however, police arrested Havel and several companions while they were mailing bundles of addressed charters. The Czech government acted immediately to stop distribution of Charter 77, but it was too late. Western European newspapers published the charter and broadcast its contents by radio to thousands of Czechs who had not known of its existence.

Arrests and Trials of Dissidents

Police released Havel soon after, arresting him one week later for attempting to undermine the government. Dr. Hájek and Professor Patoèka were not arrested, but officials questioned them repeatedly. The elderly Hájek died of a brain hemorrhage after his questioning by state police. Other charter signers lost their jobs, their passports, or—like Havel—were pressured to leave the country.

The news media did not reveal the contents of Charter 77, but it still constantly criticized it and the signers. Havel even filed a libel suit against a state-employed radio announcer who claimed that the playwright had been paid by the West to act as a spy. Havel also filed a request for release and carelessly told his jailers that he intended to resign as a charter spokesman someday. The state media then announced that Havel had turned his back on the charter.

Earlier Czech Communist administrations might have attempted to combat Charter 77 with executions. However, in the late 1970s, the Czech judicial system generally pretended to honor the human rights contained in the country's constitution. Formally charging the Charter 77 organizers was a problem, because there were no legal grounds for doing so. Instead, Havel and three others came to trial for smuggling a banned text abroad.

On October 18, 1977, the government tried and convicted the group of having harmed the international interests of the Czech Republic. Havel faced fourteen months in prison, which could be postponed for three years.

Havel Stands Firm

During this time, Havel helped to found the Committee for the Defense of the Unjustly Persecuted. It was also known by its Czech initials, VONS. The group kept track of arrests that violated human rights, filed complaints, and offered financial aid to the families of people put in prison for their dissident activities. The group also smuggled criticisms of government policy to Czech publications in other countries.

The government struck back in May 1979. It accused Havel and five others of attempting to harm the state. Since Western media, such as the Voice of America and Radio Free Europe, had broadcast the group's statements, the state accused the defendants of helping foreigners produce anti-government propaganda.

The Second Trial

Havel's second trial began on October 22, 1979. Only twelve family members could enter the tiny courtroom. More than one hundred supporters, foreign diplomats, reporters, and international human rights activists were denied entry. Police arrested some of those who waited outside, and beat others. When the trial began, they carried one of the defendants' wives from the courtroom for attempting to take notes.

The trial lasted only two days. The court found all six defendants guilty. Their sentences ranged from two to five years in prison. Havel received a four-and-a-half-year sentence. Despite international pressure from sources as different as the French Communist Party and Pope John Paul II, Havel remained in prison until March 1983. Then he was released because of illness.

Another Havel Trial

The Czech people's unhappiness with the government remained. On August 21, 1988, the twentieth anniversary of the Soviet army's seizure of Czechoslovakia, 10,000 Czechs marched in the streets of Prague. When the demonstrations continued even after the anniversary had passed, state security forces responded ferociously. By October, thousands of peaceful demonstrators were facing attacks by the police in the worst public unrest since 1968.

Another politically important anniversary came in January 1989. Twenty years had passed since a student named Jan Palach burned himself to death to protest Soviet occupation. On January 9, Havel received an unsigned letter from a student claiming to represent a group of Charter 77 supporters. The writer declared that he intended to follow Palach's example by burning himself to death in Prague's Wenceslas Square on January 15. Havel wrote a reply, urging the student not to kill himself. When Havel requested that the local media help him by publicizing his appeal to the student, he was ignored. The playwright turned to foreign broadcasters for help. Radio Free Europe and Voice of America aired his message. In a radio interview, Czech state security thanked Havel for saving the student's life. Before the interview ended, Havel mentioned that date and time of the upcoming Palach memorial.

Havel went alone to Wenceslas Square on January 16 to watch the memorial. As he left, he was arrested for interfering with the police's attempts to clear the square. By the time Havel's case reached the court on February 21, 1989, the government had also charged him with trying to create a riot by publicizing the Palach memorial.

The new proceedings against Havel were as cruelly absurd as before. One witness who testified against him proved not even to have attended the memorial in Wenceslas Square. A secret police major produced a pile of photographs of Havel at the demonstration, while at the same time stating that the playwright had not been tailed by security forces. For his part, Havel used the trial as an opportunity to repeat his political convictions. "I do not feel guilty," he said. "But if I am sentenced, I will accept the punishment as a sacrifice for a good cause, which is nothing in the face of the ultimate sacrifice of Jan Palach, which we sought to commemorate."

Havel was found guilty and sentenced to nine months in jail. This time, Havel's imprisonment caused a backlash. More than 3,800 people signed a petition for his release. This pressure caused his captors to reduce Havel's sentence by one month. He was released for "good behavior" on May 17, after serving less than a third of his sentence.

Czech Democratic Reforms Grow

Increasing political freedom in the Soviet Union left Czech Communists feeling isolated. Their leaders could not count on support, either, from

After Václav Havel was sentenced to nine months in prison, an outraged public presented authorities with 3,800 signatures on a petition demanding Havel's release. He served less than one-third of his original sentence and left jail on May 17, 1989.

other Eastern block countries. Most of them were getting rid of their own repressive governments by 1989. Public rejection of Communist political candidates promising to reform the existing system finally convinced the Czech government that new leaders would have to be freely elected.

Havel urged adoption of democratic reforms and religious freedom with a petition titled "Just a Few Sentences," which 40,000 Czechs signed. On November 27, 1989, ten days after police had violently attacked a huge demonstration in Prague, millions of Czechs protested with a work stoppage that shut down the entire country. A new party called Civic Forum was hastily organized as a political opponent of the Communists.

The structure of the Communist government began to fall apart. Civic Forum took control of ministerial posts and the parliament. Alexander Dubcek, who had been removed as president of Czechoslovakia by the invading Soviet army in 1968, was elected as chairman of parliament. Only a president was lacking. The only candidate that Civic Forum and the remaining Communists could agree on was Václav Havel. On December 29, 1989, he became the first non-Communist president of Czechoslovakia in more than forty years.

When Slovakia decided to separate from the Czech Federal Republic in July 1992, Havel resigned. He did not want to preside over the

TREASON

breakup of a country he had struggled to rescue for democracy. When elections took place later that year, however, he became the president of the new Czech Republic, created by the territorial division. President Havel was inaugurated on February 2, 1993.

Suggestions for Further Reading

Gawdiak, Ihor, ed. *Czechoslovakia: A Country Study.* Washington D.C.: U.S. Government, 1989.

Havel, Václav. *Disturbing the Peace.* New York: Alfred A. Knopf, 1990.

Havel, Václav. *Open Letters: Selected Writings, 1965–1990.* New York: Alfred A. Knopf, 1991.

Kiriseová, Eda. *Václav Havel: The Authorized Biography.* New York: St. Martin's Press, 1993.

Anatoly Shcharansky and Alexandr Ginzburg Trials: 1978

Defendants: Anatoly Shcharansky and Alexandr Ginzburg

Crimes Charged: Shcharansky: treason, anti-Soviet agitation and propaganda, espionage; Ginzburg: anti-Soviet agitation, propaganda

Chief Defense Lawyers: Shcharansky acted as his own lawyer; the name of Ginzburg's lawyer was not reported

Chief Prosecutors: Pavel N. Solonin in the Shcharansky trial; the name of the prosecutor in Ginzburg's trial was not reported

Judges: Shcharansky trial: P. P. Lukanov; the name of the judge in Ginzburg's trial was not reported

Places: Shcharansky: Moscow, Soviet Union; Ginzburg: Kaluga, Soviet Union

Dates of Trials: Shcharansky: July 10–14, 1978; Ginzburg: July 10–13, 1978

Verdicts: Guilty

Sentences: Shcharansky: three years' imprisonment and ten years in a hard-labor camp; Ginzburg: eight years in a hard-labor camp

SIGNIFICANCE: The trials of Shcharansky, Ginzburg, and other activists were intended to frighten members of human rights and Jewish emigration movements in the Soviet Union. Instead, international protest helped make them the most important trials since the years of Stalin's reign.

TREASON

Two important protest movements developed in the Soviet Union in the 1970s. Although each group had its own goals, they shared some members. Political dissidents, like Alexandr Ginzburg, wanted to reform Soviet society. They pressed for freedoms spelled out in the 1975 Helsinki human rights agreement, which had been signed by the Soviet Union and Western countries. Minority religious groups, including many Jews, had less interest in reforming the Soviet Union than in leaving it entirely.

The second group became known as "refuseniks" because the Soviet Union refused to let them leave for Israel or the United States. The state allowed tens of thousands of Jews to leave for the reason of "family reunification." However, the government retained and punished most outspoken refuseniks. Application for a permit to leave the country resulted in immediate job dismissal. It also met with criticism in the press or an order to report for duty in the armed forces. Refusal to respond to such an order often resulted in trial and imprisonment.

Soviets Harass Jewish Activists

Anatoly (also called Natan) Shcharansky was a brilliant mathematician whose 1973 application to leave the country resulted in his losing his job at the Oil and Gas Research Institute and in his imprisonment. His outspokenness, work as a translator, and meetings with visiting foreign diplomats all cast light on the official harassment of Soviet Jews. Shcharansky also worked for the larger dissident movement (a movement of those who disagree with established politics or religion), in 1976 joining Helsinki Watch, a group that watched for Soviet human rights abuses. As a result of his work, Shcharansky's reputation increased.

The refuseniks' peaceful determination that the state should not harass Jews simply for wanting to leave the country became a source of embarrassment for the Soviets. On March 4, 1977, a letter to the official Soviet newspaper, *Izvestia,* accused Shcharansky and three other Jewish activists of spying. To their shock, Sanya Lipavsky, a Jewish doctor who had taken part in refusenik activities for over a year, signed the letter.

The secret police arrested Shcharansky in the capital city of Moscow on March 15, 1977. For sixteen months, he was questioned daily. On July 7, 1978, the state announced that it would try him for treason and for participating in anti-Soviet activities and propaganda. The first charge, if proven, could result in the death penalty.

Shcharansky's Trial

Anatoly
Shcharansky
and
Alexandr
Ginzburg
Trials: 1978

When Shcharansky's trial began three days later, secret police filled the courtroom. No spectators were permitted. Shcharansky, however, threatened to remain silent unless they allowed one spectator. To prevent this embarrassment, the Soviets allowed his brother, Leonid, to be that spectator. Foreign diplomats, the Western media, and the supporters of the defendant could not enter the courtroom. Soviet press officers passed out reports of the trial twice a day. Their version of events differed greatly from that of Leonid Shcharansky.

Shcharansky was relieved when he learned he could dismiss the lawyer assigned to him by the court. He was no longer subject to the death penalty, because Soviet law did not permit it in cases where a defendant acted as his own lawyer. Shcharansky could not have most of the materials and witnesses he requested, but he still did a powerful job defending himself.

The state introduced the spying charge on the second day of the trial. The charge grew out of Shcharansky's relationship with *Los Angeles Times* correspondent Robert Toth, for whom Shcharansky had done translations. The state had expelled Toth after Shcharansky's arrest and accused him of collecting information for the Central Intelligence Agency (CIA) of the United States. After his return to the United States, Toth submitted documents denying any connection with the CIA, but the court rejected them. The prosecutors tried to call Shcharansky's mother to testify against her son, but she refused. The most negative testimony the prosecutors were able to come up with was a statement that Shcharansky was a messy housekeeper.

When the chief prosecutor summed up his case, he repeated almost none of the testimony given by prosecution witnesses. Instead, he criticized social problems in the West and the Zionist movement (the plan for settling a Jewish national or religious community in Palestine). He requested a sentence of three years in prison, followed by twelve years in a hard-labor camp.

Shcharansky's final statement lasted for more than a day. He accused *Izvestia* of declaring him guilty even before his arrest. He declared that by forbidding him to answer charges made against him in closed session, the court prevented him from properly defending himself. He explained that the Jewish wish to leave the country was a cultural process, not a political rebellion.

The court sentenced Shcharansky to three years in prison and ten years in a hard-labor camp. The world responded with outrage. The administration of U.S. President Jimmy Carter pressed for Shcharansky's release.

Ginzburg's Trial

On the same day that Shcharansky's trial began, Alexandr Ginzburg went to trial in another city. The charges against him of anti-Soviet agitation and propaganda grew out of his friendship with the exiled Russian writer Alexandr Solzhenitsyn. In 1974, Solzhenitsyn had organized a fund to aid the families of political prisoners in the Soviet Union. Ginzburg managed the fund, which came partly from the publishing fees paid for Solzhenitsyn's book about the labor camps, *The Gulag Archipelago,* which was banned by the Soviets but was a bestseller in other countries. This activity, together with Ginzburg's membership in Helsinki Watch, led to his arrest on February 3, 1977.

Ginzburg had spent time in jail twice before. In 1960, he served two years in jail because he was the editor of an underground literary magazine. In 1968, he and two others were convicted of smuggling abroad the story of the trial of Yuli Daniel and Andrei Sinyavsky, two writers accused of "anti-Soviet slander." Ginzburg's conviction that time earned him five years in a hard-labor camp.

This time Ginzburg faced a possible ten years in prison and five years of exile in Siberia. On July 13, he was sentenced to eight years in a hard-labor camp. His supporters doubted his fragile health could survive this. Yet on April 17, 1979, Ginzburg and four other political prisoners were exchanged for two Soviet spies being held in the United States.

Shcharansky Finally Reaches Jewish Homeland

Shcharansky completed his prison term, then went to a far-off labor camp in April 1980. When he went on a hunger strike, the authorities offered to release him if he would sign a request on grounds of ill health. He refused.

Appeals for Shcharansky's release continued until the liberal Soviet General Secretary Mikhail Gorbachev gained power. On February 11, 1986, officials took Shcharansky from prison, stripped him of Soviet citizenship, and allowed him to walk to freedom across a bridge connecting East and West Berlin. From there he traveled to Israel to join his wife, Avital, and children in Jerusalem. Shcharansky is now part of a political movement called (in translation) both "Israel on the Rise" and "Israel for Immigration."

Anatoly
Shcharansky
and
Alexandr
Ginzburg
Trials: 1978

Anatoly Shcharansky meets his mother, Ida Milgrom, on August 25, 1986, a few months after his release from a Soviet prison.

FRIENDS OF ALEKSANDR SOLZHENITSYN

Anatoly Shcharansky and Aleksandr Ginzburg both faced trial for anti-Soviet speech. They were inspired by Russian writer Aleksandr Solzhenitsyn. At the time of their trials he had been in exile for four years. Solzhenitsyn had won worldwide fame for his novels *The First Circle* and *Cancer Ward,* highly critical portrayals of life under Stalin. Solzhenitsyn's reputation grew in 1970, when he received the Nobel Prize in literature. In 1974, the Soviets arrested and deported him to West Germany. Eventually he settled in the United States, in Vermont, where he remained a symbol of anti-Communism. He returned to his country in 1994, after Communist rule in his homeland was ended in 1989.

Suggestions for Further Reading

Gilbert, Martin. *Shcharansky: Hero of Our Time.* New York: Viking, 1986.

Jerusalem Post. Anatoly and Avital Shcharansky: The Journey Home. New York: Harcourt Brace Jovanovich, 1986.

Scammell, Michael. *Solzhenitsyn: A Biography.* New York: W. W. Norton, 1984.

Shcharansky, Natan. *Fear No Evil.* New York: Random House, 1988.

Jiang Qing and the Gang of Four Trial: 1980

Defendants: Jiang Qing, Chen Boda, Huang Yongsheng, Jiang Tengjiao, Li Zuopeng, Qiu Huizuo, Wang Hongwen, Wu Faxian, Yao Wenyuan, and Zhang Chunqiao

Crimes Charged: Counterrevolutionary acts, including sedition and conspiracy to overthrow the government, persecution of party and state leaders, suppression of the masses, and plotting to assassinate Mao and foment a counterrevolutionary armed rebellion

Chief Defense Lawyers: Ma Rongiie, Jiang representing herself

Chief Prosecutors: Huang Huoqing and twenty-three special prosecutors

Judges: Jiang Hua and a special thirty-five-judge panel

Place: Beijing, China

Dates of Trial: November 20–December 29, 1980

Verdicts: Guilty

Sentences: Jiang Qing, Zhang Chungiao—execution, reduced to life imprisonment; Wang Hongwen—life imprisonment; Yao Wenyuan—twenty years' imprisonment; Chen Boda, Huang Yongshen, Li Zuopeng, Jiang Tengjiao, Qiu Huizuo, Wu Faxian—sixteen to eighteen years' imprisonment

SIGNIFICANCE: The trial of the Gang of Four ended the radical program of political and cultural reform of China's late Chairman Mao Zedong. The Communist Party was then able to pronounce him officially a brave revolutionary who made "grave blunders" in his later years. The final result was not only a lessening of Mao's importance, but also the suicide of his imprisoned widow.

TREASON

In 1963, Mao Zedong, the seventy-year-old chairman of the Chinese Communist Party's Central Committee, launched his Cultural Revolution. Its goal was to destroy the governing class that had become powerful within the Communist Party. Mao himself had created this group by urging country peasants to destroy the landlords who had long been the Chinese ruling class. After more than a decade of governing, the Communist leaders had grown increasingly inflexible and impatient with criticism. Mao thought the revolution he had given rise to had decayed.

Ten Million Red Guards

This time, Mao turned not to the peasants, but to young students to lead the revolution. By September 1966, the young people were calling themselves "Red Guards" and marching and demonstrating across China, crying "Long live the Red terror." They told people to put an end to old ideas, old customs, and old habits. Numbering over ten million, the Red Guards often destroyed entire museums trying to separate from the past.

By January 1967, Mao was replacing officials with inexperienced young people. The established People's Liberation Army, that others in the government called to fight the Red Guards, itself split into a number of different segments. In the summer of 1968, sensing civil war, Mao broke up the Red Guards, believing he had destroyed his opponents and secured his own control of the Communist party organization. His goal—to rule China by himself—seemed close.

Meanwhile, Mao's fourth wife, Jiang Qing, who was twenty-one years younger than he, was becoming an accomplished politician herself. She wanted not only to bring Western clothing and culture to China, but also to gain power. She and Lin Biao, who had commanded the Communists' Fourth Army in the 1930s, decided to work toward seizing control of the country. By April 1969, Jiang and Lin were members of the Communist Party's governing body, and Lin was named as Mao's heir.

Gang of Four

In August 1970, Lin and Jiang and their supporters announced at a major party conference that Lin, not Mao, was the true leader of the Chinese people. A year later, Lin and Jiang attempted to overthrow the government. They failed. Lin and his wife and other supporters fled for the Soviet Union aboard a military aircraft. They were reportedly shot down over Mongolia. Jiang escaped arrest because she had managed to hide her part in the attempted coup.

As Mao lost control, Jiang secretly led the fight to succeed him. However, in the summer of 1973, she and her followers, now called the "Gang of Four," became the true insiders. All of China became aware of them a year later when Mao publicly warned his wife and her three close allies—Wang Hongwen, Yao Wenyuan, and Zhang Chunqiao—to stop seeking power.

Arrest and Imprisonment

Mao died on September 9, 1976. Within a month, the Gang of Four and its supporters were arrested. Political posters and cartoons were published, showing Jiang as a fox (a Chinese symbol for a woman of loose morals), an empress, and a snake.

The Gang of Four remained in prison for several years while officials declared the Cultural Revolution a disaster and tried to end the "myth" of Mao's successful transformation of China into a twentieth-century power. Memorials to Mao were banned, and his portraits were removed from the Great Hall in Beijing's Tiananmen Square.

As a final blow to Mao's historical status, the Gang of Four (now totaling ten individuals) was brought to trial. They were charged with "persecuting to death" more than 34,000 people, as well as abusing 730,000 others. Other charges included plotting to attack Mao's train during a 1971 tour, attempting to seize power in a rebellion in Shanghai just after Mao's death, and training a large force to oppose the regular army. Six others, all dead, were also listed among the defendants.

The start of the trial was delayed in the belief that Jiang would confess (the Chinese legal tradition places value on the accused's confessing guilt as a sign that justice has been done). She refused, insisting that whatever she had done during the Cultural Revolution had been done at Mao's request. Zhang Chunqiao also refused. The others confessed.

Trial Begins

The trial opened on November 20, 1980, before 600 representatives of the nation, in an air force auditorium in western Beijing. The foreign press was not admitted, but five-minute excerpts from the trial were televised. Jiang Qing was led into the courtroom, her arms held by two matrons wearing pistols.

TREASON

Wang Hongwen, member of the "Gang of Four" and former vice chairman of the Chinese Communist Party, testifies at his trial on November 25, 1980.

Jiang testified for the first time on November 26. Speaking softly, she denied conspiring with the three other leading defendants to keep Mao from appointing Deng Xiaoping, who had since assumed power, as first deputy prime minister in 1974. Her testimony, however, was contradicted by two women who had been aides to Mao and whose whereabouts had not been known since Mao's death.

The next day, prosecutors demanded that Zhang reply to charges that he had harassed several of the Chinese leaders. Looking angry and skeletal, he refused to answer, even after the judges warned him he could be convicted even if he did not speak. Zhang and Jiang continued to be the only defendants who did not confess.

Outbursts From Jiang

Tensions increased when former general Jiang Tengjiao testified. With the aid of forty people impersonating Red Guards, he had raided the Shanghai homes of actors and writers, looking for love letters Jiang Qing had written during the 1930s when she was an actor. When the prosecutors then began to question her about the persecution of chief of state Liu

THE GREAT LEAP FORWARD

When the Chinese Communist Revolution took place in 1949, China was a largely rural country. Mao's first priority was to industrialize China so that it could compete in the modern world. In 1958, he established a program known as the Great Leap Forward, a disastrous attempt to create Chinese industry virtually overnight. The result was mass starvation. The failure of the Great Leap Forward led to Mao's replacement as chairman by Liu Shao-Ch'I. The Cultural Revolution, in turn, enabled Mao to attack Liu and re-establish his own position.

Shaoqi and his wife during the Cultural Revolution, Jiang reversed her plea of innocence. She admitted that she had personally directed the campaign against Liu. She claimed, however, that she had acted on orders from Mao.

On December 12, Jiang was bitterly attacked by the widow of a former movie director. He had been tortured to death because of Jiang's suspicions that he had one of her love letters dating from the 1930s. Jiang repeatedly interrupted the woman's testimony, resulting in her being expelled from the courtroom. On December 23, she attacked the judges, calling them fascists and Nationalist Chinese agents. This time she was charged with contempt of court and warned that her behavior could lead to a heavier sentence.

"I Am Prepared to Die!"

Summing up the case, the prosecutor said that while Mao's "great contributions" to China would not be forgotten, it was clear that Mao was also responsible for the Chinese people's "plight" during the Cultural Revolution. When the prosecutor then asked that Mao's widow be given the death sentence, she condemned the court and was dragged from the courtroom shouting, "I am prepared to die!"

On January 25, 1981, Jiang was sentenced to death, but her sentence was suspended for two years. Again she was dragged out of court, all the while calling for the overthrow of Deng, who had gained power after

TREASON

Mao's death. Zhang Chunqiao received the same sentence. Wang was sentenced to life imprisonment and Yao to twenty years. The others were given sixteen to eighteen years behind bars. There was no appeals process.

On January 25, 1983, the sentences of Jiang and Zhang were reduced to life in prison. Early on the morning of May 14, 1991, after a total of seventeen years' imprisonment, served before and after the trial, Jiang, then seventy-seven years old, committed suicide in prison. On October 5, 1996, Yao was freed. Wang and Zhang remained in jail.

Suggestions for Further Reading

Bloodworth, Dennis. *The Messiah and the Mandarins: Mao Tse-tung and the Ironies of Power.* New York: Atheneum, 1982.

Bonavia, David. *The Chinese.* New York: Lippincott & Crowell, 1980.

Chang, Jung. *Wild Swans: Three Daughters of China.* New York: Simon & Schuster, 1991.

Cheng, Nien. *Life and Death in Shanghai.* New York: Grove, 1980.

Clayre, Alasdair. *The Heart of the Dragon.* Boston: Houghton Mifflin, 1985.

Dimond, E. Grey. *Inside China Today: A Western View.* New York: W. W. Norton, 1983.

Hoyt, Edwin P. *The Rise of the Chinese Republic: From the Last Emperor to Deng Xiaoping.* New York: McGraw-Hill, 1989.

Lawson, Don. *The Long March: Red China under Chairman Mao.* New York: Crowell, 1983.

Salisbury, Harrison E. *The New Emperors: China in the Era of Mao and Deng.* Boston: Little, Brown, 1992.

Terrill, Ross. *Mao: A Biography.* New York: Harper & Row, 1980.

Tiananmen Square Dissidents Trial: 1991

Defendants: Some eighty-seven students, workers, and intellectuals, including Bao Zunxin, Chen Lai, Chen Xiaoping, Chen Yanlin, Chen Ziming, Guo Haifeng, Kong Xianfeng, Li Chenghuan, Li Shuntang, Li Yuqi, Liu Gang, Liu Xiaobo, Liu Xiaojing, Lu Xiaochun, Ma Shaofang, Pang Zhihong, Ren Wanding, Wang Dan, Wang Haidong, Wang Juntao, Wang Youcai, Xue Jianan, Yang Junzhong, Yao Junling, Yu Yongjie, Zhang Ming, Zhang Qianjin, Zhang Yafei, Zheng Xuguang, and Zhou Wanshui

Crimes Charged: Counterrevolutionary propaganda and incitement, subversion against the People's Government, overthrowing the socialist system, organizing attacks against the army, disrupting public order, conspiring to overthrow the government, arson, looting, larceny, and blocking traffic

Chief Defense Lawyers: Kiang Jian for Wang Dan, others undisclosed by Chinese government

Chief Prosecutors: Undisclosed

Judges: Undisclosed

Place: Beijing, China

Dates of Trials: January 5, 1991 (Kong Xianfeng, Li Yuqi, Ma Shaofang, Pang Zhihong, Xue Jianan, Wang Youcai, Zhang Ming, Zhang Qianjin, Zheng Xuguang); January 9 (Chen Lai, Guo Haifeng, Li Chenghuan, Yao Junling); January 15 (Bao Zunxin, Li Shuntang, Liu Xiaojing, Lu Xiaochun, Wang Haidong, Yang Junzhong, Yu Yongjie, Zhou Wanshui); January 16 (Liu Xiaobo); January 23 (Wang Dan); February 4 (Chen

TREASON

Yanlin, Zhang Yafei); February 5 (Chen Xiaoping); February 6 (Liu Gang); February 11 (Chen Ziming); and February 12 (Wang Juntao)

Verdicts: Guilty

Sentences: Imprisonment, including time already served: Chen Ziming; Wang Juntao—thirteen years; Ren Wanding—seven years; Liu Gang—six years; Bao Zunxin—five years; Guo Haifeng, Wang Dan, Wang Youcai—four years; Kong Xianfeng, Ma Shaofang, Zhang Ming—three years; Xue Jianan, Yao Junling, Zhang Qianjin, Zheng Xuguang—two years; Chen Xiaoping, Li Yuqi, Liu Xiaobo, Pang Zhihong, and sixty-five others—no imprisonment beyond time already served

SIGNIFICANCE: The trials of dissidents who survived the bloody military crackdown on demonstrations in Beijing's Tiananmen Square proved, once again, the power of the totalitarian (dictatorial) state. Pro-democracy activities were ended almost overnight. The trials provided Western democracies, where an accused individual is innocent until proven guilty, with a view of a judicial system where guilt is assumed and where, according to one study, judges hand down guilty decisions in 98 percent of cases.

The unrest began with the death of Hu Yaobang on April 15, 1989. Hu had become a hero to Chinese liberals two years earlier when he had to resign as general secretary of the Chinese Communist Party because he had not put an end to student unrest. On April 17, 500 demonstrators marched into Beijing's Tiananmen Square to lay wreaths for Hu before the Great Hall of the People, the government's headquarters. The next day, the crowds in the square numbered as many as 10,000.

Police tried to break up the crowd. It only got larger. On April 19, the Square held between 20,000 and 40,000 students, older intellectuals, and workers. By April 21, the date of the memorial service for Hu, the crowd had reached 100,000, despite a government's warning not to assemble.

The assembly had already become a giant rally for democracy. Demonstrators demanded political reforms such as freedom of the press, free speech, freedom of assembly, more funding for education, publication of amounts paid to party leaders, and the restoration of Hu's reputation.

"A Grave Political Struggle"

To support the rally that continued in the square, university students in Beijing stopped going to classes on April 24. In response, the government issued warnings and outlawed three committees organized by the students.

The rally continued through May, bringing Beijing to a standstill on May 17 during a summit meeting between Chinese and Soviet leaders. On May 20, martial law was declared, meaning an order was given for the suspension of all civil rights for the pretense of public safety. To prevent troops from entering Tiananmen, the demonstrators set up roadblocks. Crowds surrounded military vehicles, begging drivers to stop. Three thousand students began hunger strikes in the square, where 200,000 were camped.

The police held back. On May 25, the state-run media called on troops to enforce martial law, and 200,000 soldiers surrounded the city. On June 1, the authorities banned press coverage of demonstrations, but the next day pop singer Hou Dejian began a hunger strike as he led a rally. That night, tanks led 10,000 unarmed soldiers on a march towards the square. Blocked by a jeering mass of demonstrators, many soldiers retreated. Some of them were in tears.

Tear Gas and Cattle Prods

The next afternoon, police and troops fired tear gas and beat protesters with electric cattle prods. The demonstrators threw bricks and rocks in return. Soon after midnight, troops moved into the square, firing machine guns and automatic rifles directly into the crowds. Many demonstrators fought back, using firebombs, pipes, and sticks and stones to destroy 180 army vehicles. By dawn on June 4, the government announced that the demonstration had ended. On June 6, it announced that 300 military and civilian people had been killed and 7,000 injured.

Arrests began immediately. By June 21, 1,500 people were in jail. On June 30, the civilian death toll rose to 300. By August, the World Bank (an agency of the United Nations that makes loans to promote investment, foreign trade, and to reduce debt) had canceled proposed loans to China, the United States government had ended high-level contacts with the country, and the United Nations had condemned the Chinese government's actions in Tiananmen Square. Amnesty International, a human rights organization, accused China of secretly executing political dissidents seized during the June demonstrations. They added that at least 1,000 civilians had been killed and 10,000 jailed as a result of the student uprising.

Trials Begin

The world first learned on January 5, 1991, that China had secretly tried the dissidents. The official New China News Agency reported that a court had sentenced nine of those who had participated in the demonstrations. China released few details of the highly secret trials to the public. The Chinese justice system considers court documents confidential, and officials usually do not release them to the defendant's attorney—if the defendant can even have an attorney. Judges, rather than juries, usually decide the fate of defendants. One study showed that Chinese courts find 98 of all defendants guilty, as the system assumes them to be.

Wang Dan's government-appointed lawyer agreed to defend him only on the assumption that he was guilty. However, the twenty-two-year-old Beijing University history student did not admit to the charges against him, instead reading from a prepared text for twenty minutes during his three-hour trial. As the trial ended, he asked one of the judges, "How was my performance?" The judge replied, "Not bad," and then sentenced Wang to four years in prison.

"What I Said before doesn't Count"

Some of the dissidents faced the death penalty. Even they refused to admit guilt. Thirty-year-old Liu Gang, a physics student, spoke for one hour during his trial. He claimed that any confession he made during his imprisonment was invalid, because guards had questioned him under threat of death: "What I said before doesn't count. What does count is what I say this morning." He received six years' imprisonment.

Nearly thirty trials took place during January and February 1991. Some said the Chinese authorities were rushing the trials through while the world's attention was on the Persian Gulf War. The longest sentences were announced on February 12. Wang Juntao, thirty-three, and Chen Ziming, thirty-eight, were each sentenced to thirteen years. The judges stated that the two had committed "very serious crimes but have shown so far no willingness to repent."

HUMAN RIGHTS ORGANIZATION

Amnesty International, the group that monitored the situation in Tiananmen Square, was founded in 1961. It serves as an international watchdog for human rights. Much of the group's work focuses on the cases of political prisoners—people who are jailed for speaking out against governments. By 1977, Amnesty International had helped to free over 10,000 prisoners, including victims of the Soviet Union who were held in gulags (prison camps) such as author Alexander Solzhenitsyn. Later that year, the group was awarded the Nobel Peace Prize.

Trials End, Punishments Continue

In mid-February, the state stopped announcing the trials and sentences. Asia Watch, a human rights organization, listed 960 people still in prison. Six months later, China announced that Wang Juntao and Chen Ziming, serving their terms in solitary confinement in cells smaller that five square yards, had both begun hunger strikes. Some others, however, were released from solitary confinement. In November, Wang Youcai, who was serving a four-year sentence, showed signs of repentance. Police released him. The state dropped charges against Han Dongfang, who had organized laborers to join the students demonstrating in Tiananmen Square. He had been held in jail without trial for nearly two years.

On October 11, 1996, China's Communist Party leaders charged Wang Dan with conspiracy to overthrow the government, a crime punishable by death. The state accused him of publishing anti-government articles abroad, accepting a University of California scholarship, and raising funds to support other dissidents. Police had already held him for seventeen months in a secret police center. This new charge meant that he would serve at least ten more years in prison before being released.

Suggestions for Further Reading

Feigon, Lee. *China Rising: The Meaning of Tiananmen.* Chicago: Ivan R. Dee, 1990.

TREASON

Human Rights in China (with John K. Fairbank, Orville Schell, Jonathan Spence, Andrew J. Nathan, and Fang Lizhi). *Children of the Dragon.* New York: Collier Books, Macmillan, 1990.

Lord, Bette Bao. *Legacies: A Chinese Mosaic.* New York: Knopf, 1990.

Salisbury, Harrison E. *Tiananmen Diary: Thirteen Days in June.* Boston: Little, Brown, 1989.

Schelle, Orville. *Mandate of Heaven.* New York: Simon & Schuster, 1994.

Simmie, Scott and Bob Nixon. *Tiananmen Square.* Seattle: University of Washington Press, 1989.

Terrill, Ross. *China in Our Time.* New York: Simon & Schuster, 1992.

Yi, Mu and Mark V. Thompson. *Crisis at Tiananmen.* San Francisco: Chinese Books & Periodicals, 1989.

WAR CRIMES

The Nuremberg Trial: 1945–1946

Defendants: Twenty-two leading Nazis

Crimes Charged: Conspiracy, crimes against peace, war crimes, crimes against humanity

Defense Lawyers: Otto Stahmer, Fritz Sauter, Alfred Seitel, and others

Prosecutors: Representatives of the United States, Great Britain, France, and the Soviet Union

Judges: Chief Judge Geoffrey Lawrence of Britain and seven associates

Place: Nuremberg, Germany

Dates: November 20, 1945–September 30, 1946

Verdicts: Nineteen of the twenty-two guilty on one or more counts

Sentences: Twelve sentenced to hang; the others received prison terms

SIGNIFICANCE: The Nuremberg trial documented Germany's appalling war crimes. It also punished some of the Nazi leaders, and established the legal principle that individuals are responsible for the wars they start.

During World War II the United States, Britain, France, and the Soviet Union were known as "the Big Four" allies. In 1945, these nations made an historic agreement. They established an international tribunal (court) to try Germany's leaders for killing at least twelve million men, women, and children. Proper courtroom procedures were to be strictly followed in order to make sure the accused had a fair trial. However, the Allies ruled out the most obvious defense strategy. The Nazis would not be allowed to use a "you did it too" argument. Allied bombing of German cities, for example, could not be offered as an excuse for Nazi crimes.

The Tribunal

The International Military Tribunal assembled in the Palace of Justice in Nuremberg, Germany, in October 1945. Nuremberg was, to this time, known for pro-Nazi activities that took place there: Nuremberg's Zeppelin Field had been the site of the great Nazi Party annual rallies of the 1930s; the anti-Jewish Nuremberg Laws had been passed in the city; a Nazi judge had tried conspirators in the 1944 bomb plot against Hitler in the Palace of Justice—the victors regarded the bombed-out city as the symbolic capital of Nazism.

Hitler, the Allies argued, had grabbed power, started a war, and murdered millions of innocent people. How had he been able to do this? Because of a conspiracy. It involved military leaders, diplomats, industrialists, and minor Nazi Party officials. The tribunal determined that

The Palace of Justice in Nuremberg, Germany, where ex-Nazi leaders went on trial before an International Military Tribunal on November 17, 1945.

conspirators can be punished even though they might not have committed a crime themselves. In addition, key Nazi groups would stand trial as criminal groups. Soldiers, police, and concentration camp personnel could all be arrested simply for belonging to these groups.

The tribunal indicted twenty-three principal Nazis on four counts, of conspiracy, crimes against peace, war crimes, and crimes against humanity. Among the accused were many top Nazis, including Hermann Goering, builder of the Luftwaffe air force and Hitler's chief deputy. Among the other defendants were Nazi foreign minister Joachim von Ribbentrop, generals Wilhelm Keitel and Alfred Jodl, weapons minister Albert Speer, minister of the economy Hjalmar Schacht, governor of Nazi-occupied Poland Hans Frank, and Walther Funk, head of the German national bank. One of the defendants, Robert Ley, committed suicide in prison before the trial began. Another, Martin Bormann, vanished. He was tried anyway.

The Allies tried only the leading conspirators; national courts would handle the thousands of lesser cases. Critics claimed the Allies were creating laws to punish crimes that had already been committed. No court had existed for punishing the guilty in earlier wars. No laws declared either the Nazi Party or the Gestapo police to be criminal groups. Goering said as much when he scribbled on his copy of the indictment: "The victor will always be the judge and the vanquished the accused." U.S. Supreme Court Justice Robert H. Jackson, who served as one of the prosecutors at Nuremberg, provided a better explanation. The Nazis, after all, had committed unheard-of acts of cruelty on a massive scale.

"Let's not be derailed by legal hair-splitters," Jackson argued. "Aren't murder, torture, and enslavement crimes recognized by all civilized people? What we propose is to punish acts which have been regarded as criminal since the time of Cain and have been so written in every civilized code."

Jackson built the prosecution's case on evidence taken from documents he called "self-proving briefs:" a large number of orders, reports, logs, letters, and diary entries that proved Nazi guilt. The Germans had recorded everything in detail. One example was recorded by Hermann Graebe, a civilian working for the German army. He left a matter-of-fact account of an incident near Dubno in the Ukraine on October 5, 1942. Out of curiosity, Graebe had followed an SS (elite guard) unit and several thousand Jewish men, women, and children to a high bank of earth that stood above a newly dug pit on the outskirts of town.

"Without screaming or weeping," Graebe wrote, "these people undressed, stood around in family groups, kissed each other, said farewells. . . . I remember a girl, slim, with black hair, who, as she passed close to me pointed to herself and said, 'twenty-three years old.'" SS executioners turned their automatic weapons on 5,000 people that afternoon. The victims were buried in the pit.

The Prosecution

The tribunal president, Lord Justice Geoffrey Lawrence of Great Britain, opened the trial in Courtroom 600 of the Palace of Justice on November 20, 1945. The two American and two British judges wore black robes. The two French judges wore sable robes with white bibs and ruffles at the cuffs. The two Soviets wore brown military uniforms with green trim. At 10 A.M. the first group of defendants—Goering, Ribbentrop, and Rudolf Hess—entered from a sliding door that opened onto the prisoners' dock in the courtroom. The reading of the indictment took all of the first day and part of the second. One after another, the accused entered pleas of not guilty. Then Jackson launched into his opening statement.

Over the next several days, the Americans introduced a mass of papers. These documents overwhelmed the judges, the translators, and the defense team. They even confused the British, French, and Soviet prosecutors. After a while, too, the documents began to take the edge off the

horror of the case. Prosecutor William J. Donovan thought it was "confused and flat from so much paper evidence."

Donovan argued hard for living witnesses to add drama to the trial. On November 29, Jackson gave in a bit, introducing a motion picture titled *Nazi Concentration Camps.* The film showed conditions in the Dachau, Buchenwald, and Bergen-Belsen death camps. One scene showed bulldozers pushing mounds of stacked corpses into open graves. Another, taken from a German film, showed SS troops leading a group of prisoners into a barn, then dousing the building with gasoline and setting it on fire.

The images seemed to stun the defendants. Taylor recalled: "Schacht turned his back to the screen to show that he had had no connection with such bestiality; Goering tried to brazen it out; the weaker ones like Ribbentrop, Frank, and Funk appeared shattered."

Until then, the trial seemed to amuse Goering. He seemed especially tickled by the prosecution's portrayal of him as the mastermind of the Nazi takeover of Austria in 1938. "They were reading my telephone conversations on the Austrian affair, and everybody was laughing with me," he said later. "And then they showed that awful film, and it spoiled everything."

The allies accused Speer and Ernst Sauckel of setting up Germany's slave labor system. Sauckel rounded up slave laborers from all over Europe. There were five million altogether. Speer, in charge of weapons, assigned workers as needed to keep Hitler's war plants running at top speed.

The laborers were half-starved and often worked to death. This was especially true of the Soviets and other Slavic peoples. Soviet workers were given three-quarters of a cup of tea at the 4 A.M. start of the workday. At quitting time fourteen hours later, they were fed a quart of watery soup and two slices of bread.

Sauckel refused to take responsibility for conditions in the barracks and factories. Speer, he said, had actually put the hands to work.

The numbers were overwhelming and difficult to comprehend. Of 5.7 million Soviet troops taken prisoner, 3.7 million died in captivity. Four million Jews died in extermination camps. The SS and other Nazi groups murdered an additional 2 million Jews elsewhere.

Once again, the weight of the papers hid the human aspect of the tragedy. The dead were men, women, and children, not just numbers on paper. At one point, an assistant U.S. prosecutor, Thomas Dodd, strayed from Jackson's plan. Dodd displayed the shrunken head of a Polish person who had been executed. The wife of the commander of the Buchenwald concentration camp had used it for a paperweight. At another point,

The
Nuremberg
Trial:
1945–1946

OPPOSITE PAGE

Head Nazis stand trial in Nuremberg, Germany, on November 22, 1945. Hermann Goering, on the left side in the box, takes notes while Rudolph Hess, seated next to Goering, watches the proceedings. Former foreign minister Joachim von Ribbentrop sits to the left of Hess. In the back row (left to right) are admirals Karl Doenitz and Erich Raeder.

WAR CRIMES

a French woman who had survived another camp took the witness stand. "One night, we were awakened by terrible cries," she testified. "The next day we learned that the Nazis had run out of [poison] gas and the children had been hurled into the furnaces alive."

Beginning on January 8, 1946, the prosecution laid out its case against the individual defendants. Admiral Karl Doenitz, commander-in-chief of Hitler's navy (1943–1954), had issued orders that German U-boats (submarines) were not to pick up survivors of ships they had sunk. He had also used slave labor to build ships. Goering had served as president of the Nazi parliament, where in 1935 he approved the anti-Jewish Nuremberg laws. He bore some responsibility for the destruction of the Jews and for the execution of escaped prisoners of war.

Wilhelm Frick had drawn up the legal code that denied Jews most of their legal rights. Julius Streicher had carried on a hate campaign against Jews in his newspaper, *Der Sturmer*. Alfred Rosenberg, the "philosopher" of Nazism in the 1930s, later served as minister of the Occupied Eastern Territories (Eastern Europe), where millions were murdered.

On March 6, 1946, the prosecution rested its case.

The Defense

The accused were held in isolation cells under twenty-four-hour guard in a prison in the Palace of Justice. They had been among the most powerful men in the world. Now, in their ill-fitting secondhand suits, they looked like ordinary people.

Of all the Nazis, Goering paid the closest attention to the trial, remaining defiant throughout. Hess and Streicher both looked as though they had lost their minds. Frank wore sunglasses for most of the trial. Keitel and Jodl, both former generals, sat stiffly at attention.

The defense case opened on March 8. Goering's testimony began five days later. He admitted to approving the Nuremberg Laws and to setting up a system of concentration camps. However, he denied that he had issued the orders for "The Final Solution"—the killing of all the Jews.

Ribbentrop took the witness stand April 1. Asked on cross-examination about the death camps, he said, "I knew nothing about that."

The prosecution had made Keitel out to be Hitler's servant, carrying out his master's criminal plans without questioning them. Now, he had a certain air of dignity as he took the witness stand. He was asked about orders bearing his signature to shoot Allied commandos and to take vengeance for their attacks. Keitel's lawyer asked: "What can you say in your defense?"

"I bear the responsibility for whatever resulted from those orders," Keitel responded. "Furthermore, I bear the moral as well as the legal responsibility."

Ernst Kaltenbrunner was head of the Nazi security office. He had signed orders that sent hundreds of thousands of people to the death camps. However, because his signature was always typewritten, he claimed he was guilty only in a formal sense. "I never saw a gas chamber," Kaltenbrunner said.

Frank, Doenitz, Baldur von Shirach (a leader of the Nazi youth movement), Sauckel, Jodl, and Arthur Seyss-Inquart oversaw the deaths of 41,000 Dutch people. Another 50,000 died of starvation. More than half of the Jews living in Holland died.

Franz von Papen, who had been chancellor of Germany before Hitler, testified after Seyss-Inquart had been questioned. Speer, a brilliant, sophisticated man, testified on June 21. He had used starving Soviets to run the Nazi war industry. Now Speer claimed that in the end he had turned against Hitler, had even tried to kill him. Still, he accepted some guilt. Hans Fritzsche, at one time the head of Hitler's radio service, testified at the end of June. With this, the defense concluded.

The lawyers' summations lasted more than a month. The defense of the seven indicted Nazi organization took another month. On August 31, the accused were each given fifteen minutes for a final statement. Goering again criticized "victor's justice." Hess spoke aimlessly. Keitel was remorseful. "I did not see that there is a limit set even for a soldier's performance of his duty," he said. "That is my fate."

The
Nuremberg
Trial:
1945–1946

HITLER'S ARCHITECT

Nuremberg war criminal Albert Speer was born in 1905. He began his service to the Nazi regime as Adolf Hitler's architect. In his famous memoir, *Inside the Third Reich* (published in English in 1972), he recounts how he and Hitler would spend hours planning enormous monuments and public buildings that were supposed to last for one thousand years. In 1942, he became Nazi minister of armaments, a post he held until the war ended in 1945. Speer served his twenty-year sentence from 1946 to 1966. He died in 1981.

Speer warned of the danger ahead. He had done much to develop rockets and other technology that would make the next world war a final one. "A new large-scale war will end with the destruction of human culture and civilization," he warned. "That is why this trial must contribute to the prevention of such wars in the future." Speer had little to say about his own guilt.

The Judgment

The judges returned to the courtroom on September 30 to deliver their verdicts. The declared the SS, the Gestapo, and the SD (a security organization) all illegal. On October 1, the tribunal announced the individual verdicts. Declared guilty on all four counts and sentenced to hang were Goering, Ribbentrop, Keitel, Rosenberg, and Jodl. Kaltenbrunner, Frank, Frick, Streicher, Sauckel, and Seyss-Inquart were all found guilty of crimes against humanity, and were sentenced to hang. If Bormann were ever found alive, he, too, would hang.

Hess, Funk, and Erich Raeder, who had served as Navy commander before Doenitz, were each found guilty on two or more counts and received life sentences. Speer was found guilty of war crimes and crimes against humanity. He received a twenty-year prison sentence, as did Baldur von Shirach, who was convicted of crimes against humanity. Konstantin von Neurath, guilty on all four counts, received fifteen years in prison. Doenitz was declared guilty of war crimes and crimes against peace, for which he received a ten-year sentence. The court acquitted Schacht, Papen, and Fritzsche on all four counts.

In early October, the Allied Control Council denied all requests for pardons. They also rejected appeals from Goering, Keitel, and Jodl to be shot rather than hanged. Three gallows, eight feet high and painted black, were put up in the prison gym at the Palace of Justice. A few hours before the execution, Goering bit into a vial of cyanide poison he had hidden in his cell. He died within minutes.

The U.S. Army executioner hanged Ribbentrop first, at a little after 1 A.M. on the morning on October 16, 1946. Keitel followed, then Kaltenbrunner, then the others. The hangings were spaced a few minutes apart, and they were clumsy. Keitel, for instance, struggled for nearly half an hour. Seyss-Inquart was the last to die, at 2:45 A.M. A few hours later, the ten bodies were taken to a crematorium near Munich and burned.

Suggestions for Further Reading

Conot, Robert E. *Justice at Nuremberg.* New York: Harper & Row, 1983.

Persico, Joseph. *Nuremberg: Infamy on Trial.* New York: Viking, 1994.

Smith, Bradley F. *Reaching Judgment at Nuremberg.* New York: Basic Books, 1977.

Taylor, Telford. *The Anatomy of the Nuremberg Trials.* New York: Alfred A. Knopf, 1992.

Tokyo War Crimes Trial: 1946–1948

Defendants: Sadao Araki, Kenji Doihara, Kingoro Hashimoto, Shunroku Hata, Kitchiro Hiranuma, Koki Hirota, Naoki Hoshino, Seishiro Itagaki, Okinori Kaya, Koichi Kido, Heitaro Kimura, Kuniaki Koiso, Iwane Matsui, Yosuke Matsuoka, Jiro Minami, Akira Muto, Osami Nagano, Takasumi Oka, Shumei Okawa, Hiroshi Oshima, Kenryo Sato, Mamoru Shigemitsu, Shigetaro Shimada, Toshio Shiratori, Teiichi Susuki, Shigenori Togo, Hideki Tojo, and Yoshijiro Umezu

Crimes Charged: Conspiracy to wage aggressive war against China, the United States, the British Commonwealth, the Netherlands, France, and the U.S.S.R.; ordering, authorizing, or permitting atrocities; disregard of duty to secure observance of and prevent breaches of laws of war; total: fifty-five counts

Chief Defense Lawyers: Somei Uzawa, Norris N. Allen, Ben Bruce Blakeney, George Francis Blewett, John Brannon, Alfred W. Brooks, Beverly Coleman, Owen Cunningham, Valentine Deale, George Furness, John Guider, Joseph Howard, Tadashi Hanai, Joseph F. Hynes, Ichiro Kiyose, Aristides Lazarus, Michael Levin, William Logan Jr., Floyd Mattice, Lawrence McManus, David F. Smith, Kenzo Takayanagi, Franklin E. N. Warren, Carrington Williams, George Yamaoka, amd Charles T. Young

Chief Prosecutors: Joseph Berry Keenan (U.S.A.), W. G. Frederick Borgerhoff-Mulder (the Netherlands), Arthur S. Comyns-Carr (Britain), John A. Darsey Jr. (U.S.A.), Robert Donihi (U.S.A.), S. A. Golunsky (U.S.S.R.), Che-chun Hsiang (China), Pedro Lopez (the Philippines), Alan Mansfield

(Australia), Henry Nolan (Canada), Robert L. Oneto (France), Ronald Quilliam (New Zealand), and A. N. Vasiliev (U.S.S.R.)

Judges: Sir William Webb (Australia), Henri Bernard (France), John P. Higgins, succeeded by Myron C. Cramer (U.S.A.), Delfin Jaranilla (the Philippines), Edward Stuart McDougall (Canada), Ju-ao Mei (China), Harvey Northcroft (New Zealand), Radhabinod Pal (India), Lord Patrick (Britain), H. V. A. Roling (the Netherlands), and I. M. Zarayanov (U.S.S.R.)

Place: Tokyo, Japan

Dates of Trial: May 3, 1946–April 16, 1948

Verdicts: Guilty

Sentences: Execution by hanging: Doihara, Hirota, Itagaki, Kimura, Matsui, Muto, and Tojo; life imprisonment: Araki, Hashimoto, Hata, Hiranuma, Hoshino, Kaya, Kido, Koiso, Minami, Oka, Oshima, Sato, Shimada, Shiratori, Susuki, and Umezu; twenty years imprisonment: Togo; seven years imprisonment: Shigemitsu; (died during trial: Matsuoka and Nagano; committed to psychiatric ward: Okawa)

SIGNIFICANCE: This was one of the most complex trials in history. Unlike the Nuremberg trials of German war criminals, most of the defendants in Tokyo—nineteen out of twenty-eight—were military leaders. In Germany, the government had controlled the military. In Japan, the military ran the government. Like Nuremberg, the Tokyo trial had no precedent (model) in international law. Rather, it was based on concepts common among the world's major legal systems.

In 1946, General Douglas MacArthur was supreme commander of the Allies in the Pacific. After the Japanese surrendered, World War II came to an end. Shortly after, MacArthur issued a declaration. Dated January 16, it called for the establishment of an International Military Tribunal for the Far East. The tribunal, or court, would try people and groups guilty of crimes against peace.

WAR CRIMES

The Allies modeled this tribunal after the one that tried the Nazis in Nuremberg, Germany. They defined crimes against peace very carefully. These were "the planning, preparation, initiation, or waging of a declared or undeclared war of aggression or a war in violation of international treaties." They covered inhumane acts against civilians. No Japanese would be charged for only fighting in the war.

"Class A" Responsibility

The Allies arrested Japanese suspected of war crimes dating back to 1931. They held hundreds of them in Sugamo Prison. Twenty-eight—those especially guilty of war crimes—were called "Class A." This group included generals, government officials, ministers of war, foreign ministers, business and financial leaders, naval leaders, and ambassadors. One philosopher and a nobleman were "Class A." Emperor Hirohito was not charged because MacArthur warned this would "cause a tremendous convulsion among the Japanese people."

The trial opened on May 3, 1946, in the former War Ministry building in Tokyo. The 1,000-seat courtroom (which included 600 seats for onlookers in the balcony) was heavily guarded. It had been wired so that English, Japanese, or Russian translations reached every seat. It was brightly lit for news cameras. Military police patrolled the courtroom in white gloves and helmets. They checked every chair for weapons, messages, or other forbidden items.

Clogs and Tailcoats

The defendants filed into their assigned seats. Some wore rumpled dress uniforms from which their medals and emblems of rank had been torn. One came in wearing wooden clogs. Another wore a tropical jungle jacket. Still another wore formal Western clothes: the traditional striped trousers and tailcoat. All eyes sought out the notorious General Hideki Tojo, who had once been Japan's highest military leader. A few months earlier, Tojo had shot himself in a suicide attempt, but now he appeared well and looked dapper in his khaki bush jacket.

Setting the tone for the trial, chief judge Sir William Webb noted that the prosecution had to prove that the defendants were guilty beyond a reasonable doubt. The court clerk then read the charges. When he reached count twenty-two—charging several of the defendants with starting a war of aggression with the attack on the U.S. military base in Pearl Harbor, Hawaii, on December 7, 1941—defendant Shumei Okawa, sitting directly behind Tojo, slapped the general hard on top of his head. He repeated the attack, then military police seized him. The court ordered Shumei to be taken to a mental ward, where he was found to be incapable of testifying on his own behalf. His ill health had been produced by disease and drug abuse.

The remaining accused all plead not guilty. Several days of debate over the court's authority then followed. Crimes against peace and against humanity did not exist in international law, the defense argued, because "war is not a crime." Four defendants argued that the court was ignoring their rights as prisoners of war. On May 17, the court dismissed all these claims.

"Declared War upon Civilization"

Prosecutor Joseph B. Keenan reminded the court that Japan had been one of the allies who, at the end of World War I, agreed that "a war of aggression constitutes an international crime." Japan had also signed the Hague Convention of 1907, barring states from starting wars "without previous and explicit warning." The Japanese had also signed the Kellogg-Briand Pact of 1920. This agreement, signed August 27, 1928, rejected war "as an instrument of national policy." Yet, said Keenan, pointing to the defendants, "they declared war upon civilization."

Keenan set out to establish that there was one key issue in the trial. This was a person's responsibility when committing crimes in the name of the state. He had a three-part trial strategy: 1) to show that the defendants had risen to power in the police-state atmosphere that dominated Japan in the 1930s, in which thought control, spying, and terrorism were common; 2) to show that the military had created "incidents" to increase their power; and 3) to show that a number of fanatics, both military and civilian, had encouraged wars by their aggressive policies towards neighboring countries.

People told the court about the military police terrorizing citizens based on how they looked. Other witnesses said the army governed the empire. All war ministers were army generals. Young Japanese spectators in the courtroom gasped when one witness described the army's invasion of Manchuria, north of China, as having been undertaken without the emperor's consent.

WAR CRIMES

The Puppet Emperor

A key witness to the conquest of Manchuria, begun in 1931, was Henry P'u Yi. He was the emperor of the puppet state of Manchukuo, set up by the Japanese. On the witness stand for eleven days, he described the brutal treatment of Manchurians by the Japanese invaders. Of the twenty-eight defendants on trial in Tokyo, twenty-four were shown to have been associated with the P'u Yi's puppet government.

Witnesses testified about several incidents staged by the Japanese in China. A 1931 incident gave Japan an excuse to invade Manchuria. In 1937, another incident resulted in the deaths of 124,130 Chinese soldiers at the hands of the Japanese. The six-week violation of Nanjing, during which 20,000 Chinese women were assaulted, left behind 43,000 corpses for the Chinese Red Cross to bury.

The prosecution turned to narcotics. Although Japan pretended to control the use of opium, it had brought in large quantities of this and other drugs. The Chinese will to oppose military occupation was weakened, and at the same time the Japanese made huge profits.

Prosecution witnesses also described how the Tokyo alliance with Nazi Germany was established and how the sneak attack on Pearl Harbor was planned. They testified about abuse of prisoners of war, including surgery performed without anesthesia and the seven-day Bataan Death march that killed more than 10,000 American and Filipino troops. Witnesses told of beheadings in the jungle and on prison ships. The numbers were overwhelming; 18,000 Filipinos were murdered in the village of Lipa; 450 French and Vietnamese were machine-gunned and bayoneted in Langson, Vietnam; dozens of young Filipino women were assaulted in Manila by hundreds of Japanese; 30,000 Burmese slave laborers were forced to build the Siam-Burma railroad, while thousands sick with cholera were simply abandoned in the jungle.

Closing the prosecution's case, Keenan turned to the defense claim that Japan had waged war in self-defense. "It is significant," he said, "that no one has claimed a threat from any power to attack or invade the Empire of Japan. . . . We reject the contention that it is self-defense for a nation to attack another because the latter refuses to supply materials of war to be used against it and its allies."

The Defense Opens

The defense opened their case on February 4, 1947. "The punishment of crimes against peace in violation of treaties," argued lawyer Kenzo

Takayanagi, "has never been known to the laws of nations." War was not illegal. The idea that those who had plotted and waged war were criminally responsible was "a perfectly revolutionary doctrine."

The defense tried to establish that Japan's motive in waging war was self-defense. The United States, it said, had been the aggressor by building up its defenses at Pearl Harbor, sending war materials to China, and demanding that Japan withdraw from Manchuria. All of Japan's military and economic development before December 1941 had been defensive, according to the defense counsel for General Tojo, who had also served as prime minister.

Tojo, cross-examined by the prosecution, accepted responsibility for his country's actions. He claimed, however, that the 1941 economic blockade by the Allies had forced Japan to start the war in order to preserve its "national existence."

The defense argued that the Western Allies had repeatedly violated the Kellogg-Briand Pact and other treaties, making these agreements "worthless." The idea that a criminal conspiracy had existed in Japan from 1928 to 1941 was absurd. In that time fifteen governing Japanese cabinets had resigned. How could they, the defense asked, have had an "organized plan"?

Tokyo War Crimes Trial: 1946–1948

General Hideki Tojo listens as Chief Justice Sir William Webb reads the court's judgment against him. After finding him guilty of war crimes, Webb sentenced Tojo to death by hanging.

WAR CRIMES

Just Following Orders

Following orders in military matters was not a crime, the defense claimed. If Japanese leaders had committed crimes, then so had Soviet, British, and American leaders.The defense ended its case on April 16, 1948. By then, the trial transcript was 48,412 pages long. Four hundred-nineteen witnesses had testified, and 779 written statements had been presented in 818 court sessions over more than two years.

The eleven judges spent seven months reviewing the evidence. On November 12, after spending a week presenting their opinion, they found twenty-five defendants guilty. (Of the original twenty-eight, two had died of natural causes during the trial, and one had been declared mentally unfit.) Seven were condemned to death, including Tojo. Sixteen were sentenced to life in prison. One was given a twenty-year sentence, and another was given seven years in prison.

The executions, by hanging, were carried out shortly after midnight on December 23, 1948. MacArthur permitted no Japanese witnesses and no photographers to be present.

Suggestions for Further Reading

Brackman, Arnold C. *The Other Nuremberg.* New York: William Morrow, 1987.

Hoyt, Edwin Palmer. *Warlord: Tojo Against the World.* Lanham, MD: Scarborough House, 1993.

Minear, Richard H. *Victors' Justice: The Tokyo War Crimes Trial.* Princeton, NJ: Princeton University Press, 1971.

Piccigallo, Philip R. *The Japanese On Trial.* Austin: University of Texas Press, 1979.

Reischauer, Edwin D. *Japan: The Story of A Nation.* New York: McGraw-Hill, 1990.

Tokyo War
Crimes
Trial:
1946–1948

Adolf Eichmann Trial: 1961

Defendant: Adolf Eichmann

Crimes Charged: Crimes against Jews with intent to destroy the people, crimes against humanity, and membership in criminal organizations

Chief Defense Lawyers: Robert Servatius and Dieter Wechtenbruch

Chief Prosecutors: Gideon Hausner, Jacob Baror, Gabriel Bach, and Jacob Robinson

Judges: Moshe Landau, Benjamin Halevy, and Yitzhak Raveh

Place: Jerusalem, Israel

Dates: April 11–August 14, 1961

Verdict: Guilty

Sentence: Execution

SIGNIFICANCE: The trial and conviction of Adolf Eichmann, the most despicable (except for Adolf Hitler himself) of all Nazi officials in the German high command before and during World War II, stands as a testament to persistence. Presumed dead after the war, Eichmann was brought to justice fifteen years after the Nuremberg trials. Furthermore, the trial was held under the jurisdiction of Israel, a country that had not existed when the crimes were committed.

On May 7, 1945, Germany surrendered—ending combat in Europe in World War II. On August 8, the "Big Four" allies (the United States, Great

Britain, France, and the Soviet Union) signed the London Agreement. This agreement established the International Military Tribunal, whose purpose was to try and punish persons who had committed war crimes for the enemy powers.

In October 1945, the tribunal began the trial of twenty-four Nazi leaders at Nuremberg, Germany. More than ten months later, four judges found three defendants not guilty on any of the counts. Seven defendants were sentenced to prison terms. The other twelve were hanged, with the exception of Hermann Goering, who committed suicide in prison, and Martin Bormann, who was tried even though his whereabouts were unknown.

The tribunal also found that several organizations were criminal. These were the SS (Hitler's special guards), the SD (the security service), the Gestapo (a secret state police force), and the leadership of the Nazi Party.

Absent from Nuremberg

Prosecutors at Nuremberg noticed that several defendants, when questioned about the Nazi program to kill all the Jews, mentioned Adolf Eichmann. When asked where Eichmann was, all guessed he was dead. Not even his photograph appeared in Nuremberg. The tribunal summed up the extent of his crimes. "Adolf Eichmann, who had been put in charge of this program by Hitler, [oversaw] the killing of 6,000,000 Jews, of which 4,000,000 were killed in the extermination institutions."

As the Nuremberg trial faded into history, the name Adolf Eichmann was all but forgotten.

Seized In Buenos Aires

Nearly fifteen years later, early in the evening of May 11, 1960, seven Israeli men stopped before a house on Garibaldi Street in Buenos Aires, Argentina, waiting for Ricardo Klement to walk from a bus to his home. They grabbed him and took him to a "safe house," where he admitted to being Adolf Eichmann. Within days, the president of Israel, David Ben-Gurion, announced to the Knesset (Israeli Parliament), that the Israeli secret service had seized Eichmann, and that he was presently in Israel.

Argentina filed a formal complaint with the United Nations against Israel for abducting one of its citizens. Israel apologized but kept Eich-

WAR CRIMES

mann. The United Nations Security Council decided that Eichmann "should be brought to appropriate justice for the crimes of which he is accused."

On April 11, 1961, the trial of Eichmann opened in the district court of Jerusalem in Israel. He was charged with crimes against Jews, crimes against humanity, and membership in criminal organizations. A bullet-proof glass case large enough for Eichmann and two guards was installed in the courtroom of the newly built Beth Ha'am, or House of the People. The building was fenced-in. Heavily armed guards were stationed on the rooftop and in the basement. All those who entered the building were carefully searched.

"Looking like a Bank Clerk"

The three judges sat high above the courtroom floor. Directly below them were translators ready to render all questions and testimony in English, French, German, and Hebrew. Glaring lights and white walls brought out the yellow color of the defendant's skin, who looked so ordinary that the press described him as "looking like a bank clerk."

Gideon Hausner, attorney general of Israel, opened for the prosecution: "With me stand six million accusers. But they cannot point an accusing finger toward the man who sits in the glass dock and cry: 'I accuse.' For their ashes were piled up in the hills of [the concentration camps at] Auschwitz and . . . Treblinka, or washed away by the rivers of Poland, their graves scattered over the length and breadth of Europe. Their blood cries out, but their voices are not heard."

Over eight hours, Hausner reviewed the rise of anti-Jewish racism and the Nazi "Final Solution" for destroying all Jews. Next, a six-volume transcript of seventy-six tapes of interviews with Eichmann was placed in evidence. Some were played. The court heard Eichmann claim he was "only a minor transport officer." They heard him offer to hang himself in public as penance.

A long parade of witnesses testified as to Eichmann's crimes. They recalled how he had bragged to six Jewish leaders in Vienna, when Nazism was just starting to take over Austria, that he would clear the country of Jews "in the shortest possible way." They also described the flight of Czech Jews from Prague after Eichmann took charge there in 1939. They remembered the forced march of Polish Jews to the Soviet border, where they were massacred. They testified about the 1942 destruction of the ghetto where Jews lived in Warsaw, Poland; only 60,000 survived out of the 500,000 originally there. In Lithuania, the Nazi "children's operation" tore youngsters from their mothers' arms. In France, Holland, Norway, and Denmark, Jews had been driven from their homes and into concentration camps. All these horrors, witnesses testified, took place under the direction of Eichmann.

Eichmann's Key Role in Atrocities

One key witness was an American judge named Michael A. Musmanno. As a naval officer in 1945, he had questioned the Nuremberg defendants. He testified that Hermann Goering "made it very clear that Eichmann was the man to determine in what order, in what coun-

Nazi war criminal Adolf Eichmann sits in a bullet-proof box during his trial on April 24, 1961.

tries, the Jews were to die." Judge Musmanno also said Nuremberg had produced evidence that any Nazi who was not willing to participate in the killing of Jews was free to volunteer to serve on the front lines of the war.

Eichmann's leadership in the concentration camps was demonstrated by testimony about Strasbourg University's Institute of Ancestral Heredity, which needed Jewish skeletons for its studies. On Eichmann's order, a scientist from the institute selected 115 men and women at Auschwitz and had them killed with poison gas to provide "fresh" skeletons.

One witness, Dean Grueber, summed up Eichmann's role this way: "Eichmann was what we called in German a *Landsknecht,* by which we meant a man who, when he puts on his uniform, leaves his conscience and his reason in the wardrobe."

Other witnesses spoke of the slaughter of Jews in Hungary and of Eichmann's agreement with Arab and Iraqi leaders to prevent Jewish children from moving to Palestine, the land that later became Israel. The gruesome acts that took place in the death camps were detailed: the endless trains bringing the victims, the shooting of naked prisoners at the edges of mass graves, the piles of bodies.

Opening Eichmann's defense, Dr. Robert Servatius explained why he had not cross-examined the prosecution witnesses. Eichmann did not dispute the facts about the Jewish Holocaust or his participation in it. Rather, he had simply followed orders. He was merely a "transmitter" with no power of his own. "I never took any decision by myself," he said, adding, "I never did anything, great or small, without obtaining in advance express instructions from my superiors." Even in Hungary in the last days of the war, he claimed, "I had only railway timetables to take care of, and even this only marginally. . . . Everything was done by my superiors."

"I Will Leap into My Grave Laughing"

On cross-examination, prosecutor Hausner asked Eichmann, "Do you consider yourself guilty of participation in the murder of millions of Jews?"

"Legally not, but in the human sense—yes, for I am guilty of having deported them."

Hausner reported a boast Eichmann had made in 1945: "I will leap into my grave laughing because the feeling that I have 5 million beings on my conscience is for me a source of extraordinary satisfaction."

Eichmann said he was then referring to only enemies of the Nazi government. Judge Raveh pursued the matter. Eichmann then admitted that he had spoken of five million Jews.

"The only front on which you were active all the years from 1937 on," asked the prosecutor, "was the fight against Jews?"

Eichmann looked at the floor. "Yes, that is true."

"The Nature of a *Subaltern*"

Defense witnesses, all former high-ranking Nazis, were promised safe passage from their German and Austrian homes to testify in Jerusalem.

All refused, but many sent sworn statements. Far from supporting Eichmann's defense that he was only following orders, most of these witnesses incriminated him. The statement of former SS and police leader Otto Winkelmann was typical: "He had the nature of a subaltern, which means a fellow who uses his power recklessly, without moral restraints. He would certainly overstep his authority if he thought he was acting in the spirit of his commander."

An even more damaging statement came from Alfred Six, a former SD general:

> Eichmann was an absolute and unconditional believer in National Socialism [Nazism]. It was his world. In case of doubt, he would invariably act according to the most extreme interpretation of the party doctrine. Eichmann had much greater powers than other department chiefs.

On August 14, 1961, the Eichmann trial ended. It had taken 14 weeks, more than 1,500 documents, 100 prosecution witnesses (90 of them survivors of Nazi captivity), and dozens of defense statements delivered from 16 countries. The three judges deliberated for four months. On December 11, they announced their verdict. Under "crimes against Jews with intent to destroy the people," Eichmann was convicted on the first four counts: 1) "causing the killing of millions of Jews," 2) placing "millions of Jews under conditions which were likely to lead to their physical destruction," 3) "causing serious bodily and mental harm" to Jews, and 4) "directing that births be banned and pregnancies interrupted among Jewish women." On the charge of "crimes against humanity," he was convicted on a wide range of charges. These included abusing Jews on racial, religious, and political grounds and taking Jewish property. He was also guilty of crimes against non-Jews. For instance, he drove thousands of Polish people from their homes and deported gypsies to the Auschwitz concentration camp. On the final three counts of membership in criminal organizations, he was also found guilty. The first twelve counts carried the death penalty.

Eichmann appealed. On May 29, 1962, Israel's Court of Appeals upheld his sentence and revised the lower court's judgment to reflect the fact that Eichmann "had received no 'superior orders' at all. He was his own superior, and he gave all orders in matters that concerned Jewish affairs."

On May 31, Israeli president Itzhak Ben-Zvi turned down Eichmann's petition for mercy. Just before midnight, after refusing to put on the customary black hood, Eichmann was hanged.

WAR CRIMES

THE BANALITY OF EVIL

The philosopher Hannah Arendt attended Adolph Eichmann's trial and described the experience in her ground-breaking book, *Eichmann in Jerusalem*. There Arendt developed a notion she called "the banality [ordinariness] of evil." Arendt was fascinated by the way Eichmann so matter-of-factly undertook such horrific tasks. In her book, she discusses the difference between the type of person who undertakes evil out of hatred, anger, or a lust for power, and the type of person who, like Eichmann, simply does a job that happens to have evil results. Arendt suggested that this more banal evil is the true product of the twentieth century, in which large dictatorships run prisons and death camps with the same detached efficiency that is used to run factories and offices.

His body was cremated. Early the next morning, a police boat carried his ashes out into international waters and scattered them in the Mediterranean Sea.

Suggestions for Further Reading

Arendt. Hannah. *Eichmann in Jerusalem: A Report on the Banality of Evil.* New York: Penguin Books, 1994.

Averbach, Albert and Charles Price, eds. *The Verdicts Were Just.* New York: David McKay, 1966.

Harel, Isser. *The House on Garibaldi Street.* New York: Viking, 1975.

Malin, Peter Z. and Harry Stein. *Eichmann in My Hands.* New York: Warner, 1990.

Pearlman, Maurice. *The Capture and Trial of Adolf Eichmann.* New York: Simon & Schuster, 1963.

Sibyll, Claus. *Eichmann Interrogated: Transcripts from the Archives of the Israeli Police.* New York: Vintage Books, 1984.

John Demjanjuk Trial: 1987–1988

Defendant: John Demjanjuk

Crime Charged: Genocide (the deliberate and systematic destruction of a racial, political, or cultural group)

Chief Defense Lawyers: Mark O'Connor, Yoram Sheftel, Paul Chumak, and John Gill

Chief Prosecutors: Michael Shaked, Yonah Blatman, Dennis Goldman, and Michael Horowitz

Judges: Dov Levin, Dalia Dorner, and Zvi Tal

Place: Jerusalem, Israel

Dates of Trial: February 16, 1987–April 18, 1988

Verdict: Guilty, overturned on appeal

Sentence: Death

SIGNIFICANCE: Israel's first televised trial was supposed to show that it had not "gone soft" on Nazi war crimes. Instead, it was a fiasco (complete failure). New evidence emerged that convinced the nation's highest court that the wrong man had been convicted.

In 1975, the U.S. Immigration and Naturalization Service (INS) investigated a list of seventy war criminals living in America. High on this list was a former Ukrainian guard known as "Ivan the Terrible." He had personally killed thousands of Jews with poison gas in the Nazi death camp at Treblinka in 1942–1943. After World War II, it seemed that Ivan had entered the United States illegally and settled in Cleveland, Ohio. In 1977, a fifty-seven-year-old Ford Motor Company auto worker named John Demjanjuk was accused of being Ivan the Terrible.

Deportation Hearing

Demjanjuk arrived in the U.S. in 1952. Six years later he changed his first name to John and became an American citizen. In 1979, the INS was shown a photocopied identification card issued to "Ivan Demjanjuk" at a Nazi training camp. Demjanjuk denied that the card was his. When several former inmates of the Treblinka camp identified the person on the ID card as "Ivan the Terrible," the INS decided to review Demjanjuk's citizenship application.

The INS hearing began February 10, 1981. After hearing testimony that the identification card was real, the court heard from some of Ivan the Terrible's victims. Only five survivors of Treblinka were still alive, and four of them flew halfway around the world to testify against Demjanjuk. All identified him as Ivan the Terrible.

Testifying on his own behalf, Demjanjuk declared he had never been at Treblinka. He said his was a case of mistaken identity, and that the ID card was a forgery by the Soviet secret police. From 1942–1943, Demjanjuk said, he himself had been imprisoned in a German prisoner of war camp in Poland.

In the end Judge Frank Battisti decided that Demjanjuk had hidden his wartime record and gained U.S. citizenship illegally. He ordered Demjanjuk's citizenship to be taken away immediately. On May 23, 1984, Demjanjuk was given thirty days to leave the country. He chose to stay and fight the order. In February 1985, the INS Board of Appeals ruled that Demjanjuk's past deprived him of the right to leave voluntarily. He was put in prison to await the outcome of Israel's request that he be sent to that country to stand trial.

On Trial in Israel

On February 27, 1986, Demjanjuk was flown to Tel Aviv, Israel, to face another trial. His U.S. trial left little doubt that he was indeed Ivan the Terrible.

The order originally sending him to Israel had said he was charged with "murder." However, when his trial began in Jerusalem on February 16, 1987, Demjanjuk was charged with "genocide." The change was important. If he was found guilty of genocide, he would be punished with death. If he was convicted of murder, he would receive life in prison.

Most of the Treblinka survivors who had testified against Demjanjuk earlier did so again. Among them was Eliahu Rosenberg, who had cleared dead bodies from gas chambers. A moment of high drama came when prosecutor Michael Shaked asked Rosenberg to "look at the defendant, if you can."

Rosenberg responded, "I request that the honorable court order him to take off his glasses."

"His glasses? Why?" asked Judge Levin.

"I want to see his eyes. May I get a little closer?"

The defense lawyers protested, but Demjanjuk removed his glasses.

Rosenberg approached to within three feet of him. Suddenly Demjanjuk put out his hand. Rosenberg knocked it away angrily, crying out, "You murderer! How dare you offer me your hand." Then seconds later, "Beyond a shadow of a doubt, it's Ivan from the Treblinka gas chambers! The man I'm now looking at. I saw the eyes. Those murderous eyes!" The courtroom broke out into chaos as Rosenberg sat back down in the witness box.

Later, the significance of this identification was lessened. It became known that in 1947 Rosenberg had described seeing Ivan the Terrible being beaten to death during an inmate revolt at Treblinka on August 2, 1943. Under cross-examination, Rosenberg now claimed that his earlier statement, which he had made in Yiddish, had not been translated properly. What he had meant to say was that he saw Ivan being beaten with "murderous blows," not that he had actually seen him killed. It was a small but important victory for the defense. The first seeds of doubt about the identity of Ivan the Terrible had been planted.

J o h n
D e m j a n j u k
T r i a l :
1 9 8 7 – 1 9 8 8

Questions of Identity

Further success came with new evidence. Maria Radivker, an investigator of Nazi war crimes, admitted that the photo display of eight men that had been shown to the Treblinka survivors had not been fair to the defendant. The photo showed only one man who (like Demjanjuk) was bald.

Helmut Leonard was supposed to be one of the state's star witnesses. During 1942–1944, he had been a clerk at the camp where the ID card allegedly issued to Demjanjuk was printed. Now he stunned prosecutors by stating that if Demjanjuk had worked at Treblinka, the ID would bear

OPPOSITE PAGE

Israeli police escort accused Nazi war criminal John Demjanjuk into Israel's supreme court on May 15, 1990. This was the second day of the appeal hearing against his sentence. Originally, the court ordered the death penalty for Demjanjuk for killing thousands of Jews at the Treblinka death camp during World War II. Later, it found insufficient evidence to convict him.

a certain assignment number. It did not. The card, even if it was a forgery, could not have belonged to Ivan the Terrible.

Still another witness who disappointed the prosecution was Otto Horn, a former Nazi sergeant from Treblinka. He said that "the photograph only resembles Ivan, and that's what I said before. . . . It could be him." This was hardly the positive identification the prosecutors had been expecting.

When Demjanjuk rose to testify on his own behalf, loud cries and hisses filled the courtroom. Speaking in Ukrainian, Demjanjuk repeated his story that in 1942–1943 he had been a prisoner of war in Poland. But Demjanjuk was a bad witness. He had a bad memory, and his halting answers made onlookers suspect that he was lying.

There was worse to come. Edna Robertson came from the United States to testify as an expert on documents. She had concluded that the ID card was a forgery. However, when the prosecution performed the same tests on other verified documents, they came up with the same results. Robertson's mistake was a major blow to the defense.

The defense team recovered somewhat with the testimony of Dr. Julius Grant. Grant was a documents expert who had, in 1983, exposed the so-called "Hitler Diaries" as fake. When he compared the Demjanjuk signature on the ID card with that of the defendant, he was convinced that the card could not be a real document that belonged to Demjanjuk.

Perhaps the most important defense witness was Professor Willem Wagenaar. He was a distinguished psychologist. He explained how memory can distort events. This distortion made it "almost certain that every survivor who pointed to one of the pictures [of the eight possible suspects] would point to Demjanjuk's picture."

Sentence: Hanging

This was not enough to convince the court. On April 18, 1988, Judge Levin delivered the verdict that Demjanjuk was Ivan the Terrible. One week later, Demjanjuk was sentenced to hang.

On May 15, 1990, a lengthy appeals process began. Recently discovered documents indicated that Ivan the Terrible was not Demjanjuk but another Ukrainian, named Ivan Marchenko. Marchenko, who looked very much like Demjanjuk, had been identified as Ivan the Terrible as early as 1976 by a Treblinka survivor.

By February 1992, more evidence had emerged to support this conclusion. Libraries in the Soviet Union contained eighty statements from

WAR CRIMES

CONCENTRATION CAMPS

Treblinka was one of several concentration camps set up by the Nazis after 1933. The camps were first used to imprison Communists, Jews, homosexuals, and other groups hated by the Nazis. These people were imprisoned without a trial. Some of the camps were organized to use prisoners for forced labor, but most were simply death camps. Eventually more than six million people—mostly Jewish and Polish—were murdered in the camps.

former Treblinka guards—made in the early 1950s—that identified Marchenko as Ivan the Terrible. In particular there was a confession from Nikolai Shelaiev, who had been captured by the Soviets and convicted of war crimes. Shelaiev had personally operated the gas chambers at Treblinka. Before he was executed in 1952, Shelaiev confirmed that he and Marchenko had worked there together. Then George Parker, who had been an attorney with the Office of Special Investigation (OSI), a division of the U.S. Department of State, made a startling claim. He said that the OSI had known this as early as 1979.

Shaked argued that even if Demjanjuk were not Ivan the Terrible, he must have been a guard at some other concentration camp. The Supreme Court judges hearing the appeal did not approve of this strategy. They pointed out that the U.S. warrant permitting Demjanjuk to stand trial in Israel had specifically mentioned Treblinka and nowhere else. Then the court heard a statement given by Marchenko's daughter, Katarina Kovalenko. She confirmed that in the early 1950s, Soviet secret police had ransacked the family home and removed every photograph of her father. This disclosure supported the assertion that the notorious ID card had been a Soviet forgery.

After a year's deliberation, on July 29, 1993, the Israeli Supreme Court overturned Demjanjuk's conviction, saying he was not Ivan the Terrible. Two months later, he was deported from Israel and returned to the United States. Once back in America, Demjanjuk fought to get back his citizenship.

Perhaps the final word on this tragedy belongs to Israeli Judge Haim Cohen: "It was a spectacle for the people. Any resemblance to justice was purely coincidental."

Suggestions for Further Reading

Loftus, Elizabeth and Katherine Ketcham. *Witness For The Defense.* New York: St. Martin's Press, 1991.

Sheftel, Yoram. *The Demjanjuk Affair.* London: Gollancz, 1994.

Teicholz, Tom. *The Trial Of Ivan The Terrible.* New York: St. Martin's Press, 1990.

Wagenaar, Willem A. *Identifying Ivan.* Cambridge, MA: Harvard University Press, 1988.

John
Demjanjuk
Trial:
1987–1988

Klaus Barbie Trial: 1987

Defendant: Klaus Barbie
Crimes Charged: War crimes, crimes against humanity
Chief Defense Lawyer: Jacques Vergès
Chief Prosecutor: Pierre Truche
Judge: André Cerdini
Place: Lyons, France
Dates of Trial: May 11–July 4, 1987
Verdict: Guilty
Sentence: Life in prison

SIGNIFICANCE: The trial and conviction of Klaus Barbie affirmed that there can be no statute of limitations on crimes against humanity.

Klaus Barbie was at one time a minor official of the German SS (Hitler's special guards). He had tortured Frenchmen who resisted the Nazis and deported French Jews to the Auschwitz death camp.

Now he struck many as a decrepit old man, who looked ordinary and wore a blank expression on his face. "Criminals rarely achieve the dimensions of their crimes," wrote journalist Jane Kramer, "and Barbie was no exception." However, one French journalist thought that Barbie had "the emaciated face of a predatory bird."

When one of his French interrogators asked Barbie what Nazism meant to him, Barbie replied, "Camaraderie."

"The Butcher of Lyons"

Barbie served as head of a section of SS police in Lyons, France, in 1943 and 1944. One of the prosecutors at the Nuremberg war crimes trials of high-ranking Nazis called positions like this "criminal public service." In that job, Barbie tracked down, arrested, and tortured members of the French Resistance who fought German occupation. The best known of these Resistance martyrs, Jean Moulin, died at Barbie's hands in Montluc Prison in 1944. Barbie also rounded up 44 Jewish children from an orphanage in the village of Izieu near Lyons and sent them to the death camps. In August 1944, he arranged for the deportation to Auschwitz of 630 Jews and members of the Resistance.

A French court convicted Nazi SS commander, Klaus Barbie—alias Klaus Altmann—of war crimes in Lyons, France, in 1987.

Barbie gained a reputation as "the Butcher of Lyons." Even so, when World War II ended, he managed to escape—with the help of U.S. Army secret information. The Americans valued him for his knowledge of French Communists who were important members of the Resistance. There is no evidence, however, that the United States knew about Barbie's role in the deportation of Jews. In any case, the Americans helped Barbie leave Genoa, Italy, for South America in 1951. In 1952 and 1954, the French tried, convicted, and sentenced him to death even in his absence.

The former SS torturer began a new life in Bolivia as the German immigrant Klaus Altmann. He hardly bothered to cover up his past, and the Nazi hunters Serge Klarsfeld and Beate Klarsfeld eventually tracked

WAR CRIMES

him down in La Paz, the Bolivian capital, in 1974. The French paid Bolivia to return Barbie with $50 million and 3,000 tons of wheat. He was taken to Lyons in 1983. Four years and 23,000 pages of testimony later, Barbie was tried on charges of war crimes (acts against the Resistance) and crimes against humanity (the deportation of Jews).

Double Charges Confuse the Issues

The double charges created a problem. By the 1980s, the time limit for carrying out death sentences handed down to absent defendants had expired. And since the time of Barbie's earlier trials, France had done away with the death penalty. The minister of justice at the time the death penalty was ended was Robert Badinter, a Jew whose father had been murdered at Auschwitz.

The problem lay in a blurring of the meaning of Barbie's acts. It is counted as a war crime to torture or kill enemy soldiers after they have been taken captive. It is a crime against humanity to arrest, deport, and murder civilians—in this case, Jews—as part of a state policy of extermination. There is a difference, critics of the proceedings argued, between killing Resistance fighters and killing Jews.

Barbie's Victims Give Details of His Crimes

The trial became a media event—partly because of the antics of Barbie's attorney, Jacques Vergès. After looking at the thick stack of papers that were the indictment, Vergès remarked: "The next thing you know, they'll say he stole the Eiffel Tower." Vergès was the son of a French colonial officer who had been forced out of service for marrying a Vietnamese woman. Vergès hated colonialism (control by one power over a dependent area or people), and in the 1950s and 1960s, he became known for his defense of those who had worked for the liberation of Algeria from French rule. Now he argued that the French had no right to try Barbie because they had committed crimes in Algeria and other former colonies. In essence, Vergès was saying that Barbie's crimes were no worse than many others.

Critics claimed that journalists showed more interest in Vergès than in the testimony of those who had survived Barbie's torture sessions and deportation to Auschwitz. Possibly the press was simply bored. Certainly there was never any question of Barbie's guilt. Still, he flatly denied the worst of the charges against him. "I never committed the roundup in Izieu," he said. (Those who worked for him had.) "I never had the power to decide on deportations." (He had carried them out, though.) "I fought the Resistance, which I respect, with toughness, but that was war and the war is over."

The trial opened on May 11, 1987, in the Palace of Justice in Lyons. Barbie, then seventy-three years old, indicated at the outset that he did not intend to cooperate. He insisted that he be called Altmann—his La Paz alias. "I can understand why the name of Barbie must be too heavy to bear," the presiding judge told him.

On May 13, Barbie announced he would no longer attend court sessions, claiming that he had been sent back to France illegally. He appeared in court only three more times: twice so victims could identify him, and at the end of the trial he showed up for the lawyers' summations, the reading of the verdict, and his sentencing. His absence, of course, robbed his victims of their chance to confront him.

Cerdini questioned one woman about her arrest. "It was the difference between seeing an accident and being in an accident," she answered. A man who identified Barbie during one of his brief, forced appearances in court burst out: "Look at him. He told me, 'You will be N and N' [*nacht und nebel,* meaning "night and fog," or exterminated] with the same expression he has now!"

Testifying on June 3, Alice Vansteenberghe recalled the day Barbie tortured her and left her crippled for life. Then she told of an incident that occurred a few weeks later. On August 11, 1944, 331 Jews and 298 others were deported to Germany. The non-Jewish men and women went to different concentration camps. The Jews went to the Auschwitz death camp.

> That morning I had left my home in the full euphoria of my living body; I never regained that feeling; I have never been able to walk again. We in the Resistance knew the risks we were taking, and I accept everything that I suffered. But in the cell where I was thrown there were other people. I saw a Jewish woman and her child, well-groomed, very blond, with a barrette in her hair. Well, one day Barbie walked in to take this mother from her child. This is not warfare—it's something unspeakable, beyond all bounds.

WAR CRIMES

The train, dodging bombs and detouring around torn-up track and bridges that had been blown up, reached Auschwitz after eleven days. Twenty-three who were being deported died on the trip. On September 7, 1944, 128 of the surviving 308 Jews were killed with poison gas. The others went to the work camp, where many of them would endure a long, drawn-out death.

The Verdict

On July 3, 1987, the jury of nine women and three men began deliberations. Following French legal practice, the three judges sat in on their discussions and voted with them. The group reached a verdict on July 4: guilty. Cerdini sentenced Barbie to life in prison. The French seemed let down by the trial. The myth of the heroism of the Resistance remained undamaged.

Piece by piece the sorry record of the Vichy government's collaboration with the Nazi destruction of French Jews had come to light in the years before Barbie came to justice. Many Frenchmen hoped the trial would clear the record somehow. Those who were disappointed in the outcome tended to blame the media for making the issues seem unimportant.

Suggestions for Further Reading

Finkielkraut, Alain. *Remembering in Vain: The Klaus Barbie Trial and Crimes Against Humanity.* Translated by Roxanne Lapidus. New York: Columbia University Press, 1992.

Kramer, Jane. "Letter from Europe." *The New Yorker* (October 12, 1987): 130–144.

Morgan, Ted. *An Uncertain Hour: The French, the Germans, the Jews, the Klaus Barbie Trial and the City of Lyons, 1940–1945.* New York: William Morrow, 1990.

Klaus
Barbie
Trial: 1987

Index

Italic type indicates volume numbers; **boldface** indicates main entries and their page numbers; (ill.) indicates illustration

Note: Trial names have been treated as titles, so that *In the Matter of Baby M* falls under "I" and "John Brown Trial" is listed under "J," while John Brown himself is listed under "B"—Brown, John.

Index

Index

Index

Index

Galtieri, Leopoldo 2:479, 481, 483
Gandhi, Indira 2:341-347, 342 (ill.)
Gandhi, Mahatma. *See* Gandhi, Mohandas Karamchand
Gandhi, Mohandas Karamchand 2:327-334, 328 (ill.); 3:774
Gang, Liu. *See* Liu Gang
Gang of Four 3:791-794
Gantt, John 2:418
Garden of Eden 3:653
Garden of Gethsemane 3:610
Garibaldi, Marie L. 1:97
Garland, Hugh A. 1:15
Garland, Judy 3:810
Garmone, Fred 2:439
Garnet, Henry 3:680, 682-683
Garrett, Helena 2:505
Garrick, Edward 2:383-384, 386
Gary, Joseph E. 2:404, 407-409
Gasch, Oliver 3:748
Gast, Gabrielle 2:375
Gaulle, Charles de 3:737, 740-741
Gavira, Gustave 2:544
Geary, John W. 2:400-401, 403
Geneva Convention 2:356
Genocide 3:768, 771, 829-831
Georgia State Board of Pardons and Paroles 2:421
Georgia Supreme Court 2:419-420
Gerber, Samuel R. 2:442, 444
German Communist Party 2:309
German Federal Court of Justice 2:325
German National Socialist Party. *See* Nazis
German Press Agency 2:464
Germany's Constitutional Court 2:376
Germany's Hereditary Health Law 1:88
Gesell, Gerhard 2:536, 540
Gestapo 3:807, 811, 823
Geyer, H. S. 1:15, 19
Gibault, François 2:491
Gibbons, Henry J. 1:118
Gibson, Dorothy 1:236
Gideon, Clarence Earl 1:170, 210-214, 211 (ill.), 212 (ill.)
Gideon v. Wainwright 1:213
Gifford, Gilbert 3:667
Giles, William B. 1:112
Gill, Arthur 1:183
Gill, Charles 1:183, 185-187
Gill, John 3:829
Gillespie, John 2:388
Ginsburg, Allen 1:144
Ginsburg, Ruth Bader 1:241, 243
Ginzburg, Alexandr 3:785-786, 788, 790
Giordano Bruno Trials 3:628-633, **629 (ill.), 630 (ill.)**
Girondins 2:392, 395
Girondists 3:697
Gitlow, Benjamin 1:121
Gleason, John B. 2:410
Glorious Revolution 3:642
Glucksberg, Harold 1:241-243
Goddard, Henry W. 2:357, 361
Goddard, Robert 2:387
Godse, Gopal 2:327, 329-333
Godse, Nathuram 2:327-328, 330-333
Goering, Hermann 2:437; 3:726, 728, 807-811, 813, 823, 825
Gofman, John 1:263
Goldberg, Arthur J. 1:136
Goldberg, Dennis 3:773
Goldman, Dennis 3:829
Goldman, Ronald L. 2:496-498, 500
Golgotha 3:612
Golos, Jacob 2:367
Golunsky, S. A. 3:814
Gompers, Samuel 1:250

Gonzalez, Leonard 3:595
Good, Sarah 3:641, 644-646
Goode, George W. 1:15
Gorbachev, Mikhail 3:788
Gordon, Bennett 1:83-84
Gordon, Lady Duff 1:256
Gordon, Peyton C. 2:523
Görisch, Dr. 2:320
GPU (Stalin's secret police) 2:315, 318
Grabež, Trifko 2:302-306
Graebe, Hermann 3:807
Graffigna, Omar 2:479, 481, 483
Graham, James M. 2:422
Grand Jury 1:40, 42-43, 116, 141, 169, 171, 202, 234, 238; 2:360, 365, 385, 499, 515, 537; 3:650, 702, 706-707
Grant, John 3:678, 681
Grant, Julius 3:832
Grant, Ulysses S. 2:521, 523
Grau, Ricardo Luis 3:768
Gray, Horace 1:29
Gray, John 2:388
Gray, L. Patrick 1:42
Gray, Ralph 1:202
Gray, Samuel 2:385; 3:645
Great Hall 3:667, 670, 793, 798
"Great Leap Forward" 3:795
The "Great Negro Plot" Trial 1:168-171
Great Temple 3:609
Greeley, Horace 1:70
Green, Thomas C. 3:704, 707
Green, William 2:383
Greene, Nathanael 3:579
Greenglass, David 2:365-367
Greenglass, Ruth 2:365-367
Greengrass, Paul 1:150
Gregory IX, Pope 3:633
Greiner, Gladys 1:190, 193
Grier, Robert Cooper 1:15, 19-20
Griffin, Cyrus 3:699, 701
Griffin, John Jr. 1:262
Griffith, J. Paul 1:210, 213
Grigat, Peter 2:459
Griggs, William 3:643
Grimes, James W. 2:521
Grindlay-Ferris, I. L. 2:485
Grinivetsky, Agnate 2:293
Grinnell, Julius S. 2:404, 406-408
Griswold, Hiram 3:704, 707-708
Griswold v. Connecticut 1:92
Grossman, Howard A. 1:241-242
Grueber, Dean 3:825
Guerre, Martin 1:61-68, 63 (ill.), 66 (ill.)
Guerre, Pierre 1:64
Guerrilla war 3:598
Guforth, John 2:398, 400
Guider, John 3:814
Guildford Four 2:452-458, 454 (ill.)
Guildford Four Trial 2:452-458, 454 (ill.)
Guillaume, Gunter 2:373, 375
Guillotine 2:392-394; 3:691, 694, 697, 729
Gulag 3:730, 788
The Gulag Archipelago 3:788
Gump, Frederick 2:415
Gunpowder plot 3:678-683, 679 (ill.), 681 (ill.)
Gunpowder Plot Trial 3:**678-683,** 679 (ill.), 681 (ill.)
Guo Haifeng 3:797-798
Guthrie, Arlo 1:144
Guy Fawkes Day 3:683

H

Ha'am, Beth 3:824
Haas, Herbert 2:416

I n d e x

Index

Index

Lane, Myles J. *2:*357, 364
Lange, Tom *2:*496-497
Langford, Edward *2:*388
Lardner, Ring Jr. *1:*129, 132, 134-135
Largo Desolato *3:*784
Latimer, George W. *3:*593, 595, 597
Laughlin, Harry H. *1:*83, 84, 87
Lautz, Dr. *2:*320
Laval, Pierre *3:*736-737, 740-741
Lawrence, Geoffrey *3:*805, 808
Laws, Bolitha J. *3:*748, 751-752, 754
Lawson, John Howard *1:*129, 131-134
Lawson, Thomas *1:*196
Lazarus, Aristides *3:*814
Leahy, William E. *2:*523
Leavitt, Joshua *1:*172
Ledher Rivas, Carlos *2:*544-546
Lee, Charles *1:*3, 5
Lee, Newt *2:*418
Lee, Robert E. *3:*706
Leibnitz, Gottfried *3:*628
Leibowitz, Samuel S. *1:*196-197, 200-201
Lemaire, Jean *3:*736
Lemlich, Clara *1:*250
Lemmle, Dr. *2:*320
Lenin, Vladimir *2:*475, 314, 475; *3:*733-734
Leningrad party *3:*731
Leo Frank Trial *2:***416-421, 417 (ill.)**
Leo X, Pope *3:*622
Leon Trotsky's Assassin Trial *2:***314-319,** 316
(ill.)
Leonard, Helmut *3:*831
Leonard, John *2:*452
Leopold, Nathan *3:*653
Letherman, Lawrence *2:*429
Levin, Dov *3:*829, 831-832
Levin, Michael *3:*814
Lewis, Guy *2:*544
Lewis, Morgan *1:*110
Li Chenghuan *3:*797
Li Shuntang *3:*797
Li Yuqi *3:*797-798
Li Zuopeng *3:*791
Libel *1:*105, 108-113, 115, 125, 136, 138, 140,
183-185, 187-188; *2:*312, 359; *3:*715, 780
Liebknecht, Karl *2:*309-313
Lieres, Klaus von *2:*467, 469
Life support *1:*227-229
Lin Biao *3:*792
Lincoln, Abraham *1:*23; *2:*517-519; *3:*596
Lincoln, Levi *1:*3, 5-6
Lindbergh, Charles *2:*431, 433-435, 437-438
Lindey, Alexander *1:*123, 125
Lingg, Louis *2:*404, 407, 409
Linke, Karl-Heinz *2:*459, 460
Lipavsky, Sanya *3:*786
Little Review *1:*123
Littleton, Martin W. *2:*410, 414, 523
Liu Gang *3:*797-798, 800
Liu Shao-Ch'i *3:*795
Liu Xiaobo *3:*797-798
Liu Xiaojing *3:*797
Living wills *1:*227
Livingston, James *3:*582
Lloyd, John *2:*509
Lobetkin, Esther *1:*250
Lockwood, Frank *1:*74-75, 183
Lodge, Abraham *1:*168
Loeb, Richard *3:*653
Logan, William Jr. *3:*814
Lohier, John *3:*619
London Agreement *3:*823
Looting *3:*768, 797
Lopez, Pedro *3:*814
Lord, Walter *1:*258-261
Los Alamos Scientific Laboratory *1:*264

Los Angeles Police Department (LAPD) *1:*235
(ill.), 236-237, 239; *2:*496, 498, 500-501
Los Angeles Police Officers' Trial *1:***233-239,** 235
(ill.), 236 (ill.), 237 (ill.)
Los Angeles riots *1:*236 (ill.), 239
Los Angeles Times *1:*240; *3:*787
Losada, Manuel Piñeiro *3:*768
Loubser, J. D. *2:*469
Louis XVI *2:*393; *3:*691-693, 692 (ill.), 697
Louis XVI and Marie Antoinette Trials *2:*393;
*3:***691-698,** 692 (ill.), 695 (ill.), 696 (ill.)
Lowell, Abbott Lawrence *2:*428
Lowrey, George H. *1:*48-49
Lozier, Clemence *2:*401
Lu Xiaochun *3:*797
Lubyanka prison *3:*734
Ludlow, James Riley *2:*398, 400
Lufthansa Airlines *2:*464
Lukanov, P. P. *3:*785
Lusitania *2:*356
Luther, Martin *1:*137-139; *2:*333; *3:*621-627, 622
(ill.), 625 (ill.), 631
Luxemburg, Rosa *2:*308-313, 309 (ill.)
Lynching *1:*200-201; *2:*301, 416, 421
Lynd, Benjamin *2:*381
Lyon, Matthew *1:*112-113, 115
Lžičař, Josef *3:*779

M

M*A*S*H *1:*134
Ma Rongjie *3:*791
Ma Shaofang *3:*797-798
Mabuti, Jantjie *2:*487-488
MacArthur, Douglas *3:*815-816, 820
Maccari, Germano *2:*477
Macharia, Rawson *1:*207-209
Maclean, Donald *1:*150
MacLeish, Archibald *3:*748, 750, 752
MacRae, Gordon *3:*699, 702
Maculano, Vincenzo *3:*634, 637
Madden, Richard R. *1:*175
Madeiros, Celestino F. *2:*429
Madison, Dred Scott *1:*19
Madison, James *1:*3-7, 6 (ill.). 115
Madison, John A. *1:*19
Madison Square Garden *2:*410-411, 413
Mafia *2:*339
Magee, Ruchell *2:*446, 449
Magistrates of Massachusetts *1:*157
Magna Carta *3:*662
Mahon, John J. *2:*439, 442
Mailer, Norman *1:*144
Main Guard *2:*383-385
Major John Andre Trial *3:***579-586,** 580 (ill.)
Malek, Wenzel *2:*302
Malesherbes, Chrètien de L. de *3:*691
Malice *1:*115, 137, 139-140; *2:*519
Malman, Myles *2:*542, 546
Malone, Dudley Field *1:*190, 193-195; *3:*648, 650,
652-653
Maltz, Albert *1:*129, 132, 134
Mammoth Oil Company *2:*525
A Man for All Seasons *3:*663
Mandela, Nelson *2:*470-471; *3:*773-778, 775 (ill.)
Mandela, Winnie *3:*777
Mandjia-Baya people *2:*495
Manete, Joseph *2:*487-488
Manhattan Project *2:*365-366
Mann, Alonzo *2:*421
Mann, John *3:*759
Mann, Thomas *1:*131
Mansfield, Alan *3:*814
Manton, Martin *1:*128
Manuel Noriega Trial *2:***542-547,** 543 (ill.)

I n d e x

Index

Index

Pine, David A. *1:*129, 133
Pinkerton guards *2:*298
Piracy *1:*172, 174-175
Pius XII, Pope *2:*370; *3:*754-755
Place de la Concorde *3:*694, 698
Plato *3:*605, 606-607
Plessy, Homer A. *1:*29-30
Plessy v. Ferguson *1:***29-32**, 31 (ill.), 36-38
Plottnitz, Rupert von *2:*459
Plum, Fred *1:*231
Plutonium contamination *1:*262
Poland Law *1:*23
Polish Communist Party *2:*308
Polish Social Democratic Party *2:*308
Politburo *3:*764
Political prisoners *1:*190, 194; *2:*447; *3:*731-732, 788, 802
Pollock, Stewart G. *1:*97
Polygamy *1:*22-24, 26-28
Pomerene, Atlee W. *2:*523, 526
Pontius Pilate *3:*608-612
Popham, John *3:*672-673, 675, 675 (ill.), 678, 682
Popov, Blagoi *3:*724
Popovič, Cvetko *2:*302, 304
Popper, Martin W. *1:*129, 133
Porter, Katherine Anne *2:*428-429
Porzio, Ralph *1:*227
Potiorek, Oskar *2:*303
Pound, Ezra *1:*124; *3:*748-752, 751 (ill.)
Powell, Laurence M. *1:*233-235, 235 (ill.), 238
Powell, Lewis *1:*41, 89, 93
Powell, Lewis F. Jr. *1:*39, 47
Powell, Ozie *1:*196-197
Pratt, Arthur *1:*24
Premužič, Konstantin *2:*302
President Andrew Johnson Impeachment Trial *2:***517-522**, 518 (ill.)
Preston, Thomas *2:*381, 384-388
Preston, Thomas A. *1:*241
Prevention of Terrorism Act *2:*453
Price, Arthur *1:*170
Price, Victoria *1:*199-201
Priddy, Albert *1:*82-84
Prierias, Sylvester *3:*622
Prince Primate of Hungary *3:*754
Princeton University *2:*409; *3:*607, 700, 821
Princip, Gavrilo *2:*302-306
Prins, Martinhus *2:*467, 470
Prinzing, Theodor *2:*459, 462-464
Pritt, D. N. *1:*204, 206-208
Privy Council *3:*680
"Process of National Reorganization" *2:*480
Proctor, Elizabeth *3:*645
Proctor, John *3:*645
The Progressive *1:*225
Protective custody *3:*729
Protestant Reformation *3:*621, 626, 628
Protesters *1:*48, 48 (ill.), 141, 191, 194; *2:*370-371, 486, 488, 549; *3:*774, 799
P'u Yi, Henry *3:*818
"Pumpkin Papers" *2:*360
Puppet government *3:*818
Purcell, William *3:*589
Puritans *1:*157, 161, 165; *3:*626, 642-643, 690
Putsch *2:*321, 323
Pyatakov, Grigori *3:*733

Q

Qianjin, Zhang. *See* Zhang Qianjin
Queensberry, Marquess of *1:*183-185, 186 (ill.), 188
Qing, Jiang. *See* Jiang Qing
Qiu Huizuo *3:*791

Quakers *1:*163-166
Quien, George Gaston *2:*353
Quill, Timothy E. *1:*241-242
Quilliam, Ronald *3:*815
Quincy, Samuel *2:*381, 385-386, 389
Quinlan, Joseph T. *1:*227, 228 (ill.)
Quinlan, Julia Ann *1:*228 (ill.), 230
Quinlan, Karen Ann *1:*227-228, 230, 232
Quisling, Vidkun Abraham Lauritz Jonsson *3:*742-747, 744 (ill.)

R

Rabinowitz, Victor *2:*357
Raby, Kenneth A. *3:*593
Racketeering *2:*542-543
Radek, Karl *3:*733
Radio Tokyo *3:*758-759
Ragland, R. W. *2:*523
Rai, Ganpat *2:*327
Raleigh, Walter *3:*672-677, 673 (ill.), 674 (ill.), 682
Ramashamola, Theresa *2:*485, 487, 489
Ramsay, Dennis *1:*3, 5
Ramsey, Cheryl *2:*503, 507
Ramsey, Donald P. *2:*422
Rand, Ayn *1:*131
Randolph, Edmund *3:*699, 702
Randolph, John *2:*513
Ransom *2:*433-436, 464-465
Raspe, Jan-Carl *2:*459, 461-465
Rauh, Carl S. *1:*52
Raulston, John T. *3:*648, 652-654
Raveh, Yitzhak *3:*822, 826
Rawle, William *1:*112, 116
Reading tests *1:*29
Reagan, Ronald *1:*131, 219; *2:*536-538
Reasonable doubt *2:*300, 387, 408, 488; *3:*816
Rebellion *1:*112, 116, 119, 159, 165, 173-174; *2:*303, 390, 457, 463, 514, 549- 550; *3:*701-702, 708, 721, 787, 791, 793
Reconciliation Commission *2:*470
Reconstruction *2:*420, 518
Red Army *2:*460, 466; *3:*731, 734, 743
Red Army Faction (RAF) *2:*460-461, 464-465
Red Brigades *2:*473-478, 474 (ill.)
Red Brigades Trial *2:***473-478**, 474 (ill.)
Red Cross *1:*83; *2:*351, 356; *3:*818
Redcoats *2:*385
Reed, Carol *3:*591
Reed, Sally *1:*181
Reed, Stanley F. *1:*33, 37
Reformation *3:*621, 626, 628, 636
Refuseniks *3:*786
Rehnquist, William H. *1:*39, 41, 47, 89, 93, 241, 245
Reichstag *3:*724-726, 728-729
Reichstag Fire Trial *3:***724-729**, 725 (ill.)
Reign of Terror *2:*392-393; *3:*697
Reilly, Edward J. *2:*431, 434-435
Reinecke, Hermann *2:*320
Ren Wanding *3:*797, 798
Republicans *1:*3, 94, 110, 113-114, 116; *2:*515, 518-519, 521; *3:*699-700
Resistance fighters *2:*351, 354; *3:*738, 838
Restoration *3:*690
Resurrection *2:*431
Reverse discrimination *1:*47, 49-50
Revolution *1:*178; *2:*403
Revolutionaries *2:*293, 295-296, 310, 540; *3:*692, 694-695, 753
Revolutionary Air Force *3:*772
Revolutionary Tribunal *2:*396; *3:*691, 695
Revolutionary War *1:*105; *2:*383, 514; *3:*699-700
Rex v. Preston *2:*381

Index

Index

I n d e x

Index

Index